Deleuze and Feminist Theory

Deleuze and Feminist Theory

edited by

IAN BUCHANAN
and
CLAIRE COLEBROOK

EDINBURGH
University Press

© The Contributors, 2000

Edinburgh University Press Ltd
22 George Square, Edinburgh

Reprinted 2001

Transferred to digital print 2005

Typeset in ITC–New Baskerville
by Pioneer Associates, Perthshire

**Printed and bound in Great Britain by
CPI Antony Rowe, Eastbourne**

A CIP record for this book is available from
the British Library

ISBN 0 7486 1120 7 (paperback)

Contents

Contents

Introduction

CLAIRE COLEBROOK

I. INTRODUCTION

Throughout *A Thousand Plateaus* Deleuze and Guattari invoke Virginia Woolf's style of writing as exemplary of a new mode of becoming. Woolf is enlisted to support one of Deleuze and Guattari's most audacious and contentious claims regarding the notion of becoming and its relation to women. It may be tactical, they argue, for women to have a 'molar politics'. And this molar politics would be concerned with a specifically female subjectivity. However, they go on to insist that this female subject ought not act as a ground or limit to the women's movement. To embrace the female subject as a foundation or schema for action would lead to *ressentiment*: the slavish subordination of action to some high ideal (Deleuze 1983: 123). (If this were the case the women's movement would cease to be a *movement*. It would have taken one of its effects – the female subject – and allowed that effect to function as a cause, a ground or a moral law.)

This is where molecular politics comes in. In addition to the grounding ideas of movements there must also be the activation, question and confrontation of those tiny events that make such foundations possible. In this double politics of the molar and the molecular, Deleuze and Guattari produce two dynamic senses of movement: a political movement as the organisation of a ground, identity or subject; and a molecular movement as the mobile, active and ceaseless challenge of becoming. Any women's subjectivity, they argue, must function, not as a ground, but as a 'molar confrontation' that is part of a 'molecular women's politics' (Deleuze and Guattari 1987: 276). Any assertion of woman as a subject must not double

1

or simply oppose man, but must affirm itself as an event in the process of becoming. This is why 'all becomings begin with and pass through becoming-woman' (277). Because man has been taken as the universal ground of reason and good thinking, becoming must begin with his opposite, 'woman'. But this becoming must then go beyond binary opposition and pass through to other becomings, so that man and woman can be seen as events within a field of singularities, events, atoms and particles:

> The only way to get outside the dualisms is to be-between, to pass between, the intermezzo – that is what Virginia Woolf lived with all her energies, in all of her work, never ceasing to become. The girl is like the block of becoming that remains contemporaneous to each opposable term, man, woman, child, adult. It is not the girl who becomes a woman; it is becoming-woman that produces the universal girl. (277)

Because the girl must become a woman, she is invoked as the becoming of becoming. Man is traditionally defined as *being*: as the self-evident ground of a politics of identity and recognition. Woman, as his other, offers the opening of becoming; and the girl thus functions as a way of thinking woman, not as a complementary *being*, but as the instability that surrounds any being. For a being – an entity, identity or subject – is always the effect of a universal becoming. What makes this becoming girl-like? Its radical relation to man: not as his other or opposite (woman) but as the very becoming of man's other. And so when Deleuze and Guattari applaud the style of Woolf, they do so not because she is a woman writer but because she *writes woman*. Her writings neither express nor represent an already given female identity; rather, through Woolf's stream-of-consciousness technique, identity is seen as the effect of a flow of speech.

Isn't there something scandalous about this invocation of Woolf and the girl for a general process of becoming? And should the women's movement really be told that it must be 'molar' or concerned with identity only for a moment on the way to a 'molecular' becoming? On the one hand, we might regard Deleuze and Guattari's elevation of becoming-woman as a final recognition of the function of feminism. Feminism has always been more than a quibble regarding this or that value or prejudice within an otherwise sound way of thinking. Feminism at its most vibrant has taken the form of a demand not just to redress wrongs *within thought*, but to think differently. This is why sexual difference may be the question of our epoch – as the opening of a possibility for thinking beyond subjectivity and identity. On the other hand, Deleuze and Guattari's invocation of Woolf and becoming-woman can also be read as a domestication and subordination. Is it really *faithful* to Woolf or the women's movement to be defined as moments within a field of becoming? Just what are Deleuze and Guattari doing when they take Woolf and the women's movement away from the concepts of identity, recognition, emancipation and the subject towards a new plane of becoming?

II. THE POLITICS OF READING: INTERPRETATION AND INHABITATION

This strategy of enlisting authors and styles of thought for specific purposes – and usually against the grain of conventional interpretation – is typical of Deleuze and Deleuze and Guattari's work. Deleuze's relation to the history of writing has been one of a curious *infidelity* (Neil 1998). Texts are read in terms of how they work, rather than what they mean. Deleuze and Guattari's reading of Kafka, for example, describes a writer of passages, flight, spatial wandering and becoming-animal against the traditional understanding of Kafka as a poet of law and negativity (Deleuze and Guattari 1986). Deleuze's book on Hume uses the Scottish Enlightenment thinker to describe a radical empiricism that exceeds the subject (Deleuze 1991a). Deleuze's book on Nietzsche draws Nietzsche away from an all too human interpretation in terms of will and the overman and defines Nietzsche as the thinker of 'a world of impersonal and pre-individual singularities' (Deleuze 1990b: 107). In his book on Leibniz, Deleuze describes a writer concerned with a multiplicity of foldings (Deleuze 1993). This is directly opposed to the traditional readings of Leibniz as the philosopher responsible for a self-contained monad that acts as the ultimate ground of being. This is what makes Deleuze's history of philosophy an inhabitation rather than an interpretation. Rather than seek the good sense of a work, a Deleuzean reading looks at what a philosophical text creates. To see a text in this way means abandoning the interpretive comportment, in which the meaning of a text would be disclosed. In contrast, one *inhabits* a text: set up shop, follow its movements, trace its steps and discover it as a field of singularities (effects that cannot be subordinated to some pre-given identity of meaning). Deleuze's enlisted authors of singularity and becoming – including Spinoza, Leibniz and Bergson – perhaps present a more alarming perversity of interpretation than the use of Woolf's high Bloomsbury stream of consciousness and the women's movement to indicate non-identity and radical becoming. What is Deleuze doing when writers like Spinoza and Leibniz can come to typify the antithesis of system philosophy? And what happens to the girl and the women's movement when they are displaced in terms of a universal becoming?

We might argue that this strategy is typical of a masculine cannibalisation of thought, and that women's non-identity and writing have always been used to shore up a male identity that refuses to acknowledge any genuine otherness. But it is this risk of contagion and contamination that has characterised the odd and unfaithful position of feminism from the outset. Feminism has never been the pure and innocent other of a guilty and evil patriarchy. It has always been obliged to use the master's tools to destroy his house, and has done so in the full knowledge that this complicity, with its corruption and contamination, is itself an action against a metaphysics that would present itself as pure, self-fathered and fully autonomous. The problem of the relation of women to the tradition might be cashed out as follows: to *not* address the male canon would reduce women to an impossible outside, silence or ghetto; but to establish itself as a *women's* movement there does need to be a delimitation of the tradition in order to speak otherwise. On the one hand, women need to address the tradition and speak to an other (a male other that does not, yet, acknowledge itself as other). On the other hand, this address cannot just take the form of a simple intervention within an adequate field, but must also attempt to open other styles or modes of address, or a new field. Thus feminism has always been marked by an *odd* relation to its other. And so when Deleuze and Guattari address feminism, as the possibility for a new form of address or relation, they are at once drawn into the difficult relation between the becoming of feminism and the identity of the tradition. Their strategy has often been one of rendering the tradition non-identical to itself. Rather than attacking a philosophy of identity and being in terms of some pure outside, they have read philosophy perversely: showing the ways in which the tradition already articulates modalities of becoming. Spinoza and Leibniz are invoked as ways of thinking a being that is nothing other than its expressions and foldings. Women writers such as Woolf are not seen as struggling to find some new and pure identity beyond the being of traditional thought, and the women's movement is no longer seen as a critical point outside the tradition.

The *contamination* of tradition, its non-identity and infidelity to itself, is affirmed when writers are read in terms of what they do, and not in terms of some pre-given model of reason or authorial intention. It is this strategy – of locating oneself within a body of thought in order to dis-organise that body – that typifies not only Deleuze and Deleuze and Guattari's work but, also, the curious place of women's writing.

III. FEMINISM AND DELEUZE

It has never been a simple matter of application or addition when feminism has addressed a body of thought. From its articulation in eighteenth-century liberalism to the present even the most faithful feminisms have questioned the efficacy of the theories that promised emancipation. Significantly, the questions feminists have directed to theory have rarely, if ever, been those of one secure body of thought relating to another. It is as though the ampersand between feminism and liberalism, feminism and Marxism, feminism and postmodernism, and so on, has always struggled to *arrive* at the second term, precisely because of the uncertain identity of feminism itself. Never a stable body of thought with a grounding axiom or system, feminism has addressed theory not merely in terms of what a philosopher might offer but also in terms of what feminism might become.

When Mary Wollstonecraft embraced the liberal ideals of reason and autonomy she never assumed that such ideals might simply provide the women's movement with an identity. On the contrary, the challenge of reason was to think what human thought might become, and how reason would be compelled to address the demands of those it had excluded. Woman, Wollstonecraft argued, 'has always been either a slave, or a despot . . . each of these situations equally retards the progress of reason' (Wollstonecraft 1989: 123). For Wollstonecraft, like so many after her, the task was one of thinking how concepts might work. Reason, she argued, was not a law imposed upon thought, but a way of understanding how thought might liberate itself from law. This way of appraising concepts – as possibilities for future thinking – characterised the work of Mary Wollstonecraft and her liberal sisters, but it has also marked feminism's relation to Western thought in general. If liberal feminists asked how liberty, equality and fraternity might be used for the project of feminism, later feminists were even more astute when it came to measuring thought's effective power.

When Mary Shelley addressed Romanticism and the late eighteenth-century discourse of the subject she seemed thoroughly aware that concepts came with attendant personae. (As Deleuze and Guattari argue in *What is Philosophy?*, philosophical concepts work by being attached to figures or personalities (1994: 73). And we might think of Romantic narcissism for example as tied to Prometheus, or scientific hubris as given through Victor Frankenstein.) Shelley's *Frankenstein* (1980) can be read as a positive repetition and 'impersonation' of the Enlightenment ideals of the autonomous subject. In Shelley's novel Victor Frankenstein's creation of his 'hideous progeny' is a thoroughly *reactive* act of becoming: a becoming that grounds itself on a notion of God-like authorship or origination. Victor likens his own monstrous creation to that of God, and he sees his replication of life as the faithful copy of an unquestioned human prototype. Not only does Shelley's novel depict the thoroughly unbecoming nature of this Romantic humanism, she also indicates an entirely different mode of becoming. In opposition to Victor Frankenstein's narcissistic self-doubling, Shelley posits another form of becoming. This other becoming is the act of narrating *Frankenstein* itself. In repeating and parodying Romantic subjectivism, Shelley shows how ways of thinking and speaking can both enable and preclude life. This other mode of becoming is active rather than reactive. To become through writing is to create an event; it is to think becoming not as the becoming *of* some being. Victor Frankenstein's monster is the reactive creation *of* man, *from* God, law and science. Shelley's text, on the other hand, is becoming itself, not the becoming *of* some being or grounding intent but the presentation of becoming itself, a becoming that *then* effects certain modes of being. Writing *Frankenstein*, with all its quotations, allusions, framed stories and multiple narrators, frees becoming from being. There is the becoming of literature – such that the monster learns what it is to be human by overhearing a narration of *Paradise Lost*. The monster's humanity or being is the effect of a way of speaking and writing.

Before Woolf's modernism, Mary Shelley already shows that, to use Deleuze and Guattari's terms, all speaking is a 'collective assemblage': 'Before the interiority of a subject, or the inner space of consciousness and the unconscious there is an utterance which creates an assemblage, an act of becoming, an unconscious and collective production' (1987: 38). A way of speaking or thinking does not belong to a subject who is the ground of thought. Rather, subjects or characters are effects of speaking styles. In *Frankenstein*

6

we are shown that the scientist's 'tragedy' is not personal but the figuration of a way of speaking or style of thought. (This is why the novel borrows from Wordsworth, alludes to Milton and quotes Coleridge. By the time Victor creates his monster there have already been a series of monstrous creations that have formed the subject of male Romanticism.) Shelley's inhabitation of Romanticism as a style of existence epitomises a strategy that has characterised the tradition of women's writing. Confronted with a body of thought and with a language that comes from elsewhere, feminism has had to pose the question of how it might think and speak otherwise. Shelley's text is one of the earliest instances of positive repetition: the inhabitation of a dominant discourse in order to open up a new site. Like Irigaray after her, Shelley repeats the discourse of the subject to demonstrate its effects, its exclusions and those points at which it exposes itself to mutation.

Between Shelley and Irigaray feminist thought has offered a series of such provocative repetitions and contestations. Simone de Beauvoir's feminism, for example, was never a straightforward accommodation of existentialism. From the outset de Beauvoir was critical of the existential subject, and undertook such criticism by narrating a subject in its relation to others (*The Blood of Others*), the other's body (*A Very Easy Death*) and one's own embodiment (*The Second Sex*). For de Beauvoir it was a question of how concepts, such as authenticity, projection and consciousness, might *work*, and what such concepts might do in terms of life and becoming. We might go on to cite a series of feminist 'engagements' with male reason, all of which have asked the question of what a way of thinking might do. We need to be careful, then, of accommodating feminist thought to the standard mode of philosophical questioning. Perhaps philosophy has always been an Oedipal struggle, with sons wresting terrain from fathers. But this struggle, as described by Deleuze, has usually proceeded by assessing a thinker in terms of some unquestioned image of thought (Deleuze 1994a: xxi). The standard idea of a philosophical quibble concerns how thinkers answer or respond to a problem whose answer is seen as there to be found, as though the question or the problem were subordinate to some good reason that philosophy would simply recognise (rather than create) (1991a: 28). But feminist questions have rarely taken this form. On the contrary, feminist questions and concepts ask what a philosophy might do, how it might activate life and thought, and how certain problems create (rather than describe) effects. What this suggests is that Deleuze's thought provides a way

7

of understanding the peculiar modality of feminist questions and the active nature of feminist struggle. When confronted with a theory or body of thought feminism has tended to ask an intensely active question, not 'What does it mean?', but 'How does it work?' What can this concept or theory do? How can such a theory exist or be lived? What are its forces?

One thing that runs through Deleuze's diverse readings of the history of thought and its concepts is an ethic of affirmation. A thought is active or affirmative if it avows its status as creative and if it realises itself as the formation of concepts and as an event of life. A thought is reactive, however, if it pretends to be the mere adherence, representation, replication or faithful copy of some prior truth or meaning. An active philosophy or theory asserts itself as force, as what it is capable of doing and willing, and is affirmative of the events it effects. A reactive theory, on the other hand, subordinates itself to some unquestioned good 'image of thought' (Deleuze 1994a: 118). In so doing, reactive philosophy mistakes the cause–effect relation. In the beginning thought confronts chaos (Deleuze and Guattari 1994: 208). Thought is a hetero-genesis or becoming. In its confrontation with chaos thought creates concepts – so that concepts are the effect of active thought, and not laws by which thought ought to proceed. A reactive philosophy misrecognises this relationship. It sees effects – concepts – as the grounds or cause of thought. Thus reactive philosophy takes certain concepts – such as the subject, man, the human, being, reason – and subordinates thought to such concepts. Of course, it would be no less reactive to *oppose* reactive thought with another *concept* of the active. On the contrary, thought must *reactivate* its concepts: see concepts in terms of effects. One can't simply identify or find active philosophy; becoming-active must be a continual challenge. (Thus when feminism takes hold of the arsenal of philosophical concepts it can't be a question of how correct or faithful a certain concept is, rather, one might ask how a concept might be made to work.)

It is in his attempt to think philosophy affirmatively that Deleuze sets himself the task of a philosophy of immanence, a philosophy also defined as a radical empiricism or a transcendental empiricism. Philosophy will be immanent or radically empiricist if it does not subordinate itself to some outside ground or (as Deleuze describes it) some plane of transcendence. Philosophy strives for immanence by continually affirming its acts of thought as *acts*, and by producing concepts in terms of what they do and effect. Such a philosophy is also therefore a radical or transcendental *empiricism*: it asserts that there is nothing beyond the given – no law or real that pre-exists and governs becoming.

To think philosophy and theory as affirmation, and to think philosophical questions in terms of the effects they create and the forces they enable provides a new way of understanding what feminist philosophy has been doing all along; for there has always been a fundamental ambivalence regarding feminism's relation to philosophy. If we were to understand philosophy as the faithful commitment to truth and good reason, then feminism could only be a deployment of a general philosophic ideal. Or, if we were to understand philosophy as nothing more than the expression of male reason, then feminism would be placed outside the possibility of philosophy. On this picture, either philosophy is the logic of truth in general (genderless), or it is one interested and delimited claim to truth (masculine). Deleuze's task was to liberate philosophy from both these notions. Philosophy ought neither be a question of fidelity to some pre-philosophical truth, nor ought philosophy be located within the point of view of an interested subject. Both definitions of philosophy, according to Deleuze, rely on the question of 'Who Speaks?' (1990b: 107). Concepts are returned to a 'good' subject in general or located within an intending subject. But this would assume that there are subjects – male or female – who *then* speak or think, whereas Deleuze will insist that thinking and speaking are trans-individual possibilities of becoming. All speaking is already a collective utterance, and all thinking is an assemblage.

This provides a way of understanding the difficult location of the feminist philosopher's voice. How can one speak in such a way as to address the current corpus of concepts while at the same time seeking to think differently? Feminism, as already indicated, has always addressed philosophy in terms not restricted to truth or the personal interest of the philosopher. Feminism has always been a question of what concepts do, how they work and the forces any act of thinking enables. This gives us a way of thinking feminism's relation to philosophy positively: not just as the exposure of male bias or interests within an otherwise good reason, but as the attempt to assess the force of concepts and to create new concepts.

IV. FEMINISM AND BECOMING-DELEUZEAN

There is a story feminism has often narrated regarding its prehistory. First came the simple adherence to liberal emancipation, as though egalitarianism in general would entail the liberation of women. Following liberal feminism came a recognition that the liberal ideal of equality would only render women *equal to men*. Accordingly, radical or difference feminism emerged with attention to women's specific identities. But the problem with this 'second-wave' feminism was its assumption that women's identity existed and was knowable. In due course, then, feminism entered a third-wave, or a deconstructive, phase: one in which women's identity was affirmed at the same time as it was recognised that such an identity was constituted rather than given, and multiple rather than simple (Moi 1985; Braidotti 1991). And it is in this third-wave, or poststructuralist, phase, that feminism encounters the work of Gilles Deleuze.

However, this standard way of thinking about feminism's history presents the picture of a series of ambivalent daughters directing less than dutiful questions to their philosophical fathers.[1] It's as though we needed Marx to challenge liberalism, Freud to challenge Marxism, and Derrida to challenge Freud. But perhaps it's better to look at feminism as a different type of theoretical heritage, where questions have always been voiced in terms of what thought might become (rather than the correctness of this or that model). Thus, feminism might not be seen as an accompaniment to the transition from liberalism through Marxism to postmodernity, but more as an ongoing and active suggestion that thought might be more than a *genealogy*. Rather than understanding itself as the unfolding or progression of reason, feminist questions have more often than not been directed to interventions, encounters, forma-tions of identity and productive becomings. To use Deleuze and Guattari's terminology, we might supplant the notion of genealogy with *geology*: the creation of new terrains, different lines of thought and extraneous wanderings that are not at home in the philoso-phical terrain (Deleuze and Guattari 1987: 41).

What all this seems to suggest is that feminism finally finds itself when it becomes Deleuzean. But this would be far from the case. Indeed, it was precisely these notions of becoming, multiplic-ity and immanence that created the most anxiety when Deleuze's work was first encountered by feminists. Broadly speaking, the con-cerns regarding the force of Deleuze's work took the form of two questions. First, just how valuable is a philosophy that does away with the subject (given that feminism is only beginning to gain some sense of identity)? Second, isn't the elevation of 'becoming-woman' not one more cannibalisation of an image of women for a flagging male reason?² Before answering these questions – if an answer is possible – we have to recognise that they illuminate the key *risks* of the Deleuzean endeavour. And there is no thought without risk. To do away with the subject is to do away with any ground or home for thought; thought becomes nomadic. For feminism, doing away with the subject places what was for a long time an emancipatory discourse on an insecure footing. If feminism has no subject, then for whom does it speak, and what is it hoping to achieve? If feminism is neither the expression nor the formation of a subject, what is it?

A Deleuzean answer is, in many ways, not so much an answer as another question. Can feminism be a subject or identity when these concepts have for so long acted to ground or subordinate thought? Perhaps, then, feminism is a becoming, and much of its history suggests that it is. But is it a becoming that can be identified with, or seen as exemplary of, a general becoming? Why is 'becoming-woman' the key to all becomings?

If becoming has traditionally been subordinated to the proper *becoming of* some prior being, then becoming has always been understood reactively, as the epiphenomenon of some present ground. There is, therefore, a connection between subjectivism and the subordination of becoming. As Nietzsche pointed out, the subject might indeed be an accident of grammar. Our statements assume a subject–predicate structure. We assume a being that does this or that; we posit a doer behind the deed (1967: 45). Rather than think the groundless event or act we tend to posit some being who then acts or a ground that then becomes. When the 'subject' emerges in modern thought this is, as both Deleuze and Nietzsche insist, no shift or terrain at all; there has always been a subject-function in philosophy: the location of thought within a speaker. And it is this structure – that there is always a subject, ground, or presence that precedes predication – that both Deleuze and Nietzsche try to overcome through a project of becoming. In so doing their main target becomes clear: man. The problem with the human is not that it is one concept among others, but that it presents itself as the origin of all concepts, as the presence from which all concepts arise or become. A becoming that is not subjected to being, or a creative concept of becoming, would need to direct itself against man. One strategy of becoming would be to think woman. For it is woman that blocks or jams the conceptual machinery that grounds man. If man understands himself, not as the effect of a concept but as the ground of all concepts and speech, how can he account for woman? This is why there can be no 'becoming man' (Deleuze and Guattari 1987: 291), for man or the human has always taken itself as the ground of becoming. Woman offers herself as a privileged becoming in so far as she short-circuits the self-evident identity of man. Thus Deleuze's celebration of 'becoming-woman' begins by turning the concept of man around (or activating a reactivism). If man is the concept of being then his other is the beginning of becoming.

Nevertheless, the questions feminism has directed to this strategy of becoming cannot be answered or allayed by appealing to the true meaning or function of Deleuze's work. Not only would such a gesture be anti-Deleuzean, it would suggest that the value and force of concepts could be determined in advance – as though concepts in themselves were good or evil, safe or risk-laden. On the contrary, the task that confronts feminism in its confrontation with Deleuze is whether a philosophy of becoming, or becoming-woman, can be made to work. And if there is no pre-determined end towards which a philosophy of becoming can direct its work, then we might also have to think a new concept of the theoretical work. Indeed, this has already begun in recent feminist writing. If thought is not directed towards an image of good thinking but sets itself the task of thinking otherwise, then feminism might less be a task of emancipation, and more the challenge of differentiation. This might provide the way of thinking new modes of becoming – not as the becoming *of* some subject, but a becoming towards others, a becoming towards difference, and a becoming through new questions.

It is in this spirit of positive becoming that the essays in this volume encounter the work of Deleuze and Deleuze and Guattari. As Verena Andermatt Conley's location of Deleuze and Guattari's work within its own post-1968 Parisian terrain makes clear, the link between woman and becoming formed part of a general movement. The fact that there are resonances between the notions of becoming-woman and Hélène Cixous's writing-woman is more than an interesting point of convergence in the history of ideas. It demonstrates that the contemporary encounter between Deleuze and feminism – explored in this volume – is more than the addition of two separate lines of thought. As Conley's essay demonstrates, questions of writing, woman, becoming, identity and style formed a philosophical and creative plane at the time Deleuze was writing. In this regard, then, the use of becoming-woman in the Deleuzean corpus would be less an act of appropriation, as it was first taken to be, and more a form of address: an encounter or event within a field of thought that was attempting to become other than itself. If Deleuze's work has, then, from its very creation already been an encounter with the question of woman, it is not surprising that so many essays in this volume are able to negotiate the event of Deleuze through the events of other acts of writing-woman. And, as Conley insists, the importance of writing in Deleuze still presents us with a challenge: can feminism be the affirmation of an event and not one more grounding narrative? This places the question of becoming as a challenge rather than a position. De Beauvoir, Cixous, Kristeva, Irigaray and Le Doeuff occupy the terrain of a question, a question also traversed by Deleuze and Guattari: if we don't yet know what woman is, how can we think what she might become?

The best way of negotiating this question is perhaps by reopening that troubled determination of women's becoming: Oedipus. The problem with psychoanalysis, despite appearances, is its negation of desire. The psychoanalyst presents his story, not as a movement or event of desire, but as the mere interpretation, recovery or revelation of the analysand's truth. Oedipus is, then, yet one more reactive figure of man: an event of thought – the story of Oedipus – is used to explain thought in general. In *Anti-Oedipus* Deleuze and Guattari did not disagree with or dispute psycho-analysis; they activated it. The story of Oedipus must itself be seen as an event of desire, and as a story alongside other stories in a field of codings and becomings. No single story can transcend or ground the field in general; the phallus is an investment among others and not the translation of all investments. In the second volume of *Capitalism and Schizophrenia*, Deleuze and Guattari nego-tiate this problem of a multiplicity of desiring events through becoming-woman. If psychoanalysis has its heritage in the geneal-ogy of the human, then perhaps a becoming woman will disrupt the inherently normalising function of the human sciences. This is the question explored by Jerry Aline Flieger, who exposes the centrality and risk of becoming woman (as becoming imperceptible) in Deleuze and Guattari's project. Set against identity politics, sub-jectivism and essentialism, 'becoming woman' precedes all 'molar' identifications; in so doing becoming seems to have lost not only its feminist but also its political force. But Flieger insists that we should not see feminist identity politics and Deleuzean becoming as mutually exclusive, or as the basis of a choice between two possi-bilities. The molar politics of identities and the molecular politics of becoming are not opposed; but the latter must be thought and confronted as the possibility and mobilisation of the former. There is nothing bad or evil about identity, or women's politics. There is some justification for the feminist worries about Deleuze's attacks on identity and macropolitics, but these need to be dealt with by activating the Deleuzean corpus – an activation begun by Flieger herself in her rereading of Freud's case study of Judge Schreber. There was always a political dimension to Freud's study (including the recognised anti-Semitism of his day) – a macropolitical dimension elided in Deleuze's critique of Freud. By retrieving and re-rereading Freud, Flieger opens Deleuze's molecular politics to other determinations, and once again activates the possibilities of the psychoanalytic corpus by producing new encounters.

We can see then what Deleuze might be made to *do* if his work is read and repeated alongside other questions. While Flieger speaks back to Deleuze through a repetition of Freud, Catherine Driscoll and Dorothea Olkowski open the Deleuzean terrain through the questions offered by Julia Kristeva and Luce Irigaray: both of whom have also troubled the notion of the subject, but in ways that are ostensibly antithetical to a straightforward affirmation of becoming. Driscoll's chapter explores the status of the girl in relation to the problem of becoming, a problem addressed by Deleuze and Kristeva, but also by Virginia Woolf and the project of modernism. Like Flieger, Driscoll also sees the notion of becoming as crucial in the deterritorialisation of Oedipus, in freeing thought from a single identity or destiny. Both Deleuze and Kristeva, she argues, were united in acknowledging that 'woman' could not be appealed to as the simple other of 'man', and that feminism might then not be one movement among others but a new way of thinking movements or becoming: no longer a movement 'owned' by identities, but a movement of desires, bodies, flows and *style*. For Driscoll, then, becoming is not the becoming *of* woman, but a becoming that exceeds the dual identities of man and woman, hence the significance of Woolf's androgyny.

Dorothea Olkowski's interrogation of Deleuze, woman and becoming also sets off from the feminist corpus. This time the negotiation is through Luce Irigaray. If Deleuze presents the horror of a loss of identity to the feminist movement, then Irigaray seems to present the other extreme risk, essentialism. It is this ostensible opposition between non-identity and essence that Olkowski pulls apart, for both Deleuze and Irigaray attempt to think beyond these sorts of dualisms. An encounter between the two might give feminist thought a new way of proceeding, such that neither the subject nor becoming would govern a feminist programme. Rather, Deleuze and Irigaray might be read in order to effect new ways of asking feminist questions: questions beyond determinations of identity, essentialism, emancipation and representation. This possibility of new questions and new problems is also explored by Claire Colebrook. It might seem that feminists would have to decide how to think sexual difference, whether to 'use' Irigaray, Derrida or Deleuze. Framing the question in this way suggests that there is some truth to sexual difference and we only need to find the right theory. What Deleuze offers, though, is a different way of thinking questions. Sexual difference is not an issue within theories. The question of sexual difference challenged just the way in which theory has been undertaken. It's not a question of finding the truth of difference, so much as asking how the concept of sexual difference has allowed thought to move, to create and to become.

But if thought is a movement and becoming, if there is an emphasis on concepts, difference and other abstractions, what has happened to that feminist concept *par excellence*: the body? As Eleanor Kaufman argues, one of the main mobilisations of the work of Deleuze in feminist scholarship has been in theories of the body. If thought is the movement of desire then thought cannot be isolated in some pure Cartesian realm. Rosi Braidotti, Moira Gatens and Elizabeth Grosz used the work of Deleuze to explode the self-presence of the subject through the notion of embodiment. However, as Kaufman insists, once Cartesian dualism is challenged we also have to rethink the notion of mind, as itself a force, becoming and event. But while Kaufman wants to draw attention to Deleuzean notions of mind as becoming, Nicole Shukin raises questions as to Deleuze's troubled relation to certain body parts. Drawing on a remark Deleuze made in an interview in which he states that he prefers to eat tongue, brains and marrow (although eating in general is boring), Shukin explores the politics and determinations of Deleuze's preferences. It is as though brain (intelligence), tongue, (speech) and marrow (bodily transportation) repeated in monstrous form the very ideals of patriarchy. What is evidenced in Deleuze's celebration of body parts, the essential boredom of eating, and the affirmation of deterritorialisations is an elision of the empirical determinations of these events: the politics of bodies and food, the patriarchal derision of domesticity and food production, and the ethnographic zeal that splits between the raw and the cooked. In this essay Shukin opens the possibility of doing Deleuzean things with Deleuze: what are the desires and figurations of this text, what positions does it carve out, and how is it placed in a broader field of desire?

Deleuze, then, is more than the presentation of a theory. His corpus is also a challenge to work, create and effect – rather than interpret. Cinema, for example, is not just the unfolding of narrative, nor the presentation of desired objects for desiring viewers; cinema is a surface of intensities, effects of colour and movement, and an event that cannot be contained within a subject's point of view. And this raises implications for a feminist politics that has, in the past, been primarily concerned with subject positions. It is this possibility of film – as event rather than representation – that is effected in Camilla Benolirao Griggers' own highly cinematic writing. Griggers does not interpret film; she creates a series of plateaus that effect new ways of looking, new effects that dislocate the standard location of film from the intending subject. Griggers stretches filmic impressions across a space of history and concepts, providing new ways of thinking film and the identities film *creates* (and not the identities it putatively represents or expresses). Griggers' mobilisation of Deleuzean concepts – from becoming-woman to Griggers' own 'Filipina-becoming' – raises the question of the future of Deleuze, the becoming of Deleuze and the problem of thinking *from* Deleuze, rather than remaining faithful to the corpus. In a similar manner Rosi Braidotti rereads Deleuze in relation to the postmodern. Deleuze is neither dismissed as one more sign of a postmodern malaise of dehumanisation. Nor is Deleuze celebrated as the harbinger of post-human cyber-liberation. Braidotti charts the conflicting possibilities for the future enabled by what her essay explores as the 'teratological' imaginary.

Elizabeth Grosz, whose work on Deleuze and the body has already transformed feminism, now uses Deleuze to address the question of transformation itself. For Grosz, the issue presented by Deleuze has moved from the specificity of bodies and desires, to the movement of the virtual. Grosz's argument is not a straightforward uncovering of a project or deep meaning in Deleuze's texts. Rather, Grosz weaves her own reading of Bergson back through Deleuze's use of Bergson to ask whether there might be a politics of the future. Given the ostensible demise of the emancipationist historicisms of Marxism, Hegelianism and liberal progressivism, it is the openness of the virtual that can now provide a way of thinking the event of a future not determined by the proper inauguration of an origin. Indeed, as Grosz's argument demonstrates, the idea

16

that the future is a thing of the past – condemned to the otiose revolutionary paradigms of the 1970s – itself needs to be re-cast. For Bergson and Deleuze the future is a thing of the past, but this is precisely because the past is not a thing. The past is the possibility of a mobile and active present. Any movement of utopianism or any politics of the future is perhaps best thought of through a Deleuzean notion of becoming, a becoming that refuses to know what or where it is, a becoming that embraces all those questions and problems that have precluded thought from being at home with itself – including the thought of woman.

NOTES

1. And, of course, even the first- to third-wave picture is more complex than the passage from liberalism, through radicalism to post-structuralism. Wollstonecraft immediately saw the need to vindicate the rights of *woman*; Marxist feminists were, from the beginning, intent on broadening the notion of production; and neither psychoanalysis nor poststructuralism were accepted without intense question and challenge.
2. The summary of this debate is given in Grosz (1993b).

1

Becoming-Woman Now

VERENA ANDERMATT CONLEY

Only recently and reluctantly have feminists taken a positive turn in the direction of Gilles Deleuze's philosophy. Where the texts of Jacques Derrida and Jacques Lacan have been a mainstay of feminist theories of subjectivity for several decades, welcoming receptions of Deleuze's philosophy have been few and far apart. The reasons for this fact may be attributed to geography: Derrida and Paul de Man were the subject of intense scrutiny in the development of the 'Yale School' of deconstruction in the 1970s that located the origins of sexual difference in enunciation. As utterers of inherited idioms, they argued, we quickly discover that language tends to mold our identity before we have anything to say about it. Only by working into an actively performative relation with language do we, as 'subjects', begin to alter its formative effects. The Yale School gained renown as a site where French theories of subjectivity (and hence, of female identity) were developed in America. The success was a function of the participants who established lines of exchange between Paris and New Haven. Deleuze, by contrast, did not travel; in the 1970s he taught in the Philosophy Department at the University of Paris-VIII and published copiously through the Editions de Minuit. Reception of his work outside of France has forcibly been slower.

If the philosopher was mentioned or discussed, it was mainly in critical terms, as exemplified in Alice Jardine's early reading, a first extensive critical assessment made available to anglophone readers (Jardine 1984). Jardine eloquently questions the expression coined by Deleuze and his intercessor Félix Guattari, 'becoming-woman', by which woman as a reality is made to disappear. Worse,

18

woman is the first to vanish while man – in their idiolect, a 'molar', or self-contained entity that contrasts the 'molecular' or more fluid virtues of generally feminine valence – remains intact. Jardine wanted to establish a woman-subject with an identity prior to the advent of any notion of becoming-other. Following Simone de Beauvoir's axiom ('one is not born a woman, one becomes one'), Jardine argued that first one is and then one risks oneself or becomes.

The status of the gendered subject has indeed been crucial to most contemporary debates that are far from reaching closure. We can recall that prior to the Yale School, in order to counter Western anthropocentrism, structuralists had evacuated the subject – Man – altogether from the horizon of the social sciences.[1] In their wake, most post-1968 philosophers and cultural theorists, though often critical of structuralism have, on the one hand, avoided going back to prestructural attachments that hold to phenomenology and ego-psychology and, on the other, have refrained from keeping in focus the full historical subject. Deleuze and Guattari, like Derrida, Cixous, Lyotard and others, are critical of neo-Hegelianism in its postwar Marxist or existentialist forms. They write not against but *away* from the negativity and sublation that had been an anathema to French feminism. They write *away* from a unified subject for whom the other is merely a mirrored reflection of the self. They search for other structures – or structures-other – unknown, not yet here, always to come, which cannot easily be identified by language. Identity for them is imposed by given codes that define the subject from spaces outside of his or her body. Never far from an 'identity card', it limits and subjects. They search for ways out, in other words, for exits or *sorties* from the confines of a disciplinary society. For them the subject, always more than the names imposed upon it, continually reinvents itself, even though *how* such reinvention is carried out varies from one individual to another.

In their analyses of continental writings of the 1970s, Anglo-Saxon feminists have often condemned the absence of subjectivity. Concepts in the continental tradition, it is often argued, prevail to the detriment of real people; relations are treated in abstraction, which seems distant from the feeling or emotion that mark subjectivity. To date, the notion of an identity that will only *subsequently* be modified continues to be the topic of much feminist theory under the influence of psychoanalysis as well as communitarian identity politics. In such a political climate, a sympathetic reassessment of Deleuze's (and Guattari's) passages on becoming-woman now comes as somewhat of a surprise. Camilla Benolirao Griggers, Elizabeth Grosz, Dorothea Olkowski, Patricia Pisters and other feminist theorists are rereading the philosophers' writings more sympathetically. Is it because they are more secure and have more of an 'identity' now? Because women have had time to think of becoming? Or, is it, as Griggers suggests, that caught in the most alienating capitalist network of forces, becoming is even more limited and, therefore, it is more important than ever to address it now? That not only men but women too are molar? (Griggers 1997). In the pages to follow I wish to reconsider the controversial expression 'becoming-woman', but rather than rehearsing the debates about its respective merit, I also wish to do minor violence to Deleuze's (and Guattari's) text by reinserting it in the political, social and cultural context of its elaboration and by following its evolution both in the philosophers' writings and in its formative milieu.

Even though Deleuze (and Guattari's) philosophy tends to eschew chronology, the elaboration of their concepts is not without context. The expression 'becoming-woman' is first developed in *A Thousand Plateaus* (in French in 1980) the second volume to the *Anti-Oedipus* (in French in 1972) subtitled 'Capitalism and Schizophrenia'. Deleuze takes as his authorial intercessor Félix Guattari, a detail that has its importance. In *Pourparlers* (1990a) Deleuze states that the second volume, published eight years after the first, had been their most poorly received book. Indeed, next to Deleuze's often arduous philosophical rereadings of Hume (1953), Nietzsche (Deleuze 1983), Spinoza (1968), Leibniz (begun in the context of Proust in 1964) and others, *A Thousand Plateaus*, emphasising becomings, rhizomatics, multiplicities, lines of flight, is set apart from the style and orientation of the properly philosophical essays. Most 'plateaus' were written in the 1970s, in the aftermath of the revolution of May 1968, when, for a brief moment, before order was re-established in France, it seemed possible to bring about other ways of being – and becoming – than those dictated by capitalist political economy.[2] *The Anti-Oedipus* had shown how Oedipus is a handmaiden to capitalist economy. By making Oedipus into some kind of a foundation, psychoanalysis, in the service of capitalism, had neutralised the unconscious.[3] It had made the latter into a theatre rather than a locus of production in conflict. It had regulated the sexes and stifled desire. After exposing some of the complicities and making *tabula rasa* of the Oedipus complex, *A Thousand Plateaus* proposes some alternatives. These plateaus open the prison of the logic of meaning and of the Oedipal subject; they focus on multiplicities, on becoming and an intensity of desire. To the Oedipal molar constructs, they oppose the nomadic Body Without Organs (BWO), multivalent, smooth and open to production on the inside as well as to making connections on the outside. For them, the social signifiers impose castration rather than some personal relation to separation that stifles the subject and prevents true becomings from happening.

There is a method in the philosophers' molecular madness. Blurring the division between subject and object, *A Thousand Plateaus* writes of desire, trajectories, molecular flows of various speeds, intensities and becoming-woman without forgetting other concepts elaborated elsewhere, particularly that of the univocality of being, in lieu of the various binary constructs such as self and other or the divided subject that have currency with other philosophers and analysts. Rather than following Saussurean linguistics with its definition of the sign based on the opposition of signifier and signified, Deleuze and Guattari take a nod to Hjelmslev's theory of language that reads utterances according to forms of content and forms of expression. When mobilised to launch a critique of Lacan, this affiliation enables them to downplay the emphasis on epistemology while focusing on ontology.[4]

Yet, by means of rhizomatics and nomadism, Deleuze does not simply argue for 'connectedness' of subjects as does Donna Haraway, who refuses Oedipus and the entire clinical apparatus (Haraway 1991).[5] He and Guattari, finding that the Freudian fact is in our era – a moment of historicisation in their work – still unsurpassable despite massive transformations in all areas, argue against Oedipus and for another psychoanalysis based on a productive, auto-poetic, unconscious.[6] Far from repeating the same scenario, the unconscious, by means of slips, parapraxes or symptoms, opens to becomings. No longer under the sway of a death drive and repetition, unconscious production is real and turned towards life.

Life as process and work in progress! The production is double, without being simply voluntary or linked to agency. Rhizomatic processes are, in other words, lines, or trajectories open to becomings. The philosopher does not state that there is no being, but the latter consists of a temporary assemblage of partial components and effects of subjectivation. Being, the moment of arrest in the roll of the dice, is always open to, and traversed by, becomings that are more than simple transformations of an existing real. Virtualities actualise entirely new assemblages in time and space.

21

Becoming (*devenir*) differs from the realising of possibles and is not entirely under the sway of rational or diurnal control.[7] As a philosopher, Deleuze deals with these concepts and their genesis through arduously creative readings of other philosophers' texts. We could follow their elaboration in the text as a form of 'apprenticeship in philosophy',[8] but here, I propose instead to contextualise the concepts that subtend the complex hyphenated expression, 'becoming-woman', by continuing to reinsert them into a complex cultural environment.

Many of Deleuze's pleas for mobility and becomings were made in a special context of May 1968 that he called an 'Intempestif', a becoming, an irruption of pure virtuality from which something new had been created (1990a: 231). From this emergent context we can read about intensity of desire, unlimited movements and metamorphoses, the doing-away with Oedipus as regulator of the subject and the socius, the critique of molar man and the insertion of the expression, becoming-woman, in which the emphasis bears on becomings, on an irreducible multiplicity rather than on woman. It is also here, in the same cultural climate, that we can reiterate the premisses of some feminist writings, such as those by Hélène Cixous of synchronous publication. Deleuze and Guattari's notion of becoming-woman emerged from the same post-1968 context as Hélène Cixous's Newly Born Woman, a concept that merits, no less than BWO, the acronym of NBW (Cixous 1975). Both undo the self-identical subject, open the self to metamorphoses and becomings. They write out of a set of historical conditions in which terms are caught. The Body Without Organs (BWO) does away with mental and physical obstacles and smoothes out space. It is not without echoes at a certain level of Cixous's Newly Born Woman (NBW), who continually engenders herself through passages of the other in herself and of herself in the other. In French, NBW reads as *là-je-une-nais*, 'here I give myself birth [sic] as one'. The concept is less machinic and more organic than the BWO, and it, too, predicated on the couple of self and other, is also open to becomings.

The writer intersects with the philosopher on several points. Cixous in *Prénoms de personne* (First names of nobody, 1974a) and in 'Sorties' in *The Newly Born Woman*, writes of unlimited becomings and of ongoing transformations of Western thought. She strives to undermine the unified subject equated with deadly forms of narcissism, as a means to changing social and political structures altogether.[9] To write oneself (out of painful situations) and to singularise through recourse to aesthetics and ethics, away from grammars of repression, were tantamount to engaging in a poetic revolution that would open the way to – the still modernist notion of – political revolution. Artists, more than theorists of all stripes, were felt to be endowed with 'radar' like antennae, more capable of 'perceiving' virtualities or structures-other. As Freud had once remarked, artists are always ahead of common men. Theories follow or sum up the more vital but inchoate works of art.

The opening sentence of Cixous's *Prénoms de personne* (1974a) has the ring of a manifesto: 'I ask of writing what I ask of desire: that it have no relationship with the logic that puts desire on the side of possession, acquisition, consumerism-consumption [*con-sommation-consumation*] which, so gloriously pushed to the end, links (mis)knowledge with death. I do not think that writing – as production of desire, where desire is capable of everything – can be or has to be defined through the border of death' (Cixous 1974a: 15). The allusions to Deleuze's *Logic of Sense* are obvious and a debt is recognised. There is infinite belief in transformations, in freeing the individual from social constraints and laws. Cixous's concern is to affirm life and to eradicate (metaphoric) death. 'It will be a question of limitless life, of all life, in these texts: a question, I say, for they all have in common this question which they answer in various ways, of the possibility of something limitless' (1974a: 15). Writing engages 'what is happening in this non-locus (*non-lieu*) that cannot really be described, represented and that the word "fiction" designates a troubling, moving adventure beyond genres and oppositions, where the real is not defined by its contrary, where the literary is not an emanation of something else to be printed, where a phantasm is not simply filling a gap, where desire is not a dream, where, in the plusreal, the elsewhere to come is announced' (1974a: 16). Writing, thus, moves *across* the bar of castration that would yoke the creative agency to collective and common sense. An excess, as the style of the excerpt shows, drives the writer across Freudian borders.

Across her readings of Freud, Kleist and others, Cixous reads how fiction actualises virtualities. She scorns representational literature that would but serve as a mirror to society, and repeat clichés to ensure further the functioning of a group. To this mercantile idea of literature based on representation of 'reality' by means of characters that mime the effects of everyday life, she proposes scenes of intensity and desire. Through a practice of grafting of words and sounds from other texts, the *thing* writes itself not as something hidden to be revealed but as an effect of surfaces grafted on to each other. A stratigraphy resembling the plan of *A Thousand Plateaus* results. In a delirious procession of masks, doubles and quotes, poets and revolutionaries enter and exit: Marx, Freud, Shakespeare, Dante, Hölderlin, Milton, Poe. Myths and their allegorical messages are exploded, castration is mocked through a rewriting of the mythological couples.

Délire, delirium, with its echoes of undoing conventional reading, crime, production of words and process, makes Cixous's text resonate with those of Deleuze. Writing at a moment when the novelty of theories outdid their divergences, she combines a notion of a desiring machine, of a positive desire, with that of the Derridean notion of same and/in other. Of importance for our purposes is her assertion of an indomitable, unlimited production of desire that capitalist society, with the help of psychoanalysis, reins in. Any access to desire then cannot come about without a change in political and libidinal economy, without a transformation of capitalism *and* of psychoanalysis. Deleuze asserts: 'The true difference of nature is not between the symbolic and the imaginary, but between the REAL element of the machinic that constitutes the desiring production and the structural ensemble of imaginary and symbolic that only forms a myth and its variants' (Deleuze and Guattari 1977: 271). For him, a delirious production replaces images fixed into myth or allegory. He declares that Oedipus is in fact literary before being psychoanalytic: 'There will always be a Breton against Artaud, a Goethe against Lenz, a Schiller against Hölderlin, in order to superegoize literature and tell us: Careful go no further!' (1977). And he adds: 'Literature must be process. At least, spare us sublimation! Every writer is a sellout!' For Deleuze and Guattari, women's movements issuing from 1969 contain the 'requirements of liberation: the force of the unconscious itself, the investment by desire of the social field, the disinvestment of repressive structures' (1977: 61). The question is not of knowing whether women are 'castrated' but whether 'the unconscious "believes" it' (61). And they ask, 'What is an unconscious that no longer does anything but 'believe' rather than produce?' (61). Deleuze and Guattari denounce literature that bears the mark of castration and subscribes to Oedipal norms. This is not to say that they write against either literature or psychoanalysis but that they argue for a different kind of literature and another form of psychoanalysis as process and invention.

That is where they intersect with the concepts guiding the

fiction of Hélène Cixous, who equally sees writing as non-representational, as process, and who argues against a literature of
commodification as well as a psychoanalysis based on castration
(Cixous 1974b). In 'Sorties' she writes: 'If there is a self proper to
woman, paradoxically it is her capacity to dispropriate herself
without self-interest; if she is a whole made up of parts that are
wholes, not simple, partial objects but varied entirely, moving and
boundless change, a cosmos where eros never stops travelling, a
vast astral space. She doesn't revolve around a sun that is more star
than the stars.'

And, she continues, 'this does not mean that she is undifferen-
tiated magma, it means that she doesn't create a monarchy of her
body or her desire. Let masculine sexuality gravitate around the
penis, engendering this centralized body (political anatomy) under
the party dictatorship. Woman doesn't perform on herself this
regionalization that profits the couple head-sex, that only inscribes
itself within frontiers' (93). Production of desire does not go back
to an origin (distinct from a source) but tends towards the mapping
of new territories: 'Not the origin: she doesn't go back there. A
boy's journey is the return to the native land, the *Heimweg* Freud
speaks of, the nostalgia that makes man a being who tends to come
back to the point of departure to appropriate it for himself and
to die there. A girl's journey is farther – to the unknown, to invent'
(93).

Cixous – like Deleuze – posits two sexes and psychic consequences
of these differences. But they cannot be reduced to the ones that
Freudian analysis designates. Starting from the relationship of the
two sexes to the Oedipus complex, boy and girl are steered towards
a division of social roles. If there are two sexes, there is no more
destiny than nature or essence. There are living structures caught
within historical and cultural limits mixed up with the scene of
History in such a way that it has been impossible to think or even
imagine an elsewhere. We are now, for Cixous, living in a transi-
tional period, one in which it seems possible to think that the
classic structure might split and open to becoming. This period, in
1968 and its aftermath, concerns the possibility of transition
towards a non-phallocentric *and* non-capitalist space outside of a
deadly and reappropriating dialectic.

Becomings will be initiated primarily by women. Since man is
called to the scene of castration more than woman and since he
has more to lose than she in the present order of things, it will be
easier for women to experiment with changes and, in the process,

to bring about changes in men. Cixous declares that the de-oedi-palisation of women, their becoming, their access to real desire – not one based on lack – does not go without a general change in all the structures of training, education, supervision, hence in the structures of reproduction of ideological results. 'Let us imagine a real liberation of sexuality, that is to say, a transformation of each one's relationship to his or her body (and to the other body). This cannot be accomplished without political transformations that are equally radical' (1974b: 83). Emphasis is on political and sexual transformation and on invention. It means that there is no invention possible, whether it be philosophical or poetic, without there being in the inventing subject 'an abundance of the other, of variety: separate people, thought-/people, whole populations issu- ing from the unconscious, and in each suddenly animated desert, the springing up of selves one didn't know' (84). Of importance, as for Deleuze, is the need to de-oedipalise, to 'de-mater-paternalize': 'One has to get out of the dialectic that claims that the child is its parents' death. The child is the other but the other without violence. The other rhythm, the pure freshness, the possible's body' (84) The girl is present in every woman. There is no dialectical progression. The body keeps its possibles, its virtualities, its power (*potestas*) in a Spinozist sense.

Cixous and Deleuze wind their critique of the full, historical (male) subject through a stringent critique of capitalism. They both emphasise becomings and militate against the Oedipal theatre that benefits those in power. Yet, clear differences are already perceptible. Now, where becoming and multiplicities in Cixous are related to a critique of metaphysics, Deleuze insists rather on an other metaphysics. For Cixous, Cartesian metaphysics separates subject and object, inside and outside, high and low. It creates social hierarchies and exclusions. It inaugurated an era which has just come to a close. She deconstructs metaphysics by reintroducing time in space and the other in the same. Deleuze, however, searches for another metaphysics. He looks to an alternative tradition, in which force is of importance in the elaboration of becoming. The concepts thus formed are not those of a wilful subject. They are defined by a communicable force in relation to which the 'subject' – such as woman – is but an effect.

Yet, both Cixous and Deleuze emphasise multiplicities and mil- itate against the Oedipal theatre that benefits those in power. Both share notions of becoming, intensity, production of positive desire, the absence of a logic of meaning, and both write against Oedipus as a masculine invention. Identity is imposed from the outside and produces arrestations, in a historical context, from which one has to turn away. The body is less the visible phenomenological entity than a locus producing an affect. Nobody knows what a body is capable of, writes Deleuze, quoting Spinoza. And Cixous echoes, as if in dialogue: Which one will I be? How far can I go? There are human beings marked men and women. They have biological bodies that are never natural but always culturally inflected, always ciphered by their surroundings. There are psychic differences of the sexes but the latter can never be entirely separated from cultural differences. Bodies are neither natural nor essential; they are marked, not determined. They are 'situated' in a context. Yet, becomings continually alter bodies and contexts on the bases of future markings. To begin, Oedipalisation along with fetishisation and castration – deterministic traits that delimit and imprison the sexes – have to be done away with. They are but words that fix terms in a universalising configuration.

Here, it is important to distinguish levels and to choose one's discourse. Both Cixous and Deleuze make it clear: philosophy or writing cannot be confused with law, government, science or religion. These are real powers. Both philosophers and poets can write against power by carrying on a kind of guerilla warfare. Since people internalise the schemas of power, they can also lead a kind of guerilla warfare against themselves (Deleuze 1990a; Cixous 1991). But fiction or philosophy can only enter in negotiation with the discourses of real power.

In Cixous as well as in Deleuze and Guattari, the 'winter years' of the 1980s downplay the exuberance of the tenor of their earlier writings. In this decade the poet and the philosopher continue to write against various forms of oppression and denounce the absence of ethics in the ideology of postmodernism. Cixous at times calls her writings of these years 'difficult joys'. The emphasis in their respective writings change. For Cixous the importance of the question of sexual difference recedes or at least is complicated by the irruption of other pressing problems that include apartheid, the gulag, political oppression in the Far East, or deception by the French state in respect to its egalitarian principles. The emphasis placed on sexuality recedes, and the limitless is less prominent. The latter is felt in the undoing of limits in the form of censorship or repression for the sake of giving voice to others. Similarly, in Deleuze there is a slowing down; the multiplicity of 'tiny sexes' takes on lesser importance, although the philosopher continues to preoccupy himself with actualisation of virtualities. *A Thousand Plateaus* continues to be a manual of polemology available to subjects who live under the regime of global capitalism as a system of immanence that continually pushes back its own limits. Rather than disengaging the social contradictions of a given society, Deleuze continues to focus on what escapes it, on what he calls its lines of flight. Here, he resonates with Cixous, who declares: *Je vole*, I steal and I fly. What one steals, or poaches, how one draws one's lines of flight will change over the decades.

Neither Deleuze nor Guattari lived long enough after the Fall of the Berlin Wall in 1989 to witness globalisation in its present stage. They sensed it coming and were among the first to denounce, what they called, the society of control. They denounced the political apathy and continued to polemicise their thought after the fall of one of the last great concrete walls. Like the creative feminist writer, they continued to undo other, invisible, walls. They never abandoned futurology for memorialisation or the kind of melancholia to which even Hélène Cixous, at times, seems to succumb. They argued for an unconscious in terms of its trajectories, lines of flight and becomings. The latter are more limited in the new era of global markets that make an equivalence between natural goods, cultural goods and money. The philosophers deplored the absence of real becomings within the present vertical and horizontal intensification of capitalist structures. Yet, they recognised that markets are here to stay. What interested them was 'the analysis of capitalism as an immanent system which does not cease to push back its own limits, and which always finds them again at a larger scale, because the limit is Capital itself' (Deleuze 1990a: 232).

Critical of technosciences that did not bring about social progress, Deleuze and Guattari denounced the lack of solidarity among humans and the absence of subjectivity inaugurated by the globalisation of the media. Humans are forced to live in a world of clichés. By means of prefabricated images, many women, feminists included, have tended also to become molar. In order to actualise becomings one has to have a vision or see the image in the cliché. Deleuze studied not its fixity but the general side of its emergence: 'Becoming is not history. History only designates a set of conditions however recent they may be, from which one turns away in order to "become," that is, in order to create something new. This is what Nietzsche calls the "Intempestif"' (Guattari 1989; Deleuze 1990a: 231). For Deleuze, May 1968 was the manifestation, the irruption of a becoming in its pure form. He added: 'Today, it is

28

fashionable to denounce the horrors of revolution. This is not new . . . One says that revolutions have a bad future. But one does not cease to confuse two things, the future of revolutions in history and the becoming revolutionary of people . . . The only chance for humans is to become revolutionary in order to conjure up shame, or to answer the intolerable' (1990a: 231).

It is in this sense that Cixous's NBW too was never quite here, always to come; it is the girl who perpetually lives in the woman: closer to the 'origin', that is, birth, and always in becoming: History as a configuration in which terms are caught, as a set of conditions from which one can turn. In Deleuze too, woman is never done with becoming, she is never done with becoming imperceptible, that is, with going back through a kind of zero degree that makes possible mutations and new becomings. Not the Histories of Feminism! Not the Future of Feminism! But the becoming feminist of women *and* men! Women and their (virtual) bodies exist only in contexts from which they continue to turn away.

In the philosopher's later work, specific references to women are rare and appear only in the context of other political issues. Women's struggles, the infrequency of allusions implies, cannot be abstracted from other political, social or ecological struggles. Like Cixous, Deleuze and Guattari distinguish between militantism and artistic creation. As Deleuze puts it: 'To write is to struggle, to resist; to write is to become, to write is to trace maps' (Deleuze 1990a: 231). Militating is done in the streets, by 'good, little soldiers' (Guattari 1989: 29). As such, women's struggles are seen as part of long-term changes (in the sense of Fernand Braudel) rather than in terms of historical continuity. It is part of an evolving complexity with moments of bifurcations and mutations. For women artists, writers, painters, filmmakers, in the present era of standardisation and slogans, at stake is always a resingularising, or particularising to the point of universalising, of, once again, becoming minoritarian, of embracing aesthetics and ethics rather than a militant reductionism.

That the women's struggle cannot be separated entirely from a capitalist economy has today been all too readily forgotten, especially in the United States, where feminists seem to speak and write of communitarian ideals and identity in abstraction. It is all important to detect how and where the capitalist machine prevents true becomings and produces molar men *and* women. In the name of 'realism' and mimesis, invention is stifled. By means of advertisement and slogans, becoming reduces images to clichés in a society completely under the spell of marketing.

How to turn away from these conditions and actualise virtualities is taken up in the second of Deleuze's two volumes on film entitled *Time-Image*. There Deleuze alludes to the revolutionary side of three women filmmakers, Chantal Akerman, Marguerite Duras and Agnes Varda. The repertoire is less 'classical' or 'popular' than, as with his choice of literature, anti-consumption. Deleuze deals with an anti-cinema that does not give the spectator the easy satisfaction of consuming images or of identifying with the screen. This cinema keeps, and shows, its links to writing and thinking. With the possible exception of Varda, none of these women film-makers is at any point truly 'militant'. Deleuze sees all three as 'revolutionary', as focusing on certain notions of becoming(-woman) in their films. These becomings are now analysed in terms of bodily attitudes and postures. The way that the feminine in Cixous was not reserved to women alone, but was also the attribute of writers like Kleist, Hölderlin and others – the very same writers also discussed by Deleuze – allows us, by shifting Cixous's reflections on to the plane of Deleuze's taxonomy of cinema, to contemplate how becoming-woman in film is not limited to women filmmakers. We can see it happening in male cinema such as that of Jean-Luc Godard. Here, for the sake of brevity, I will limit myself, to conclude, to some of Deleuze's comments on Chantal Akerman.

In the *Time-Image*, Deleuze classifies women filmmakers under the chapter entitled 'Cinema, Body, Brain and Thought' (Deleuze 1989). Deleuze discusses the body in philosophy and in cinema: '"Give me a body, then:" this is the formula of philosophical reversal' (189). And he again repeats Spinoza's injunction:

'We do not even know what a body can do': in its sleep, in its drunkenness, in its efforts and resistances. To think is to learn what a non-thinking body is capable of, its capacity, its postures. It is through the body (and no longer through the intermediary of the body) that cinema forms its alliance with the spirit, with thought. 'Give me a body, then' is first to mount the camera on an everyday body. The body is never in the present, it contains the before and the after, tiredness and waiting. Another way of mounting a camera on the body would be, instead of following it, to make it pass through a ceremony. (189)

These two poles, the everyday and the ceremonial body, are discovered in alternative cinema. Attitudes and postures pass into the everyday theatricalisation or a ceremony of the body. Of importance

30

is the passage from one pole to the other, from attitudes to 'gestus', in Deleuze's idiolect or his poaching of the term, a Brechtian notion referring to the link or knot of attitudes between themselves, insofar as they do not depend on a previous story, a pre-existing plot or a traditional action-image (Deleuze 1989: 191–3).[10] The 'gestus' is the development of attitudes themselves, and, as such, carries out a theatricalisation of bodies. The story should be secreted by the characters and not the other way around. Deleuze notes the cinema of the bodies in relation to French post-New-Wave women filmmakers in general and Chantal Akerman in particular. We are, of course, reminded of Cixous and Ariane Mnouchkine's collaboration of epic theatre:

Female authors, female directors, do not owe their importance to a militant feminism. What is more important is the way they have produced innovations in this cinema of the bodies, as if women had to conquer the *source of their own attitudes and the temporality* which corresponds to them as individual or common gest. (Deleuze 1989: 196–7)

Since the new wave, Deleuze writes in 1986, 'every time there was a fine and powerful film, there was a new exploration of the body in it' (196). Here Deleuze discusses Akerman as a female director possessing a certain specificity and Spinozist signature:

Akerman's novelty lies in showing in this way *bodily attitudes* as the sign of states of body particular to the female character, whilst the men speak for society, the environment, the part which is their due, the piece of history which they bring with them (*Anna's Rendezvous*). But the chain of states of the female body is not closed: descending from the mother or going back to the mother, it serves as a revelation to men, who now talk about themselves, and on a deeper level to the environment, which now makes itself seen or heard only through the window of a room, or a train, a whole art of sound . . . The states of the body secrete the slow ceremony which joins together the corresponding attitudes, and develop a female gest which overcomes the history of men and the crisis of the world. (196)

Deleuze undoes masculine and feminine paradigms: the body is not to be overcome nor does one think through the body. Rather, one must plunge into the body to reach the unthought, that is (material) life. Here, Deleuze again rehearses his well-known triad – affect, percept, concept – in the context of a woman's becoming. Once again, he insists that all is not language and makes the case for a pragmatic philosophy. To think is to learn what a non-thinking body is capable of, its capacity, its postures. To become, women – as individuals or as a collective group – must conquer the source of their attitudes and the temporality that corresponds to it. We could put Deleuze's pronouncements side by side with Cixous's preoccupations with a bodily voice that goes far beyond the wilful, legislating subject.

Anna's Rendezvous (1978) shows the states of Anna's body during her passage through Germany. She is tired; she is waiting; she is hungry. She has everyday encounters: an encounter with a man (her producer), she meets an old woman friend who confides in her by recounting scenes from her marriage to the condition of Jews in postwar Europe. Her producer talks to her about his failed marriage and problems of the environment. She strikes up chance conversations on trains, has an incestuous night with her mother, and finally returns to her apartment where there are many recorded messages waiting for her on what was then a newfounded memory-machine, the telephonic answering and recording device. The ceremonial passage of Anna's body makes others talk. Her empathy makes them confide in her. Representation or movement is limited to the journey itself, the countryside seen from a train window, the walking in and out of hotels, the movement to and from train stations. Anna does not as much become herself than she enables others to become through this slow ceremony and everyday occurrences.

Now what about Akerman's *A Couch in New York/Un divan à New York* (1997)?[11] The film-poem-ballad, a kind of 1990s update of *Rendezvous*, deals with a transatlantic journey now taken by plane. The film avoids what Deleuze had called Akerman's 'excessive stylization' of her minimalist period and develops further her turn to the burlesque as in *Toute une Nuit* and other subsequent films. *A Couch in New York* is a film about the conditions of living in contemporary, capitalist New York but nonetheless, like the origins that have been stated above, about becomings. Featured are two well-known actors, Juliette Binoche and William Hurt. The former, contrary to most movies made by male directors, is not cast like a tragic or castrating character as in *Blue* or *Damage*. Unlike her cosmetic roles in those films, she is not camouflaged under heavily made-up features. She is cast as a young woman, even with girlish residues. With little dressing-up and shot in diaphanous ways, Binoche leaves behind all the familiar features that have characterised her.

She herself is in becoming in this film. She plays Beatrice, a dancer who swaps her Parisian apartment in a popular and colourful neighbourhood with an established New York psychoanalyst's expensive but sterile apartment on Fifth Avenue and 86th Street. She goes to New York as he comes to Paris. We see her riding in a taxi and enjoying the New York sky while he is trying to stop all the flows and fill all the gaps in her Paris apartment. However, the film is no simple travel narrative, nor an advertisement for *Architectural Digest* or Crate and Barrel's products. The only space shown is that which is connected to the bodies. Outside any real deixis, the space is composed from bodily attitudes that form the gest. The analyst, who is supposed to be able to make flows pass between bodies, is seen sitting on Beatrice's bed, all buttoned up. He discovers her through the accounts of her lovers, whom she had temporarily fled in order to find the source of her own attitudes. He reads in Kafka's *Diaries* lying next to Beatrice's bed, a passage about lemonade, hay and youth. Though he understands the words, he cannot understand the poetry. Over time, through her, he will be able to enter into a kind of becoming. At the other end, Beatrice, in her (his?) bathrobe and barefooted, receives his patients and, by showing them empathy, makes them feel better. Men are lying down on the bed or on the couch. They are uptight or catatonic. Beatrice's graceful postures make them talk and reveal themselves to themselves. The comment on New York and America is made through the men's narratives that could be the stuff of realist TV dramas that are never shown. Any residue of narrative realism, expensive apartment, chic interior, is quickly dismissed when the apartment becomes a neutral space. The patients are seen mainly going up and down the hallway, or in and out of elevators. Beatrice's postures and attitudes serve as a revelation to the male patients, including the analyst who is equally affected and transformed by her.

The movie can be said to be a contemporary version of *Rendezvous d'Anna*, but now, the young woman is less alienated and more capable of finding a source of pleasure and enjoyment in the world. Her bodily movements are freer and quicker than in *Rendezvous*. She is in sharp contrast to the men in New York, who live in a system that suppresses pleasure and becomings. A certain capitalist system produces molar men and women, such as the analyst's fiancée, whose face caked under a cosmetic and plastic grin are tributes to her molarity and general condition of unhappiness. Their neurotic discourses contrast with Beatrice's face, her gestures and her stammering words. She does all the wrong things and goes against the rules of psychoanalysis although this behaviour seems to improve the patients' state.

The film has a strong anti-Oedipal take. In humorous and graceful ways, castration is mocked and incest encouraged. A certain psychoanalysis with its emphasis on Oedipus goes along with a capitalist regime that blocks flows and prevents becoming. Male and female bodies in postures on the bed or in the analyst's chair are part of a ceremony that has become burlesque. In addition to the attitudes of the body, there is more emphasis on the female face, a moving face unfettered by makeup. It's not the marketed, clichéd face of advertisement (Griggers 1997). The girlish openness of Beatrice's face and eyes have an ongoing sense of wonder of the world, an openness that will enable the men to turn away from their present condition. Not only do the patients feel better, but so do the dog and the plants. In the process of affecting them, Beatrice is also transforming herself.

In a review in the *New York Times* (21 March 1997), Janet Maslin calls the movie fluff. Or is it grace? Is it that we can no longer recognise grace because we are so superegoised? *A Couch in New York* is a remake of the minimalist *Rendezvous d'Anna* as a burlesque ballad: The bodies, the talk about things that are never shown; the descent from, and going back to, the mother; the face and the visionary look that uncovers all the hidden things. Beatrice sees below the clichés and helps others to accede to new ways of perceiving.

In *Rendezvous*, allusions abounded to history, to the holocaust and the environment, to the sense of alienation in postwar Europe. *A Couch* functions at a different level. It is about New York here and now, and its molar structures and its lack of a condition of becoming in a postmodern, capitalist society. Akerman does not show social contradictions but certain conditions. She also draws some lines of flight, those of young people, of women, of poetry and love. And love, like grace, cannot be marketed even if it is present in a production of dominant cinema.

One could find a similar focus on everyday pleasures and becoming throughout Cixous and Mnouchkine's theatre. In their epic plays about Cambodia, India or France they use a certain poetry of everydayness and mime to criticise discourses of power, to enter into guerilla warfare with them. Their theatre equally works on attitudes and states of the body. Theatre, even more than film, enables them to stage an opera of voices in such a way that vocal modes precede or replace the characters.

Though the post-1968 euphoria in which early pronouncements on women has clearly subsided, both Deleuze and Cixous continue to advocate the importance of becoming. Less than to a wilful, legislating subject, becoming is linked to the body, the body into which, according to Deleuze's reading of Akerman, one must plunge in order to reach life. To write is to resist, asserts Deleuze.[12] In philosophy or poetry, this resistance necessitates an ongoing turning away from present conditions. This continues to be of interest to feminists and women, who, in the present climate of globalisation, are faced with dangers of molarisation. Real becomings are made more difficult in a society of advertisement. They are facilitated through an aesthetics and singularisation, a breaking away from the norm and the continual invention of different social relations (changes in the relations to one's body, between couples).

At one level, women will have to look carefully, each for herself, whether she wants to adopt Deleuze's theory of univocality of being, of a new metaphysics, or whether she wishes to retain a more deconstructive model of self and other, or even, *à la* Lacan, espouse a divided subject. On a more general level, we have tried to show how, by contextualising and generalising the concept, we can reinsert 'becoming-woman' first in a post-May 1968 era and point to its similarities with concepts used at the time by 'feminist' writers such as Hélène Cixous. We then followed the evolution of the concept in Deleuze's work, with yet another reference to Cixous, in order to see how it can function in today's conditions. We can conclude by saying that though Deleuze emphasises different concepts at different times, he continues to work along rhizomatic processes and lines of flight from a productive rather than theatrical unconscious. Of importance, for him, is the reversal of traditional philosophical formulation. The body does not separate thought from itself, one must, to the contrary, plunge into the body in order to reach the unthought of life. In his view, the 'being' of each woman is always temporary. An effect of subjectivation, it cannot be separated from a context and is always exceeded by becomings that can neither be completely controlled nor foretold. Similar to Cixous's concept of NBW, becoming-woman entails a continuous turning away from one's present conditions, an ongoing actualisation of virtualities. In the present time of vertical and horizontal intensification of capitalism into strata more and more unconscious, actualisation of true virtualities – other than those based on 'I consume, therefore I am' – is more and more difficult. It is, therefore, all important for women to remain vigilant, to avoid a becoming molar of feminisms, to turn away continually from present contexts and to continue to draw new lines of flight.

NOTES

1. The last chapter of Claude Levi-Strauss's *Tristes Tropiques* (1955) envisions a world that will ultimately be bereft of human presence. Michel Foucault ended *Les Mots et les Choses* (1966) with the celebrated image of the name of 'man' disappearing into the sands of a beach on which it was written.

2. Deleuze will later distinguish between an *'intempestif'* like May 1968 and the slow, inexorable transformation from a disciplinary society to one of control. (See *Pourparlers* (1990a), 'Postscriptum': 240–7.)

3. Deleuze and Guattari develop their anti-Oedipal stance in the context of a disciplinary society. They extend their critique, though somewhat briefly, to societies of control that, under the sign of marketing, make real desire impossible. Their pronouncements on movement and desire are not to be confused with many contemporary celebrations of dizzying movements and gliding across surfaces in cyberspace. Deleuze and Guattari make it clear: computers and cybernetics are not simply part of a technological evolution, they are part of a deeper restructuring of capitalism.

4. Deleuze and Guattari's critique of Lacan is elaborated throughout their work. They repeatedly denounce Lacan for asserting that all is language and for making use of Saussurean linguistics. To develop a theory in which all is not language, Deleuze and Guattari turn to Charles Sanders Peirce's semiotics and, especially, Louis Hjelmslev's glossematics. From the latter, they derive an immanentist perspective of the sign that cannot be reduced to the opposition signifier/signified. They favour Hjelmslev's reciprocal presupposition of content and expression, both having their form and substance, rather than a hierarchical subordination between signifier and signified, form or content. Deleuze and Guattari focus on semiotic experimentation of collective agencies rather than on linguistic expression of individual persons. They also reject the instance of the letter in favour of an incidence of the social signifier on the individual. There is no latent content that will be made manifest. To the contrary, for Deleuze, 'the map expresses the identity between the act of traversing and the traversed itinerary. It confounds itself with its object, when this object itself is movement' (*Critique et clinique*, 1997: 61). Thus, a psychic map can no longer be distinguished from the existential territory it engenders. Subject of enunciation and object of knowledge coincide.

5. Patricia Pister makes the connection between Deleuze and Haraway in 'Cyborg Alice; or, Becoming-Woman in an Audiovisual World', (Pister 1997) *Iris* 23 (Spring 1997): 148–63. It is important to remember though that Deleuze remains sympathetic towards certain aspects of psychoanalysis, like that of the unconscious. His criticism bears mainly on the later Freudian elaborations around the id, the ego and the superego.

6. In *Empirisme et Subjectivité: Essai sur la nature humaine selon Hume* (1953), Deleuze already addresses his political and philosophical project that will consist in distinguishing between theories of institutions and theories of law. For Deleuze, the negative is outside of the social (needs) and society is essentially positive and inventive (original means of satisfaction). He differs from those advocating theories of law that put the positive outside of the social (natural rights) and the social in the negative (contractual limitations).

7. Crucial to all of Deleuze's work is the well-known triad, affect (new ways of feeling), percept (new ways of seeing) and concept (new ways of knowing). They are working simultaneously and continually flowing into one another. Of importance is that affect escapes language and functions at the level of the real and life. Deleuze, again, sets himself apart from Lacan, for whom the real, outside of language, is unattainable. Accompanying this triad, and of equal importance, is the couple virtual/actual. Just as affect becomes percept, so virtualities can be actualised. The virtual is different from the possible, which is already present, waiting to be realised.

8. The expression is the subtitle of Michael Hardt's book, *Gilles Deleuze* (1993).

9. The unified or full subject enters into a dialectical relation with an object in a deadly battle that ends in the death of one of the terms. The aim of the struggle is recognition of the victor by the vanquished.

10. For Brecht, 'gestus' is the essence of theatre. It cannot be reduced to plot or 'subject' and is generally social (Brecht 1978).

11. 'Divan', means both couch and poem in French. A curious coincidence, no doubt, couch in English also refers to a 'rhizomatous grass growing between cracks' (*OED*). The obsessive male protagonist is imagined by the female actress as 'never having a single piece of grass on his vest'.

12. Writing here is taken in a strong sense of creation, singularisation and aesthetics, not simply of reproduction.

2

Becoming-Woman: Deleuze, Schreber and Molecular Identification

JERRY ALINE FLIEGER

The true religious force in the world is the world itself . . . an aesthetic tough, diverse, untamed,
incredible to prudes, the mint of dirt,
Green barbarism turning paradigm.

Then let a tremor through our briefness run,
Wrapping it in with mad, sweet sorcery
Of love; for in the fern I saw the sun . . .

Wallace Stevens[1]

Paradox is the pathos or the passion of philosophy.

Gilles Deleuze (1994a: 227)

I. IS FEMINISM 'BECOMING' TO DELEUZE?

Gilles Deleuze is the poet-philosopher of immanence, advocate of the material world; laureate of intensity, of energies manifest in organic and inorganic life. His philosophy engages the reader in a difficult adventure; for Deleuze asserts that the innovative thinker 'elaborates a punctual system or a didactic representation, but with the aim of making it snap, of sending a tremor through it' (Deleuze and Guattari 1987: 295). Just so, Deleuze's own work sends a tremor through philosophy; provocative and unsettling, it both valorises and performs what Deleuze calls a 'deterritorialization' or 'line of flight' away from habits of thought and perception.

But this body of work reflects more than an impressive pyrotechnics of the imagination. Deleuze is nothing short of daunting in his

38

erudition, treating with astounding facility, by turns, complex philosophies; the ethnographic history of the entire human socius; the consequences of capitalism; the techniques of cinema; the debates of linguistics; and the aesthetics of artists. He is also fluent in the idiom of science, and engaged in constant dialogue with scientific theory, past and present. Thus we could envisage any number of titles for a volume of essays on Deleuze – 'Deleuze and Philosophy', 'Deleuze and Aesthetics', 'Deleuze and Science', 'Deleuze and Politics', 'Deleuze and Cinema', 'Deleuze and History', 'Deleuze and Psychoanalysis', perhaps even 'Deleuze and Guattari'.[2]

But the coupling of 'Deleuze and Feminism' gives one pause. Far-reaching as his cultural analyses are, Deleuze's strange world of abstract machines, apparatuses of capture, tribal despots, and ambulant war machines seems to be pretty much a male realm – as feminist critics Rosi Braidotti, Anne Balsamo, and Luce Irigaray have pointed out; his nomad, his smith, his warrior-chief are all seemingly masculine constructs, armoured, aggressive, moving in a high velocity, sometimes high-tech environment.[3] Is 'Deleuzean feminism' an oxymoron?

Perhaps. But a thinker as important as Deleuze cannot simply be dismissed on the grounds of androcentrism; especially since the feminist theoretical endeavour is always, in patriarchal culture, a revisionist undertaking. In order to consider the odd couple of Deleuze and feminism, and finally to argue for the importance of that coupling for feminist and psychoanalytic theory, I shall reconsider here a concept elaborated in both volumes of *Capitalism and Schizophrenia* – the concept of 'becoming'. I focus here on one essay that has attracted the attention of a number of feminist theorists, since it discusses the vicissitudes of 'becoming-woman'.

Curiously, in spite of the centrality of the notion of 'becoming-woman' in Chapter 10 of *A Thousand Plateaus*, there is no reference to woman in the title: 'Becoming-Intense, Becoming-Animal, Becoming-Imperceptible'. The conspicuous omission may be deliberate, since Deleuze argues that 'becoming' itself aims at a kind of erasure, tending towards 'imperceptibility'. In any case, the essay does seem to be written from a masculine subject position, suggesting that 'becoming-woman' is the paradigmatic instance of changing one's perspective, one's very essence, one's very status as 'one'.

But more problematic is Deleuze's assertion that 'becoming-woman' is a phase in a journey of diminishment – a step on the road to 'becoming-imperceptible': 'If becoming-woman is the first quantum, or molecular segment, with the becomings-animal that link up with it coming next, what are they all rushing toward? Without a doubt, toward becoming-imperceptible' (Deleuze and Guattari 1987: 279). If Deleuze is indeed saying that becoming-woman is the first and necessary step towards attaining a desirable state of 'imperceptibility' ('imperceptibility is the immanent end of becoming, its cosmic formula'), it is not surprising that the formulation has caused some alarm for feminists.

Deleuze himself poses the crucial question:

But what does becoming-imperceptible signify, coming at the end of all the molecular becomings that begin with becoming-woman?[. . .] What is the relation between the (anorganic) imperceptible, the (asignifying) indiscernible, and the (asubjective) impersonal?

A first response would be: to be like everyone else. (Deleuze and Guattari 1987: 279)

This response, of course, offers little to dispel feminist objections, although 'being like everyone else' is arguably a formulation of one practical feminist goal, implying equality of opportunity and full participation in society for women as an unmarked term, 'like everyone else'. Yet Deleuze is not concerned here with carving out a singular identity with something like full rights, because his agenda does not directly address the status of individual as citizen. Indeed, he seems to be resolutely opposed to any form of what we have come to call identity politics, presumably since this politics necessitates 'territorializing' – staking out one's turf in the social hierarchy. In fact 'identity' itself is a notion that Deleuze wants to undercut or complicate, as do other poststructuralists, because it implies a struggle for territory or centrality of position, pride of place.

But Deleuze concedes that real women do need to struggle collectively for a place from which to speak: 'it is indispensable, of course, for women to conduct a molar politics, with a view to winning back their own organism, their own history, their own subjectivity: "we as women" makes its appearance as a subject of enunciation' (Deleuze and Guatttari 1987: 276). However, Deleuze goes on to qualify this 'macropolitics' of the female subject in an unfortunate and even hackneyed way, cautioning that 'it is dangerous to confine oneself to such a subject which does not function without drying up a spring or stopping a flow' (Deleuze and Guattari 1987: 276).

In spite of this worn-out essentialist approximation of the (non-subjectified) woman with 'spring' or 'flow', it is important to note that Deleuze's emphasis on becoming does not privilege Man;

it critiques Man as the 'molar' paradigm of identity and subjectivity, opposed to 'molecular' immanence. Indeed, throughout his work, Deleuze opposes the notion of 'molecular' to that of the 'molar'. To put it simply, the molar register concerns whole organisms, subjects, forms, and their interaction, including social action; while the molecular register considers non-subjective being on the level of chemical and physical reactions, intensities, in a radically material 'micropolitics'. The molar is transcendent, the molecular immanent. The molar register (society, family, politics) is important, but it is the molecular which is privileged in the essay on becoming, and at many points in the work: 'Yes, all becomings are molecular: the animal, flower, or stone one becomes are molecular collectivities, haeccities, not molar subjects, objects or form that we know from the outside . . . there is a becoming-woman, a becoming-child that do not resemble the woman or child as clearly distinct molar entities' (Deleuze and Guattari 1987: 275).

In other words, for Deleuze becoming-woman is not a 'macro-political' project concerning female subjects. This is already potentially disturbing from a feminist perspective, though not as troubling as Deleuze's apparent consignment of 'molar' women to the sexual and reproductive roles marked out by patriarchy, as though the 'molar' were immutable: 'What we term molar entity is, for example, the woman as defined by her form, endowed with organs and functions and assigned as a subject' (275).

Predictably, this problematic distinction between the molecular and the molar woman, with the attendant dismissal of the 'macro-political' level, has not gone uncriticised by feminist theorists. In a trenchant recent attack, for example, Anne Balsamo categorises Deleuze and Guattari with other practitioners of 'panic postmodernism', reiterating the familiar feminist scepticism about the liberating potential of ascendant technological developments in areas such as body imaging, assisted reproduction, plastic surgery and virtual sexuality in disembodied cyber space (Balsamo 1996). Balsamo echoes the sentiment of many feminists, even those sympathetic to postmodernism, who question the erasure of the body in millennial culture. She cites Alice Jardine's caveat about postmodernism: 'even while remaining wary of totalizing notions like Truth, [women] must lend continual attention – historical, ideological, and affective – to the place from which we speak' (Jardine 1985: 37).

It is not surprising, then, that Deleuze and feminism have often been cast in adversarial positions: 'The place from which we speak' is not, to be sure, a central concern for Deleuze (the feminine 'we' is evoked only once in his text). Moreover, Balsamo and other feminist critics are probably correct in complaining that however vigorously Deleuze advocates 'becoming-woman', the starting-point for that transformation is Man. Nor does Deleuze pose the celebrated query of psychoanalysis: what does woman want? For he is not interested in woman as individual entity:

All we are saying is these indissociable aspects of becoming-woman must first be understood as a function of something else: not imitating or assuming the female form, but emitting particles that enter the relation of movement and rest, or the zone of proximity, of a micro-feminity, in other words, that produce in us a molecular woman, create the molecular woman. (Deleuze and Guattari 1987: 275)

This creation of the 'microfeminine' molecular woman is unsettling, by virtue of the proximity of molecular 'woman' to 'child', to 'beast' and to the idealised nature of 'springs and flows'. Deleuze goes so far as to assert that real women do not even enjoy an advantage in the trajectory of 'becoming-woman':

We do not mean to say that a creation of this kind is the prerogative of the man, but on the contrary that the woman as a molar entity has to become-woman in order that the man also becomes- or can become-woman. (Deleuze and Guattari 1987: 275–6)

In this particular paradox (woman herself must become-woman) – the real molar woman seems to drown in the cosmic molecular soup. Alas, microfeminity would seem to be the molecular helpmate of macromasculinity in these co-ed adventures in intensity.

II. FACE-OFF: 'EITHER' DELEUZE 'OR' FEMINISM?

We fall into a false alternative if we say that you either imitate or you are. What is real is the becoming itself, the block of becoming, not the supposedly fixed terms through which that which becomes passes. (1987: 238)

In an apparent anticipation of feminist objections to his text on 'becoming-woman', Deleuze argues that a clear-cut distinction between the sexes itself is reductive:

[Sexuality] is badly explained by the binary organization of the sexes, and just as badly by a bisexual organization with each sex. Sexuality brings into play too great a diversity of conjugated becomings; these are like *n* sexes, an entire war machine through which love passes. (278)

In other words, gendered sexuality implies territories, 'either/ or', 'his' and 'hers'. For Deleuze, however, love observes no such boundaries, it is a mix-up, an intense, transgressive phenomenon, a 'war machine' without bellicosity.

This is not a return to those appalling metaphors of love and war, seduction and conquest, the battle of the sexes and the domestic squabble . . . : it is only after love is done with and sexuality is dried up that things appear this way. What counts is that love itself is a war machine endowed with strange and somewhat terrifying powers[. . .] Sexuality proceeds by way of the becoming-woman of the man and the becoming-animal of the human: an emission of particles. (278–9)

While this formulation might seem only to reassert a cliché (love as transformative intensity), Deleuze is strikingly original in arguing that 'becoming', in love or other transgressive processes, is not a question of interaction between individual subjects, but of multiple assemblages: 'These multiplicities with heterogeneous terms, cofunctioning by contagion, enter certain assemblages; it is there that human beings effect their becomings-animal' (242). These 'assemblages', also called desiring machines, are always the over-lapping of 'heterogeneous terms in symbiosis', and that multiplicity 'is continually transforming itself into a string of other multiplicities, according to its thresholds and doors' (249). So becoming-woman does not aim at the emancipation of a homogenous collectivity (women), an aggregate of same-sex subjects with a shared 'identity', struggling to gain political and economic rights; it aims at tensile transformation and transgression of identity.

Indeed the outcome of any Deleuzean 'becoming' is not empha-sised, for becoming is a process, a line of flight between states which displaces and disorients subjects and identities. This 'betweenness' (*entre-deux*) is experienced, not attained. (In this formulation, Deleuze's thought owes an explicit debt to Maurice Blanchot's notion of '*entretien infini*', a philosophical treatise on 'entertaining' desire between points, in an 'infinite conversation' (*entretien*) which is also an infinite diversion from goal ('entertainment'); whereby desire perpetuates itself (Blanchot 1969).) In fact, what we call 'being in love', a revealing term, is certainly a molecular identifica-tion, a commingling in a line of flight. In Deleuze's 'molecular' and material rendering of love, this intertwining becomes textile, 'a string of multiplicities', where 'a fiber strung across borderlines constitutes a line of flight or deterritorialization', where 'the self is only a threshold, a door, a becoming between two multiplicities' (Deleuze and Guattari 1987: 249).

Deleuze might then have no quarrel with feminism and its goals for the individual and collective female subject, but his 'becoming-woman/animal/intense' is not concerned with the same level of experience as is the 'becoming-ourselves' which is feminism. He invokes an 'altogether different conception of the plane':

Here, there are no longer any forms or development of forms; nor are there any subjects or the formation of subjects. There is no structure, any more than there is genesis. There are only relations of movement and rest, speed and slowness between unformed elements . . . There are only haecceities, affects, subjectless individuations that constitute collective assemblages. (266)

Deleuze gives a name to this plane, where nothing subjectifies, where no 'one' is oneself: 'We call this plane which knows only longitudes and latitudes, speeds and haecceities, the plane of consistency or composition (as opposed to the plan(e) of organization or development)' (266). On this fibrous plane, it is a question not only of being strung out but also of hanging together, in a textured multiple viscosity. One example Deleuze gives of this kind of consistency is the tribal ritual of identification with the sacred totemic animal, where 'becoming' is not mimetic, but transformative:

Becomings-animal are basically of another power, since their reality resides not in an animal one imitates or to which one corresponds but in themselves, in that which suddenly sweeps us up and makes us become – *a proximity, an indiscernibility* that extracts a shared element from the animal. (279)

Again we see traces of an important theorist of the time, Georges Bataille, whose work focuses on the notion of ritual as transgression, with transformative powers that abolish boundaries between individuals (Bataille 1957). But whereas theorists like Bataille and Blanchot stay in the realm of the human, Deleuze's great originality resides in his inmixing of planes or phyla – animal with plant and with human – and his explanation of 'transgression' in molecular terms, which apply to non-organic phenomena as well as to human and animal life.

In a further elaboration, Deleuze opposes the transgressive molecular 'becoming' to the whole notion of 'majoritarian' memory. The majoritarian has to do with a punctual form of thought, specifically, the submission of the line to the point, which Deleuze calls 'arborescent', 'hierarchical', or linear organization, an ordering that traces origins, family trees, genealogy, and thus implies status, progress, and ends. But becoming is process, not status or place: 'A becoming is always in the middle, one can only get it by the middle. A becoming is neither one nor two [points], nor the relation of the two, it is the in-between, the border or line of flight or descent running perpendicular to both' (293). This kind of crystalline intersection of planes of consistency is termed 'rhizomatic': a column of ants, a river, a crystal, a tangle of vines, a weather system; all are entities that are non-individuated, non-representational, anti-memory. In human society, this kind of entity is also called 'minoritarian':

Why are there so many becomings of man, but no becoming-man? First because man is majoritarian par excellence, whereas becomings are minoritarian; all becoming is a becoming-minoritarian . . . In this sense women, children, but also animals, plants, and molecules, are minoritarian. It is perhaps the special situation of women in relation to the man-standard that accounts for the fact that becomings, being minoritarian, always pass through a becoming-woman. (291)

Deleuze of course recognises that 'minoritarian entities – the child, the woman, the black – have memories', but he insists that 'the Memory that collects those memories is still a virile majoritarian agency treating them as "childhood memories," as conjugal or colonial memories . . . one does not break with the arborescent schema, one does not reach becoming or the molecular, as long as a line is connected to two distant points, or is composed of two contiguous points' (293).

This is an interesting twist in the familiar critique of Western 'binary oppositions' elaborated by poststructuralist writers (notably Derrida, Barthes, Lyotard, and the feminist writers Julia Kristeva and Hélène Cixous). Binary oppositions, for Deleuze, are based on 'centrisms' not unlike the 'logocentrism' that Derrida and others criticise. Like the other poststructuralists, Deleuze insists that all binaries privilege one term as standard: '"white", "male", "adult", "rational", etc., in short the average European, the subject of enunciation' (292). In other words, these characteristics take majoritarian Man as the centre and make territory of all else:

Following the law of arborescence, it is this central Point that moves across all of space or the entire screen, and at every turn nourishes a certain distinctive opposition, depending on which faciality trait is retained: male-(female), adult-(child), white-(black, yellow, or red); rational-(animal). (292)

To undo this identification with the central face of the majoritarian, one has to first decentre 'oneself', become unwound, strung out, 'minoritarian', de-faced: becoming-woman is a first shift, destabilising the conventions of the Total. Seen in this way, becoming-woman is an active minoritarian ethics, opposed to the majoritarianism dominant in pragmatism and rationalism, but also opposed to 'identity politics' of any sort:

This is the opposite of macropopolitics, and even of History, in which it is a question of knowing how to win or obtain a majority . . . There is no history but of the majority, or of minorities as defined in relation to the majority. (292)

'Imperceptibility' is thus not a function of invisibility or lack of importance; it is a function of a recomposition, a radical change in consistency, where the connecting 'thread' is not one of subjective identity:

There is a mode of individuation very different from that of a person, subject, thing or substance. We reserve the term haecceity for it. A season, a winter, a summer, an hour, a date have a perfect individuality lacking nothing, even though this individuality is different from that of a thing or a subject. They are haeccities in the sense that they consist entirely of relations of movement and rest between molecules and particles, capacities to affect and be affected. (261)

This is a radical atomistic materialism, where even seemingly abstract notions like 'winter' become functions of material differences and intensities, 'capacities to affect and be affected'.

However, as John Mullarkey has convincingly shown, Deleuze is not always simply anti-molar and pro-molecular; indeed, Mullarkey argues that the impression that Deleuze simply wants to do away with 'macropolitics' may have given rise to some of the anti-Deleuzean reaction among feminists: 'the misimpression that Deleuze would dissolve molar beings into anonymous molecular flows has brought him much criticism from at least one quarter, namely, feminist philosophy' (Mullarkey 1997: 445). While it is debatable whether the impression of Deleuze as 'anti-molar' is actually a misimpression, it is surely the case that the face-off with feminism based on oppositional posturing, 'either/or' logic (advocating 'either' the individual subject 'or' the molecular haecceity) is a false problem. For Deleuze discounts antagonistic either/or face-offs. In fact, he is interested in taking the face off faciality itself, since majoritarian thinking marks the face as male, white and adult.

In spite of the merits of this strategy, it is hard to deny that the 'becoming-woman' passage finally does relegate 'woman' to an enabling term, and one which already inhabits the primary term (Man). But Deleuze's molecular woman is not the Eve of the myth of origin, who is a secondary being, the 'fruit' of arborescent organisation, originating inside man at the foot of the genealogical tree, named by Man and transcribed in majoritarian memory. On the contrary, Deleuze's woman is unnamed, anti-memorial. It would seem that 'woman' is not even a noun in his lexicon: the 'woman' of 'becoming-woman' is a qualificative, adjectival term, outside of the game of subjects and objects. (In the term 'becoming-woman', 'woman' has the same syntactical force as the adjective 'intense' or 'animal', as in 'animal magnetism'.) The most important term in 'becoming-woman' is neither noun nor adjective, but the verbal gerund, designating 'becoming' as a line of flight, moving towards excess, other, exteriority. Deleuze's world is not in stasis; hence woman is not a goal or a term, but a potential, a valence.

So in a way, feminists like Balsamo are justified in accusing Deleuze of considering 'woman' as excess, exterior and threatening to the system. But Deleuze explicitly devalorises the system, and considers 'excess' or exteriority as a gateway to the anti-systemic, the transgressive. For Deleuze, it is a change in ways of being and thinking that will effect a true 'becoming', rather than perpetuating habits of thought that support 'majoritarian' business as usual. Deleuze asserts that 'Man constitutes himself as a gigantic memory, through the position of the central point,' a monument to his own centrality, while the minoritarian or molecular is anti-memory (293). Thus the point of any becoming is, in a sense, to lose face, to become imperceptible, in order to counteract the very notion of individual stature.

III. THE POLITICS OF CROSS-DRESSING

> In a way, we must start at the end: all becomings are already molecular. That is because becoming is not to imitate or identify with something or someone. (292)

Perhaps the most interesting commentary on 'becoming-woman' in Deleuze is his treatment of Freud's famous case study, based on the memoirs of the 'paranoid' Dr Schreber (Freud 1911: 3). For

Schreber left a compelling record of his illness, his astounding transformation from staunch citizen, state authority and husband, into a 'female' concubine of God. In an elaboration on the illness of 'paraphrenia', (paranoia, with schizophrenic aspects) Freud diagnoses Schreber's hallucinations as symptoms provoked by repressed homosexual feelings first towards his strict disciplinarian father, and later towards a father-figure, his doctor. Freud surmises that Schreber's illness is an unconscious defence against these feelings; whereby the homosexual cathexis is projected on to an external source. Schreber then experiences this projection as aggressive amorous persecution emanating from God Himself: the deity demands that Schreber submit to him sexually by 'becoming-woman'.

Deleuze is categorical in his critique of Freud's analysis, claiming that it leaves out all social context (the rising anti-Semitism and proto-fascism of the era). In other words, he actually criticises Freud for leaving out the 'molar' level in his analysis; yet at the same time he attacks Freud for being too molar, hierarchical and reductive: 'the entirety of this enormous (social) content disappears completely from Freud's analysis: not one trace of it remains, everything is ground, squashed, triangulated into Oedipus; everything is reduced to the father, in such a way as to reveal in the crudest fashion the inadequacies of an Oedipal psychoanalysis' (Deleuze and Guattari 1977: 89). In *Anti-Oedipus* Deleuze insists that a true politics of psychoanalysis would consist in undoing the familial reduction in order to 'analyze the specific nature of the libidinal investments in the economic and political spheres' (1977: 105). Yet to be fair, we must note that Deleuze himself refrains from a political analysis in the Schreber case – 'All this happens not in ideology, but well beneath it' (105) – focusing on the molecular register of Schreber's experience:

There is a schizophrenic experience of intensive quantities in their pure state, to a point that is almost unbearable . . . like a cry suspended between life and death, an intense feeling of transition, states of pure, naked intensity stripped of all shape and form. These are often described as hallucinations and delirium, but the basic phenomenon of hallucination (I see, I hear), and the basic phenomenon of delirium (I think . . .) presuppose an I feel at an even deeper level, which gives hallucinations their object and thought delirium its content. (18)

Schreber is saturated by an amorous God; in an experience that Deleuze insists is real, on the level of molecular intensity:

Nothing here is representative; rather, it is all life and lived experience: the actual, lived emotion of having breasts does not resemble them, it does not represent them, any more than a predestined zone in the egg resembles the organ that it is going to be stimulated to produce within itself. Nothing but bands of intensity, potentials, thresholds. And gradients. A harrowing, emotionally overwhelming experience, which brings the schizophrenic as close as possible to matter, to a burning, living center of matter. (19)

In other words, Deleuze wants to shift the 'familial' nosology of Freud's account of paranoia, to a commentary on the material nature of schizophrenia as a molecular intensity.[4]

This is in itself a worthwhile project, but his critique of Freud is based on an incomplete account of Freud's position. Freud in fact does not simply neglect the question of Schreber's identification with the whole 'minoritarian' aspect of the repressive majoritarian society. For Freud, Schreber's experience of transformation to 'woman' is accompanied by an identification with the Jews in anti-Semitic Germany. Indeed, one could reproach Deleuze himself with reducing the Schreber case to an oppositional 'either/or' frame: Schreber is 'either' a paranoid (in Freud's molar version) 'or' a schizophrenic (in Deleuze's molecular account), influenced either by social factors (family, ideology) or by molecular intensities.

In a recent study which both draws on and critiques Deleuze's reading of the Schreber case, Eric Santner has set an original socio-political reading of paranoia in the frame of Freud's theory, demonstrating how the macropolitics surrounding Schreber and the micropolitics of his 'becoming-woman' are interrelated, not opposed (Santner 1996). Santner refers to Deleuze's negative characterisation of the paranoid as the artist of large molar aggregates, organised crowds; for Deleuze, paranoia is a 'molar' disease provoked by repressive power and totalising vision; whereas 'schizophrenia' is the manifestation of the immanent and material.[5] For Santner however, as for Freud, paranoia is not merely a familial/ideological effect, and a socially conditioned one, it is also a very real trans-formation of the self in response to real conditions (for Freud, psychic reality is 'real'). Santner's analysis is thus both molar and molecular, societal and elemental. The repressive father of child-hood coincides with the social authority, the judge who swears Schreber in as President of the Senate, thus literally 'investing' him with authority. Tellingly, it is this investment as an insider in disci-plinarian power that sets off Schreber's delirium: he hallucinates that the investing judge publically denounces him as a 'sham', jokester, con man (Luder); he thus feels exposed in his shameful hidden psychic identity (as Jew, woman, homosexual – the non-powerful others with whom he unconsciously identifies, in his 'becoming-intense'). Santner's reading of Schreber's paranoia is consistent with Deleuze's injunction to look for the 'schizzes and flows' well beneath ideology, but Santner, unlike Deleuze, does not reject the role of the family – Santner shows, as does Freud, that the symptom of becoming-woman is overdetermined, 'either' familial 'or' ideological 'or' social, all at once; not constrained by binary 'either . . . or' exclusions.

This approach is paradoxically more consistent with Deleuze's stated objectives than is Deleuze's own anti-Freudian reading. For throughout his work Deleuze repeatedly promotes the use of 'disjunctive synthesis', or 'inclusive disjunction', which allows impossibilities to coexist in the paradoxical formulation 'either . . . or . . . or', rather than privileging one term in a binary exclusion ('either . . . or'). In *Anti-Oedipus*, Deleuze first proposes the deployment of 'the unknown force of the disjunctive synthesis', an immanent use that would no longer be exclusionary or restrictive, but 'fully affirmative, non restrictive, inclusive':

A disjunction that remains disjunctive and that still affirms the disjoined term, that affirms throughout their entire distance, without restricting one by the other or excluding the other from the one, is perhaps the greatest paradox. 'Either . . . or . . . or,' instead of 'either/or'. (Deleuze and Guattari 1977: 76)

Cast in these terms, Santner's argument shows a nuanced understanding of Freudian overdetermination as an instance of Deleuze's own project (the disjunctive logic of 'either . . . or . . . or'), rather than an 'explanation' of one event by another. This is another way of saying that Santner refutes Deleuze's simplistic characterisation of paranoia, suggesting instead that paranoia may be in this case a creative (unconscious) solution to fascistic conditions, as well as a symptom of a personal crisis of legitimisation. It is also a symptom of disjuncture in the socius itself. Thus, in this poetics of paranoia, Schreber's symptom is both reactive, to a misogynist and anti-Semitic moment that characterises 'the secret history of modernity', and active, aesthetically enabling, as a manifestation of the modern. In this account, Schreber's fantasy is a 'becoming' which provides solutions to an impossible social impasse, the demand that he become 'majoritarian':

Schreber's cultivation of an ensemble of 'perverse' practices, identifications, and fantasies, allows him not only to act out, but also to work through what may very well be the central paradox of modernity: that the subject is solicited by a will to autonomy in the name of the very community that is thereby undermined . . . Schreber's phantasmatic elaboration of that paradox allows him to find his way back to a context of human solidarity without having to disavow this fundamental breach of trust, without having to heal it with a final and definitively redemptive solution. (Santner 1996: 145)

Both Santner and Freud see the ideological climate as partially determinative of the 'distribution of intensities', while in Deleuze we are left with the troubling dismissal of ideology in Schreber's case, since his putative subject is the molecular transformation at another level altogether, which claims to study intensities non-politically, 'on behalf of a new order: the intense and intensive order' (Deleuze and Guattari 1977: 85).

Yet even while the specific political valence of the new order remains unclear, Deleuze's contribution to the study of paraphrenia lies precisely in his postulation of a transformation at a material level, 'real' rather than hallucinatory, a function of differential intensity. In this notion of intensity lies the connection between Deleuze's micropolitics and his molecular science.

We are also of a mind to believe that everything commingles in these intense becomings, passages, and migrations – all this drift that ascends and descends the flows of time: countries, races, families, parental appellations, divine appellations, geographical and historical designations, and even miscellaneous news items. (1977: 84–5)

The mechanics of becoming are finally material forces, the interplay of matter and energy, the ebb and flow of intensity, literally at the molecular level. In fact, in *Difference and Repetition* Deleuze states that intensity is a direct measure of difference, and difference is the 'sufficient cause' of everything:

Everything which happens and everything which appears is correlated with orders of differences: differences of level, temperature, pressure, tension, potential, difference of intensity . . . The reason of the sensible, the condition of that which appears, is not space and time but the Unequal itself, disparateness as it is determined and comprised in difference of intensity, in intensity as difference. (Deleuze 1994a: 222–3)

The difficulty in apprehending intensity as difference is that intensities hide or masquerade in the things which harbour them:

'Intensity is difference, but this difference tends to deny or cancel itself out in extensity and underneath quality' (223). (That is, the coffee in the mug cools, and we 'perceive' a loss in intensity in the liquid, but the heat goes somewhere else, it is displaced, not cancelled out. Difference remains.) Of Schreber's experience, Deleuze writes:

[These pure intensities] come from the two preceding forces, repulsion and attraction, and from the opposition of these two forces. It must not be thought that the intensities themselves are in opposition to one another, arriving at a state of balance around a neutral state . . . In a word, the opposition of the forces of attraction and repulsion produces an open series of intensive elements, all of them positive, that are never an expression of the final equilibrium of a system, but consist, rather, of an unlimited number of stationary, metastable states through which a subject passes. (Deleuze and Guattari 1977: 19)

Here, we recognise the outlines of modern 'far from equilibrium theory', which does not see intensity as evened out or levelled, but as energy permanently in flux, motivating transitions in matter, the motor of 'becoming'. In fact, our notion that energies tend to dissipate, says Deleuze, is merely a habit of 'good sense'; good sense essentially distributes or repartitions: '"on the one hand" and "on the other hand" are the characteristic formulae of its false profundity or platitude. It distributes things. It is obvious, however, that not every distribution flows from good sense; there are distributions inspired by madness, mad repartitions. Perhaps good sense even presupposes madness in order to come after and correct what madness there is in any prior distribution' (Deleuze 1994a: 224). It is interesting to note here the idea of 'madness' as corrective, also inherent in Santner's discussion of Schreber, as well as yet another Deleuzean affirmation of the 'disjunctive synthesis', which decentres ('either . . . or . . . or'), rather than effecting a balanced distribution ('on the one hand, on the other hand').

And while Deleuze's analysis is not political in the sense of the work of Santner, there is actually an ethics of force and intensity in Deleuze, based on a contrast between active and reactive force. In his essay on Deleuze, John Mullarkey comments on this contrast:

Deleuze describes reactive force as separating 'active force from what it can do,' while active force '. . . goes to the limit of what it can do.' Significantly, the separation of a force from what it can do is Deleuze's definition of slave morality. (Mullarkey 1997: 449)

Mullarkey's observation on Deleuze's ethics of intensity suggests one oblique way in which feminist analyses may rejoin the materiality of 'micropolitics'. 'Man' in his majoritarian state harbours forces subject to a repressive ideology, a slave morality; in Man, 'force is impeded in what it can do'; while 'woman' is the marker of a more active force which motivates the differential flow of becoming – a line of flight away from majority, faciality, centrality. Deleuze's notion of becoming-intense suggests that crossing the line is an actualisation of Schreber's repressed active force. He can act by becoming-woman, while he can only react as a (powerful, majoritarian) man, enforcing the authority of the reactionary system which seeks to invest him. By becoming-woman, Schreber rejects the masculine 'vestment' of power, and dons a fanciful, feminine habit.

IV. DELEUZEAN FEMINISM: NO-MAN'S LAND

[Becoming] constitutes a zone of proximity and indiscernibility, a no-man's land, a nonlocalizable relation sweeping up the two distant or contiguous points, carrying one into the proximity of the other. (Deleuze and Guattari 1987: 293)

Although the Schreber case provides a fascinating instance of 'becoming' on both the molar and molecular levels, it is unlikely to answer feminist objections to Deleuzean theory, because it still foregrounds 'becoming-woman' as a means to an end for Man, however 'real' is Schreber's 'virtual' experience of womanhood. But in another important example Deleuze elaborates becoming in a way that transcends gender distinctions: commingling two different strata – plant and animal – in a 'rhizomatic' organisation. In the first chapter of *A Thousand Plateaus*, Deleuze cites a becoming (in a reference to Proust) which is not a one-way trajectory, as in man-to-woman; but a mutual transformation:

The orchid deterritorializes by forming an image, a tracing of a wasp, but the wasp reterritorializes on that image. The wasp is nevertheless deterritorialized, becoming a piece in the orchid's reproductive apparatus. But it reterritorializes the orchid by transporting its pollen. Wasp and orchid, as heterogeneous elements, form a rhizome. (10)

In other words, this rhizome results from a kind of material identification, which frees 'identification' itself from the notion of representative signification or mimesis:

It could be said that the orchid imitates the wasp, reproducing its image in a signifying fashion (mimesis, mimicry, lure, etc.). But this is true only on the level of the strata – a parallelism between two strata such that a plant organization on one imitates an animal organization on the other. At the same time, something else entirely is going on: not imitation at all but a capture of code, surplus value of code, an increase in valence, a veritable becoming, a becoming-wasp of the orchid and a becoming-orchid of the wasp. (10)

In the mutual capture of orchid and wasp, Deleuze observes 'the aparallel evolution of two beings that have absolutely nothing to do with each other'. For there is no subordination of one term to the other: 'There is neither imitation nor resemblance, only an exploding of two heterogeneous series on a line of flight composed by a common rhizome that can no longer be attributed to or subjugated to anything signifying' (10). Deleuze also suggests that this 'aparallel evolution' – where there is a lateral connection, an alliance, rather than a filial, hierarchical one – introduces a new evolutionary schema, emphasising symbiosis and synergy, not intergenerational mutation or survival of the fittest: 'More generally, evolutionary schema may be forced to abandon the old model of the tree and descent' (10).

Thus surprisingly, in this avowed enemy of psychoanalysis, we find something like the notion of Lacanian intrication of one being in another (as in the Lacanian axiom, 'our desire is the desire of the Other'); where entities are complicated not because of sameness (narcissistic identification), but because of difference (Otherness). For Lacan as for Deleuze, desire is productive, causing heterogeneous elements to overlap in what Lacan calls the 'signifying chain'. Deleuze, however, rejects the notion of signification, but this is not as opposed to the Lacanian psychoanalytic account as he (like many others) seems to think. For the signifying chain is not just language, as it is often misunderstood – it is, rather, an elaboration of the drive that Freud calls 'the compulsion to repeat', associated with the death drive. In fact, in 'Beyond the Pleasure Principle', Freud discusses a movement driven by something remarkably like Deleuzean difference: intensities that, in a sense, do not satisfy or annul desire, but feed desiring production, perpetuating actions that are 'meaningful' only by dint of their repetition, in response to a compulsion to repeat (Freud 1920). For Deleuze, this kind of self-feeding chain reaction can be described as a punctual line, always in the middle, 'far from equilibrium' (to use the language of modern physics) always throwing each organism out of its isolation and individuation, in an act of commingling. Even sexual life is seen not as an activity of one gendered subject upon another, but as a reciprocal capture and mutual 'becoming', where neither term simply conquers, 'mimes' nor even 'lures' the other.

The line or block of becoming that unites the wasp and the orchid produces a shared deterritorialization: of the wasp, in that in becomes a liberated piece of the orchid's reproductive system, but also of the orchid, in that it becomes the object of an orgasm in the wasp, also liberated from its own reproduction. (Deleuze and Guattari 1987: 293)

In other words, Deleuze insists that the 'rhizome' is anti-hierarchy, not an imitation or tracing, but a mapping and a connection. The wasp-orchid effects a disorientation and reorientation of each organism, a dislocating identification which 'forgets' the past of the organism, opening it to becoming-other:

The line-system (or block-system) of becoming is opposed to the point-system of memory. Becoming is the movement by which the line frees itself from the point, and renders points indiscernible: the rhizome, the opposite of arborescence, a break away from arborescence. Becoming is an antimemory. (Deleuze and Guattari 1987: 294)

The wasp-orchid is an animation of a fundamental idea in Deleuze: the concept of heterogeneous couplings with maintained difference, an encounter but not an assimilation, a paradoxical identification that dislocates identity. Already, in *Anti-Oedipus*, Deleuze introduces the theme and variation of that strange and different pair, the flower and the insect, when he comments on Proust as an example of a syntactical figure, the disjunctive synthesis: 'Here all guilt ceases, for it cannot cling to such flowers as these. In contrast to the alternative of the "either/or" exclusions, there is the "either . . . or . . . or" of the combinations and permutation where the differences amount to the same without ceasing to be different' (69–70). This particular 'variation' on the orchid-wasp identification 'theme' harbours a reference to the figure of disjunctive synthesis, 'either . . . or . . . or', which we encountered in the Schreber case. Indeed, this inclusive disjunction permeates Deleuzean thought, furnishing the verbal equivalent of the 'love' which links heterogeneous elements in a movement maintaining difference. The figure of 'either . . . or . . . or' is, for Deleuze, 'the greatest paradox', and the most productive if difficult linkage.

It is as 'the greatest paradox' that the disjunctive synthesis holds a particular place in Deleuzean syntax, since Deleuze celebrates paradox itself as 'the passion of philosophy' (Deleuze 1994a: 227).

Moreover, paradox and disjunction are inherent in the very notion of rhizome: a conjunction that does not imply genealogy, but alliance. Interestingly, Deleuze invokes the same paradoxical syntax when speaking of Schreber: '[The schizophrenic] is not man and woman. He is man or woman, but he belongs precisely to both sides . . . The schizophrenic is dead or alive, not both at once, but each of the two as the terminal point over which he glides . . . like the two ends of a stick in a nondecomposable space' where 'even the distances are positive'. In this same passage Deleuze asserts in fact that 'it would be a total misunderstanding of this order of thought if we concluded that the schizophrenic substituted vague syntheses of identification of contradictory elements for disjunctions, like the last of the Hegelian philosophers . . . He is and remains in disjunction; he does not abolish disjunction by identifying the contradictory elements by means of elaboration; instead, he affirms it through a continuous overflight spanning an indivisible distance.' Thus Schreber is transexual, 'he is trans-alivedead, trans-parentchild. He does not reduce two contrarities, to an identity of the same' (Deleuze and Guattari 1977: 76–7). In another vegetal example, Deleuze insists that the schizophrenic 'does not confine himself with contradictions; on the contrary he opens out, and, like a spore case inflated with spores, releases them as so many singularities that he himself had improperly shut off' (Deleuze and Guattari 1977: 77).

The disjunctive synthesis allows the linkage of these infinite maintained differences, the release of 'improperly shut off' singularities, as material variations on a material theme. Indeed, an axiom of Deleuzean thought is that there is infinite difference in every repetition: 'Rediscover Mozart and that the "theme" was a variation from the start' (Deleuze and Guattari 1987: 309). In fact, like the work of the artists he admires and invokes – Proust, Mozart, Kafka, Woolf – Deleuze's own work is cast as theme and variation (in matter, since Deleuze describes even Mozart's music as molecular flows). In Deleuzean variation, the transvestitism of Schreber, the cross-pollination of orchids, the 'becomings' of intensity and animality are all elaborations of difference and repetition, various and reiterated. If we rediscover Deleuze himself in these terms, we find that the theme of 'becoming-woman' is a variation on molecular intensity from the start, at the level of matter and energy. In this experience 'one's entire soul flows into this emotion that makes the mind aware of the terribly disturbing sound of matter' (Deleuze and Guattari 1977: 19).

56

Deleuze's own writing is filled by this 'disturbing sound of matter'; and it is 'rhizomatic', overdetermined, thanks to the 'disjunction' of Schreber, Freud, Proust, flower, insect, God and molecule. The very incommensurability of these linked terms may bring us full circle to the opening question: is it possible to map Deleuzean thought with feminism? Can these two parallel evolutions, 'having nothing to do with each other', produce intersecting coordinates, in a disjunctive synthesis? I believe that they can, through the mediation of an unlikely ally: Freud.

I have argued elsewhere that Freud and Deleuze are far more compatible in their theory than the invective of *Anti-Oedipus* would suggest. But the disjunctive synthesis of Freud–Deleuze depends, among other things, on their respective work on wit and humour, which suggests yet another facet of the Deleuzean–feminist rhizome for which Freud's thought could serve as a conductor.

V. IS DELEUZEAN FEMINISM A JOKE?

> The art of the aesthetic is humour, a physical art of signals and signs determining the partial solutions or cases of solution – in short, an implicated art of intensive qualities. (Deleuze 1994a: 245)

If Deleuze were here today to comment on an edition entitled 'Deleuze and Feminism', he might well respond with humour; for he valued the function of wit in all productive disjunctions. Moreover, Deleuze's formulation of humour as the 'implicated art of intensive qualities' comes very close to Freud's analysis of the 'economics' of joking as a play of differences, and the spirit of joking as a transgressive transfer of intensities. (Freud: 'Jokes always have something forbidden to say' (Freud 1905: 130–2).)

For Deleuze, the spark of wit resides not in rigidity but in movement, 'differential partial solutions' that do not enforce conformity but more often subvert it: 'The first way of overturning the law is ironic . . . , the second is humour, which is an art of consequences and descents, of suspensions and falls . . . Repetition belongs to humour and irony, it is by nature transgression or exception, always revealing a singularity opposed to the particulars subsumed under laws' (1994a: 5). For Deleuze, this art of partial solutions deploys contrasts, at once maintained and resolved, which resemble disjunctive syntheses, a play of flexible syntheses (as in a pun, where one meaning of a word evokes other meanings, rather than excluding them: 'either . . . or . . . or'. Deleuze speaks of freeing the 'point' from linearity, 'with the aim of making it snap, of sending a tremor through it' (Deleuze and Guattari 1987: 295). This sounds very much like Freud discussing the 'point' or punch of a joke, which recruits a kind of absurd disjunctive logic to produce just this kind of seismic 'snap'.

Freud also specifically valued the disjunctive synthesis as a technique of wit, as a way of expressing impossible, incompatible, or forbidden truths. In fact, Freud explicitly calls on the figure of inclusive disjunction to make his point about the technique of the famous 'kettle' joke. (A kettle-borrower is accused by the lender of burning a hole in the borrowed vessel. The borrower defends himself with three arguments which cancel each other out, with comic effect: (1) I never borrowed the kettle; (2) it was already damaged when I borrowed it; and (3) I gave it back undamaged.) Freud concludes: 'A. was treating in isolation what had to be [logically] connected as a whole . . . We might say A. put an "and" where an "either, or" would suffice' (Freud 1905: 62; Flieger 1991). In other words, the absurd joke avails itself of 'either . . . or . . . or' reasoning to send a tremor through normal logic and push it to the 'point' at which laughter breaks out.

It is perhaps both ironic and humorous to find the author of Oedipus and the author of *Anti-Oedipus* on the same page, as it were, when it comes to this art of differential intensities. Indeed, Freud and Deleuze themselves produce a kind of disjunctive synthesis, when their two bodies of work are mapped together, demonstrating the value of unlikely junctures: what Deleuze calls a 'schizoid' experience, enacted in the juncture of the orchid and wasp, and the 'material' experience of Schreber is indeed a deterritorialised kind of 'wit', in the Freudian sense of an encounter of intensities which transforms all participants.

If Freud reterritorialises Deleuze's becoming as 'wit', Deleuze in turn reterritorialises the Freudian unconscious, transforming it from a repository of repressed 'wishes' to an interaction of intensities. Similarly, he transforms Freud's notion of 'identification' from a 'molar' imitation, to something 'molecular'. For Deleuze, this molecular identification is linked to 'simulation', a travesty of identity:

[Simulation] expresses those nondecomposable distances always enveloped in the intensities that divide into one another while changing their form. If identification is a nomination, a designation, then simulation is the writing corresponding to it, a writing that is strangely polyvocal, flush with the real. (Deleuze and Guattari 1977: 87)

Can Deleuze then 'identify' with feminism, in this revised sense of 'simulation'? In determining whether the work of Deleuze may be mapped with feminism, one must of course first consider which feminism one wants to 'map'. Some feminists will certainly continue to object to what they see as the cooptation of 'woman' in Deleuze's work by an essentialist formulation which does seem to exclude real women. However, cultural feminists, such as Judith Butler, who see gender as a largely performative effect, will probably welcome the Deleuzean notion of 'becoming' (Butler 1990, 1993). This is especially true of 'cross-dressing' as a kind of performance or masking, which characterises the mutual lure of the orchid and the wasp.

But the productive disjunction between Deleuze and feminism is more material than thematic, literally material, since it 'strings' them together, while maintaining separation. In its 'strangely polyvocal' quality, 'flush with the real', Deleuze's writing of simulation is textured, textile, tensile and textual (as in the Latin *textere*: to weave): it intersects with the '*l'écriture féminine*' practised by feminists writing in France, at about the same time. (One thinks, for instance, of the explosively subversive writing of Cixous in 'The Laugh of the Medusa' (Marks and de Courtrivon 1981) or the sensual lyric and charged prose of Irigaray in *This Sex Which is Not One* (1985a), or the material intensity of Kristeva's evocation of maternity in 'Stabat Mater' (1986).) These theorists highlight the subversive nature of *l'écriture féminine*, which is a practice that they do not limit to women writers; this mode of writing is reminiscent of Deleuze's 'becomings', in that it seeks to take language/thought and make it 'snap', passing a tremor through it. Certain essays of Julia Kristeva, for example, actually refer to the 'molecular' and profoundly material, corporeal nature of women's experience (as in the lyric and violent passages of 'Stabat Mater', written with the same exultation, and difficulty, and with the same 'molecular' atomised material sense of 'becoming' as, say, Deleuze's chapters on 'faciality' and 'rhizome'. Kristeva's graphic and lurid passages on becoming-mother are imbued with the transformative experience of becoming-other. Indeed, like Deleuze's own writing, one could say of Kristeva's essays ('Soleil noir', 'Le Temps des femmes' (Kristeva 1975)) that they '[belong] to the realm of physics'; where the body and its intensities 'are not metaphors, but matter itself' (Deleuze and Guattari 1977: 283). In all of these cases, the writing is certainly polyvocal. (One of Kristeva's works is titled *Polylogue* (1975), rehearsing a multiple internal voice curiously 'flush with the real' which it maps in the rhythms of the body.)

In other words, the feminists of immanence are proximate to what Deleuze calls 'the terribly disturbing sound of matter': Luce Irigaray, who calls for a fluid, non-monolithic embodied writing; Kristeva, who fashions a non-representative semiotics of the *chora*, the voice at the 'molecular' level; or Cixous, who calls for woman to explode everything with laughter, or, perhaps just as comically, to 'write with her milk'. It is this immanence, this materiality, this call to the experience as lived by the body, that may link a certain feminism with the molecular becomings of Deleuze. In her essay 'Women's Time', in fact, Kristeva writes of pregnancy in just these terms, as a becoming which saturates the cells, the molecules, the very atoms of the maternal body, no longer just one-self, but a self in an altered state, linked by the cord that binds with an alien other.

I shall close by suggesting one other mapping of Deleuze with feminist theory which might allow us to think of Deleuze as a 'millennial' thinker. For high-tech 'millennial' feminism – in the work of thinkers like Donna Haraway, Roseanne Stone, or Avital Ronell – seems to be in a kind of disjunctive synchrony with Deleuzean becoming (Haraway 1991; Stone 1995; Ronell 1989, 1994). Haraway's cyborg, for instance, is itself a disjunctive synthesis of sorts, a monstrous Frankensteinian coupling which commingles and inter-wires human and machine, human and animal. In her later work, dealing with 'engineered' species of mice with human genes, the distinction between 'phyla' is further blurred (Haraway 1996). Of course Haraway is only one of many important thinkers talking about cybernetics, but what is so striking about Haraway's formulation is that it lacks the dystopian tenor of other millennial commentaries: she welcomes this permeability of animal-machine-human, as an opportunity for feminism, or for living beyond the boundaries imposed by a too-strictly constructed and observed gender, claiming that cyborg society is a 'post-gender world'. While at the moment, I think there is nothing like this 'post-gender' society anywhere in sight, Haraway's notion of a hybrid, post-gender world is not inconsistent with Deleuze's trajectory of implicated serial becoming: woman-child-animal. And Freud could join the club: like Haraway's human-machine, Freud's paraphrenic man-woman belies a single identity: in his becoming, man-woman is no longer a binary opposition but a binary apposition, whereby majoritarian man is de-positioned.

In other words, Haraway's permeable boundaries promote contamination in the sense of pollination, and cross-connecting, culminating in hybrid organisms that change our view of evolution itself. For thinkers like Haraway and Deleuze, the masculinist agon of evolution no longer suffices to explain being, since it describes a hierarchy culminating in 'Man', the hero of the narrative of the survival of the fittest. 'Millennial' thinkers like Deleuze and Haraway promote instead a cross-gendered game of lure and alliance, where the surviving of the fittest becomes the conniving of the wittiest – as when the orchid 'dresses' to fool the wasp. In this molecular play of intensities, the orchid is a transvestite, luring the wasp with a material wit.

But the joke is on no one, for in becoming-other, every 'one' loses face and identity, and finds creative solutions, ways to gain pleasure. Paradoxically, one finds 'survival' at the expense of 'identity', by becoming-other.

Yet there is nothing tame about Deleuze's universe, however ludic and sympathetic: its intensity comes from passion. After all, for Deleuze, 'Paradox is the passion of philosophy', its self-sacrifice, its becoming-intense, its self-irony. In Deleuze's work, philosophy is wittily transvesting itself so that its subject becomes its object ('man') and in so doing loses a centred identity. For the ultimate modern philosophical paradox is that modern 'man' loses 'man-hood', his majoritarian identity, by becoming-intense, but this loss is enabling, and energising. The Deleuzean transformation – becoming less (perceptible) by becoming-other – is becoming to him, like Schreber's flamboyant finery.

I will close with Deleuze's reference to Viriginia Woolf, who says that it is necessary to 'saturate every atom' in order to be 'present at the dawn of the world':

> To reduce oneself to an abstract line, a trait . . . and in this way enter the haecceity and impersonality of the creator. One is then like grass: one has made the world, everyday/everything, into a becoming, because one has made a necessarily communicating world, because one has suppressed in oneself everything that prevents us from slipping between things and growing in the midst of things . . . Saturate, eliminate, put everything in. (Deleuze and Guattari 1987: 280)

This passage highlights a productive irony: here Deleuze cites a feminist icon, the very emblem of 'identity' for woman, the original tenant of a 'room of one's own', claiming to put down roots, a 'plot' or place from which to speak. But Woolf is also Deleuze's chosen poet of deterritorialisation, of itinerant moves, of becoming-imperceptible, 'like grass', articulating an inarticulate politics of the 'point' which destabilises and sends a tremor through any party 'line'. We are reminded that Deleuze's non-linear politics is 'the opposite of macropopolitics, and even of History' because all history is majoritarian (Deleuze and Guattari 1987: 292).

Deleuze seems to be saying that activism must be at the level of intensities, always far from equilibrium, shaking things up: 'A punctual system is most interesting when there is a musician, painter, writer or philosopher to oppose it, who even fabricates it in order to oppose it, like a springboard to jump from. History is made only by those who oppose history (not by those who insert themselves into it, or even reshape it)' (Deleuze and Guattari 1987: 295).

Deleuze's 'fabrication' would seem to exclude any effort to solve the problems of history by intervention, revolution, or persuasion. We thus seem to be left with a quietism as problematic as the formulations on becoming-woman with which we began. But at another level – at the level of disjunction, saturation with matter, location in 'real bodies', and the valorisation and mobilisation of difference as a force that 'does what it can do' – Deleuze may speak to the strongest impulses of feminists who seek to deterritorialise rather than codify, who seek to change the very rules and terms of being oneself – to being beside oneself, passionately and radically – struggling with the paradox of becoming equal while insisting on being different.

Perhaps some feminists have always understood that history is made only by those who oppose history: those not in line but out of line, who refuse to play the game, or who play the game wittily in order to alter its rules. Deleuze and feminism may seem to be at odds, from the perspective of the concerns of real women. But like the orchid and the wasp, the relation of Deleuzean thought and feminist thought may be 'mapped' or interwoven in a kind of productive disjunction. It is perhaps neither a matter of window-dressing, masquerade and cosmetic solutions, nor of conflict and irreconcilable differences, but a matter of paradox.

NOTES

I should like to thank Manuel De Landa for his helpful insights concerning Deleuze's concepts of intensity and non-linearity. De Landa elaborates his interpretation of Deleuze's materialism in *A Thousand Years of Non-Linear History* (1997).

1. The first citation is quoted from Michael Hofmann's review essay, 'The Emperor of Nonsense', *The New York Times Book Review* (21 December 1997: 9). Hofmann's reference to Wallace's materialist aesthetics is based on the journal entry of 10 August (1902), in *Wallace Stevens: Collected Poetry and Prose* (Stevens 1997: 929). The second quotation is from 'Sonnet VI' (Stevens 1997: 485).

2. The co-author of many of Deleuze's works is Félix Guattari. However, for the sake of brevity and consistency, I will attribute the ideas here to 'Deleuze' rather than to 'Deleuze and Guattari', because the argument is rooted in the poststructuralist thought of *Difference and Repetition* (1994a), of which Deleuze was the sole author.

3. For a critique of 'becoming-woman' as a term associated with the nomad in Deleuze's text, see Rosi Braidotti, *Nomadic Subjects: Embodiment and Sexual Difference in Contemporary Feminist Theory* (1994b). Luce Irigaray refers to Deleuze's masculinist tendencies, as well as Lacan's 'phallic' bias, in *This Sex Which is Not One* (1985a). Elizabeth Grosz's critique of 'rhizomatics' appears in 'A Thousand Tiny Sexes: Feminism and Rhizomatics' (1993b).

4. Deleuze insists that all becomings, including Schreber's transformation, are real, even while he is not a real woman. This may be explained as an actualisation of the 'virtual': 'The virtual is opposed not to the real but to the actual. The virtual is fully real in so far as it is virtual. Exactly what Proust said of states of resonance must be said of the virtual: "Real without being actual, ideal without being abstract"; and symbolic without being fictional. Indeed, the virtual must be defined as strictly a part of the real object – as though the object had one part of itself in the virtual into which it plunged as though into an objective dimension' (Deleuze 1994a: 208–9).

5. Recent work by political psychoanalytic thinkers, such as Jean Baudrillard and Slavoj Žižek, follow Deleuze's characterisation of paranoia as the disease of the totalitarian socius, recalling the Frankfurt School's doctrine linking eroticism with the 'mass psychology' of the fascist. See Freud's analysis of the identificatory relation between the masses and the charismatic church/army leader in 'Group Psychology and the Analysis of the Ego' (Freud 1921).

3

The Woman in Process:
Deleuze, Kristeva and Feminism

CATHERINE DRISCOLL

There was an interval.
(Virginia Woolf, *Between the Acts*, 1988)

INTRODUCTION

Gilles Deleuze and Julia Kristeva are problematic figures in contemporary feminist theory with apparently opposed views on the influence of the psychoanalytic model of the subject in late modernity. Any analysis of Deleuze's and Kristeva's relations to modernity and subjectivity must also raise their contradictory references to gender and sexual difference, and probably evoke the antagonistic interdependence of feminism and psychoanalysis as crucial ideological forces in the twentieth century. First, I want to compare Deleuze's and Kristeva's positions on the constitution of the gendered subject of modernity through their position in relation to psychoanalysis, a comparison enabled by considering Elizabeth Grosz's use of both Kristeva and Deleuze towards a feminist philosophy of difference with its own particularly tense relation to psychoanalysis. Second, I want to suggest that it is crucial to this comparison that in their accounts of body, desire and subjectivity both Deleuze and Kristeva produce 'the girl' as an impossible figure of anticipation and escape within the Oedipal framework, and thus within dominant understandings of how the subject is constituted. Feminist uses of Deleuze have not yet sufficiently addressed the significance of the girl in his work, as an assemblage which moves through and escapes the foundational territory of the Oedipalised family which feminist theory has inherited from psychoanalysis.

I want to consider what the process located in 'woman' is for Deleuze and Kristeva by considering how they place the girl as a pivotally difficult figure for the process of constituting the subject. Deleuze and Kristeva, despite professing dramatically opposed positions on the constitution and reproduction of the subject, take comparable positions in relation to the proposition 'woman'. For Deleuze, woman is a position in relation to the majority (or dominant set of social norms) which must be engaged in order to interrogate or escape that norm, by both women and men. In response to Lacan's claim that woman, as such, does not exist, Kristeva similarly argues that 'if the feminine *exists*, it only exists in the order of signifiance or signifying process, and it is only in relation to meaning and signification, positioned as their excessive and transgressive other that it *exists*, *speaks*, *thinks* (itself) and *writes* (itself) for both sexes' (1986: 11). Both Kristeva and Deleuze emphasise this constitution in language, and in the final section I will consider their reference to Virginia Woolf as example of how both 'woman' and the 'signifying process' encounter Oedipal organisation. Woolf's engagements with both feminism and modern subjectivity, and her assemblages of subject positions which escape Oedipal frames, might be useful to considering what Deleuze's thought offers feminists.

DELEUZE AND PSYCHOANALYSIS

The Deleuzean century (Foucault 1984: 165) has been crucially influenced by psychoanalysis and what Kristeva describes as the 'Copernican revolution' begun by Freud's recognition that the self-aware subject (the Cartesian paradigm, among others) is in fact divided and contradictory. Deleuze's philosophy consistently engages with the psychoanalytic subject's processes for overcoming disunity through a developmental schema culminating in the Oedipal complex and its putatively predictable effects. While Deleuze also critiques the unified subject of Western philosophy, he finds the Oedipalised template for identity at least equally oppressive. From psychoanalysis Deleuze takes as his principle target the colonisation of the unconscious by Oedipus, describing the Oedipalised unconscious – one in which repression has been instituted as necessary for existence – as an entirely interested invention: 'the plane of the Unconscious remains a plane of transcendence guaranteeing, justifying, the existence of psychoanalysis and the necessity of its interpretations' (Deleuze and Guattari 1987: 284).[1] The Oedipus complex develops and affirms a set of oppositions including masculine and feminine, subject and object, presence and lack. Psychoanalysis expresses these structures by reference to the Other: the term in relation to which objects are recognised, and the concept which opposes and constitutes the subject. Deleuze rejects this pattern – the subject and, its structural antithesis, the Other; I and it – for a model of subjectivity and desire which is mobile and connective rather than oppositional. Deleuze also rejects the centred subject of language and history, but in favour of a multiplicity that does not simply multiply the normative subject. Identity for Deleuze does not require any binary opposition to or within the self, and yet the modes of subverting normative models which he privileges – figures like the girl, nomad, or becoming-woman – themselves suggest alterity to a norm. While this appears entirely amenable to feminist critique, these figures have seemed difficult for feminists, even those who would employ Deleuze in critiques of psychoanalysis, because he often takes up such figures without reference to women or gender, or rejecting reference to them.

Alice Jardine argues that 'For Deleuze, psychoanalysis is the last avatar of the anthropological representation of sexuality' (Jardine 1985: 135), and Foucault also points to Deleuze's attack on 'The poor technicians of desire – psychoanalysts and semiologists of every sign and symptom – who would subjugate the multiplicity of desire to the twofold law of structure and lack' (1977: xii). But Deleuze's use of apparently feminised concepts to disrupt hierarchies suggests his relative tolerance for Lacanian rather than Freudian psychoanalysis, as the norm the hierarchies he addresses constitute linguistic rather than behavioural structures: 'the form under which the majority is based [is] white, male, adult, "rational," etc., in short the average European, the subject of enunciation' (Deleuze and Guattari 1987: 292). It is even arguable that Deleuze and Guattari privilege Lacan's mirror-stage as an exemplary, though not necessary, totalisation of the body. Reference to this mirror-stage appears in several of Deleuze's definitions of this majority or normative subject, including this 'average European', demonstrated, they argue, by 'The faciality function' (1987: 292). A strange hiatus in their escape from the organisation of the subject occurs in *A Thousand Plateaus*' assertion that 'small amounts' (bits and pieces?) of subjectivity must be retained in order to engage with the world (1987: 160). This tolerance continues to critique Oedipal effects. Indeed this preference for Lacan might rest on his ambivalence concerning the work of Oedipus, or any comparable template for desire. Deleuze argues that Oedipal models are not just prescriptive – if you negotiate your Oedipal complex in the right way you will be normal – but constrictive: every action or power relation can be explained under the Oedipal code, and every desire, however far beyond the Oedipal triangle, can fall back on to that model for its explanation or correction. In these ways psychoanalysis reduces 'every social manifestation of desire to the familial complex' (Seem 1977: xviii), and the mother's body and father's name are left as the surfaces upon which desire is recorded.

Deleuze thus interrogates the psychoanalytic assumptions concerning relations between sexes, bodies and power that have been crucial to feminist theory, producing new terminologies which disrupt a 'commonsense' connection of these to 'inner selves'. A number of binary oppositions central to psychoanalysis have dominated feminist theory: including male and female sexes, masculine and feminine genders, subject and object, presence and lack, and mind and body. Across these oppositions feminist theory, especially since Simone de Beauvoir's *The Second Sex* (1972), has debated what, historically and/or essentially, a woman is. For de Beauvoir the problem of sexual difference was solved by existentialism, by the transcendence of consciousness over the gendered body, and it is arguable that Kristeva's invocation of overcoming gender prioritises this term in the same dualism. As I suggested above, Deleuze's understanding of subjectivity does not organise the self into more or less innate binary oppositions and is thus useful for a feminist theory which would consider conjunctions of body and identity without relying on transcendence. Transcendence reinforces the body–mind division which imposes on feminist theory a particular interpretation of experience, whether interested in how women might avoid assignation to the side of the body in that division, or privileging woman as a position which destabilises that division. As Moira Gatens suggests, this division is already unstable: 'mind is constituted by the affirmation of the actual existence of the body, and reason is active and embodied precisely because it is the affirmation of a *particular* bodily existence' (1996a: 57). Yet the mind–body division remains the precise scene of a psychoanalytic discourse which continues to delineate the concerns of much feminist theory, as Grosz suggests in the introduction to *Volatile Bodies* (1994a), and a feminist reading of Deleuze would inevitably be some kind of reply to this dominance. The difficulty of feminists using Deleuze, I would argue, has less to do with his deployment of gender, or any obscurities or contradictions, than with the fact that he does not just critique but rejects the descriptive power of psychoanalysis.

Deleuze himself appropriates psychoanalysis to respond to the modern centrality of the self. Little attention has been paid to whether Deleuze's earlier uses of psychoanalysis effect continuities across his work, for example, the relation between the little girl of *The Logic of Sense* and the becoming-woman of his work with Guattari. In *The Logic of Sense*, the girl retains a fixed oppositional relation to Oedipus:

> In its evolution and in the line which it traces, the phallus marks always an excess and a lack, oscillating between one and the other and even being both at once. It is essentially an excess, as it projects itself over the genital zone of the child, duplicating its penis, and inspiring it with the Oedipal affair. (Deleuze 1990b: 227)

Yet the *Capitalism and Schizophrenia* books articulate Deleuze's criticisms of psychoanalysis, and his later opposition to psychoanalysis seems to render his work incompatible with Kristeva's, who is not only a psychoanalytic theorist but a practising analyst. But it remains too easy to insist on this opposition, which cannot address the continuities between many of Deleuze's and Kristeva's accounts of modernity, subjectivity, language and gender. These continuities suggest not that feminism might now have overcome debates over psychoanalysis, but instead that feminism, including poststructuralist feminism, remains more complexly implicated in the psychoanalytic project than those debates usually recognise.

PSYCHOANALYSIS, FEMINISM, IDENTITY

It appears self-evident now that feminists are also interested in critiquing the Oedipal subject. But much contemporary feminist theory assumes a psychoanalytic model by collapsing all difference into an identity constituted by gender; emphasising familial centres for social reproduction and prioritising consciousness. Psychoanalytic models presume that desire and language, reproduced in the nuclear family, are templates for one another: a stratification which organises bodies and identities. Kristeva's alignments of linguistics or literary technique and familial patterns endorse just this model. As Kristeva's repeated engagement of the two attests, feminism and psychoanalysis are closely entwined not only by their responses to each other, but in belonging to the same period of redefining relations between gender and cultural reproduction. Theories of how identity is embodied and articulated are also central to both.

While Deleuze and Kristeva disagree concerning the usefulness of psychoanalytic models they agree on the undesirability of deploying the category 'woman' in cultural analysis. While Kristeva's writings on what a woman is and on the impossibility of feminine subjectivity are not homogenous, her earliest challenges to feminism have not been redirected or qualified in later work. In the well-known essay 'Women's Time' Kristeva writes:

[T]he apparent coherence which the term 'woman' assumes in contemporary ideology, apart from its 'mass' or 'shock' effect for activist purposes, essentially has the negative effect of effacing the differences among the diverse functions or structures which operate beneath this word. (1986: 193)

Referring to the feminine, Kristeva asserts here, 'we can speak only about a structure observed in a socio-historical context and not about essences' (1986: 199). And yet, without any need for reference to the essence of woman, the trans-historicism of this structure allows gendered figures to pass unanalysed or endorsed through Kristeva's account of the subject.

Both Kristeva and Deleuze would also agree with the central feminist assertion that the body and politics are inextricably intertwined. But while Kristeva remains invested in some distinctions of the body from the social, Deleuze's use of identity is not distinguishable from politics, unlike theories which hold subjectivity as prior to actions. In psychoanalysis the public and private are tautologically interdependent – penis envy is the public imprinted on the private, the law of the father the public made analogous to the private. Grosz's discussion of embodied subjectivity in *Volatile Bodies* takes up both Deleuze and Kristeva in critiquing this tautology and in support of her thesis that mind and body fold into one another, but their roles in her account are very different. Grosz's turn from 'the inside out' to 'the outside in' turns away from the visible materiality of the body in psychoanalysis, neurophysiology and most phenomenology towards the invisible materiality of the body mapped by Nietzsche, Foucault and Deleuze. Grosz's turn is particularly articulated against psychoanalysis, moving towards a body without any organs to be cathected and hierarchised in its models of development, a project described as 'rewriting the female body as a positivity rather than as a lack' (1994a: 61). Grosz's broader relationship to psychoanalysis is problematic, including a movement away from and return to psychoanalysis as the most useful, at least most accurately descriptive, account of desire, if not the body. Grosz claims that feminists who critique Freud as well as those who endorse him

agree that his account of sexual difference, with its references to the phallic mother, the castration complex and the Oedipus complex, provides an accurate description of the processes which produce masculine and feminine subjects within our Western, patriarchal, capitalist culture. Their disagreements arise regarding . . . the necessity of the domination of the phallus. (Grosz 1994a: 57)

But *Volatile Bodies* marks Grosz's influential move away from psychoanalysis, furthered in her collection *Space, Time and Perversion* (1995).

While Grosz's account of Kristeva is consistently ambivalent, acknowledging Kristeva's antagonism towards some forms of feminism and endorsement of the Lacanian model for gendered subjectivity and desire, it is in *Volatile Bodies* that this ambivalence is most evident, given that Grosz had prioritised Kristeva in accounting for relations between feminism and psychoanalysis in her previous texts. Here Kristeva is employed entirely with reference to her theory of abjection, as the position from which she might be thought to turn away from the 'subject/object and inside/outside oppositions' (Grosz 1994a: 192). For Kristeva, though, while the body does found identity, it is as that from which identity separates itself, and the abject only compromises these oppositions by reinforcing them. For Kristeva, because she is a psychoanalyst, desire is a broad pattern of social and pre-social forces, and one which underlies political movements and ideas, including feminism. As in Lacanian theory more widely, body and desire are formed together, but according to a pattern which precedes them.[2] Kristeva's use of 'woman' is as distant from any biological determinism as Grosz desires, but it moves in a very different direction – from the inside out, Grosz might suggest. Grosz prioritises Deleuze as an alternative to psychoanalysis in this regard, but within the same paradigm, also expanding on feminist critiques of his work. From *A Thousand Plateaus* she draws the following:

Questions related to subjectivity, interiority, female sexual specificity, are thus not symptoms of a patriarchal culture, not simply products or effects of it, but are forces, intensities, requiring codifications or territorializations and in turn exerting their own deterritorializing and decodifying force, systems of compliance and resistance. (Grosz 1994a: 180)

But Grosz's 'sexual difference' and her account of relations between bodies and identities are compatible with psychoanalysis and phenomenology (1994a: 203), and how Deleuze belongs to such an intersection remains unrealised.[3] What Kristeva's understanding of the subject's constitution across boundaries between dualist terms will not admit is an analysis of power as it is practised rather than according to its origins, an emphasis Deleuze refers to Foucault (Deleuze 1988: 71).

Like Grosz, Ian Buchanan notes that Deleuze and Guattari's thought on the body focuses on the problem of what a body can do (Buchanan 1997: 74):

We know nothing about a body until we know what it can do, in other words, what its affects are, how they can or cannot enter into composition with other affects, with the affects of another body, either to destroy that body or to be destroyed by it, either to exchange actions and passions with it or to join with it in composing a more powerful body. (Deleuze and Guattari 1987: 257)

In thinking about the body as action and affect rather than cause and effect (Buchanan 1997: 74), Deleuze disallows the primacy that the sexed body mostly retains in feminist theories of the body. The body without organs is the body without hierarchised organs such as penis, phallus, vagina, even mouth; 'opposed not to the organs but to that organisation of the organs called the organism' (Deleuze and Guattari 1987: 158). The organism is the unification of the body, the conceptualisation of the body as unified, and it is difficult to conceive of gender or sexual difference as other than such organisations. The organisation of the body is a delimitation of what the body can do. But for Deleuze some things a body does – like becoming-woman or being a girl – are not so easily organised into delimited hierarchies, into relations to norms or majorities; they can even defer or defy normative or majoritarian organisation. The Body Without Organs is the site for these processes: it is a

limit; a tendency; a becoming that resists the processes of overcoding and organization according to the three great strata or identities it opposes: the union of the *organism*, the unification of the *subject*, and the structure of *significance*. The BwO resists any equation with a notion of identity or property: 'The BwO is never yours or mine. It is always *a* body'. (Grosz 1994b: 201)

These strata emphasise links between subjectivity and signification, between being (organised) and language, but it will be useful to further consider what kind of a body and process this is.

DELEUZE, KRISTEVA, THE GIRL

Deleuze and Guattari acknowledge their own use of dualisms as a territory through which they move 'in order to arrive at a process that challenges all models' (1987: 20). The two clear differences between Deleuze and Kristeva, then – the structuring of their analysis and their model of the subject – both depend on their relation to psychoanalytic structures, the poststructural elements of which complicate without undoing its dualisms. I have argued that this is a difficulty for feminists who want to avoid reference to the inevitability of any binary opposition. I want now to consider how Deleuze might avoid that reference, and what alternative might be located in an engagement of Deleuze and Kristeva.

The idea that the subject is not only structured but predictable because of that structure is the basis for the therapeutic undercurrent of psychoanalysis (not necessarily directed to a therapeutic end). All of Kristeva's analyses are negotiations of dualisms, and rely on a foundational, and sometimes apparently naturalised, dualist structure for subjectification and the linguistic order which constitutes it.[4] Gender is central to that structure, and while Kristeva calls for the dissolution of gender she also relies on its inevitability for the structure of her analyses. From the earlier concepts of dialogue and semiosis to her widely appropriated conceptions of abjection and the Symbolic Order, Kristeva's work conforms to what Foucault called 'the twofold law', while emphasising the moments in which oppositional structures are breached. Moreover, Kristeva explains such structures and breaches as exchanges between maternal and paternal, prelinguistic and linguistic oppositions. Indeed, the passionate moments of undoing or threatening order which she privileges require that order, exist within that order, and do not structurally challenge it. Exemplarily, the abject and the carnivalesque name the structural permeability of structure: the foundational failure of boundaries. But neither the carnival nor abjection threaten the subject as a structure, only individuals.

Deleuze rejects all predicable structures, his dualisms are not dichotomies but movements and effects.[5] This process is exemplified in the figure of becoming-woman, or the little girl, and I want to turn now in more detail to the girl's role in psychoanalytic models of subjection and in locating distinctions between Deleuze and Kristeva that are more productive than their opposition over psychoanalytic description.[6] Feminist discussion of Deleuze's becoming-woman tends to focus on the woman but, like the becoming a wolf which Deleuze and Guattari turn against Freud, becoming-woman 'is not a question of representation' (Deleuze and Guattari 1987: 32). For Kristeva also, the semiotic and related figures are not feminine in any sense which links them to women representatively or has a privileged relation to women, and yet they are indisputably feminised. Deleuze explains this as the 'incorporeal': the little girl and the woman named in becoming are detached from corporeal causes, they are 'a way of being' (Deleuze 1990b: 147). As Grosz points out, Deleuze utilises 'the girl as the site of a culture's most intensified disinvestments and re-castings of the body' (Grosz 1994a: 174–5). For Deleuze, however, the girl is not a free agent or only a radical singularity. She consists in relations between statements and visibilities, in power relations (Deleuze 1988: 79). Grosz does not mediate between Deleuze's and Kristeva's versions of this girl figure so much as divert them towards what might become a Deleuzean critique of Kristeva. While Grosz engages directly with Deleuze and Guattari's use of the girl she only refers in passing to its relation to the girl in psychoanalysis and does not refer at all to Kristeva's use of the girl. Yet in emphasising how the girl avoids some of the clear boundaries of psychoanalysis which Grosz associates with Kristeva, such a critique is implied.

Kristeva maps the girl's difficulties in direct relation to the Oedipal family, and Deleuze's figure of the girl also moves in relation to territories. Indeed it is as a daughter that the girl delineates the proprietary succession which she escapes: after all, 'How could lines of deterritorialization be assignable outside of circuits of territoriality?' (Deleuze and Guattari 1987: 34). As both Kristeva and Deleuze also suggest, the girl is a sexuality, if she is not a figure for sexuality. However, while sexuality within the nuclear family – 'sexuality' never having been anywhere else, as Foucault has argued – is predominantly patterned on the triangle of parents and child, even if its Oedipal formation is symptomatic rather than causative, the daughter does not belong to this triangle. As Luce Irigaray explains, the daughter can become neither the father nor the mother, given that the mother is not a subject. But Kristeva considers the girl only in relation to the mother's exclusion from the symbolic, describing the girl's love for the mother as 'like black lava' lying in wait for the girl 'all along the path of her desperate attempts to identify with the symbolic paternal order' (1986: 157). For Kristeva, in comparison to this girl's struggle with her body's exclusion, the body is 'stolen first' from the boy by its relegation to the place of mother or woman.

Kristeva's theories of subjectivity always return to this relation to origin and the gender order, insisting that

[T]he first 'other' with whom 'I' – the son – initiate a genuine dialogue is above all the other sex; [the mother] is therefore doubly justified in constituting this pole of alterity through which the allocution constitutes itself, and which fiction is going to usurp, absorb, and dissolve. (1984: 320)

If the son's identification with the father does not extend to a daughter, and the daughter is not continuous with the mother, it is unclear what such fiction will do for her. The girl perpetuates the territorialising force of Oedipus and the nuclear family by her very liminality to such developmental orders and processes. *A Thousand Plateaus* contends that

The body is stolen first from the girl: Stop behaving like that, you're not a little girl anymore, you're not a tomboy, etc. The girl's becoming is stolen first, in order to impose a history or prehistory upon her. The boy's turn comes next, but it is by using the girl as an example, by pointing to the girl as the object of his desire, that an opposed organism, a dominant history is fabricated for him too. The girl is the first victim, but she must also serve as an example and a trap. That is why, conversely, the reconstruction of the Body without Organs, the anorganism of the body, is inseparable from a becoming-woman, or the production of a molecular woman. Doubtless, the girl becomes a woman in the molar or organic sense. But conversely, becoming-woman or the molecular woman is the girl herself. (1987: 276)

But in what sense does this little girl defer or escape becoming woman? As Grosz recognises, this incorporates psychoanalytic accounts of the boy's Oedipalisation (1994a: 175), where a girl also must not become the woman as mother. Certainly it retains the girl's role as opposing and defining the boy's development. Yet *Anti-Oedipus* describes what will be called becoming-woman as 'the real production of a girl born without a mother, of a non-oedipal

74

woman (who would not be oedipal either for herself or for others)'
(1977: 471–2).

Becoming-woman specifically deterritorialises the organised
body and Oedipalised desire, and in doing so it draws on Deleuze's
prior conception of 'the little girl' in *The Logic of Sense*. But if there
is a deployment of the little girl in becoming-woman there is no
simple causal connection between them. The little girl does not
become a woman as molar or majoritarian identity – as a gendered
identity, that is, one which is fixed in relation to the majority – and
she remains separate from that proposition, 'woman', which neither Deleuze nor Kristeva want. According to *A Thousand Plateaus*:

The girl . . . is an abstract line, or a line of flight. Thus girls do not
belong to an age, group, sex, order or kingdom: they slip in everywhere,
between orders, acts, ages, sexes: they produce *n* molecular sexes in
the line of flight in relation to the dualism machines they cross right
through . . . The girl is like the block of becoming that remains contemporaneous to each opposable term, man, woman, child, adult. It is
not the girl who becomes woman; it is becoming-woman that produces
the universal girl. (1987: 276–7)

Becoming-woman is a way of understanding transformative possibilities – the ways in which identity might escape from the codes
which constitute the subject.

While feminists discuss becoming-woman when they consider
Deleuze's usefulness, surprisingly little has been done with the
concept becoming-woman in feminist analysis. For Grosz, perhaps,
the fold has been a more useful figure – 'the inside as the operation
of the outside' (Deleuze 1988: 96) – taken up it seems, although
she does not cite it directly, in her conception of the Möbius strip
as a model for rethinking relations between body and mind. Grosz
has described Deleuze's model of subjectivity as a 'flat subjectivity,
a subjectivity composed of planes, surfaces, matter rather than
emotions, attitudes, beliefs' (1993b: 53). This model is both a critique, arguing that Western philosophy's account of subjectivity,
'in its effort to preserve the identity of the One, hardened the
ontological difference between Being and becoming' (Boundas
1993: 5), and an alternative which could be figured as the girl's
impossible relation to the subject's origin. Kristeva represents the
girl as a trap or failure for exactly the same reasons. It is because
neither women nor girls become the subject that becoming-woman
produces an identity which is not an outcome of a process but is
that process itself. While becoming-woman is not a reference to

women, covering the same terrains as 'becoming-animal', having been named as woman and girl this line of flight continues to evoke the 'minority' aspects of women and girls and should have a special relevance to feminists. The status of women as 'minority' is not unproblematic in Deleuze's work. In *Cinema 2*, he argues that the minority is 'still to come' (Deleuze 1989: 196), while in *Kafka: Toward a Minor Literature* Deleuze and Guattari (1986) explicitly employ women as a metaphor for the minor.[7] But even if becoming-woman or women as minority do continue to have a metaphoric function for Deleuze, women are not excluded from deploying the minor, or women, and the minor may be still to come in the same way that 'becoming', for Deleuze, is never finalised, but always in the middle or in process.

DESIRE AND LANGUAGE: BETWEEN THE ACTS

Deleuze's critique of the psychoanalytic subject is inseparable from his approach to language insofar as he recognises the constitution of the subject in language. Like psychoanalytic theorists, Deleuze claims that relations of desire produce subjectivities, but not according to a developmental schema where a subject is causally produced as the producer of desire. For Deleuze these subjectivities are temporary and mobile, produced contingently by connections and disconnections between bodies and desires, rather than a foundational sense of the self. This production is dispersed across heterogeneous processes of desire that Deleuze and Guattari call desiring machines, always 'Producing, a product: a producing/ product identity' (1977: 7) from among their group flux of 'associative flows and partial objects' (287). Such an organisation of flows and partial objects resembles Kristevan psychoanalysis, particularly in her account of abjection. Deleuze's understanding of such flows and objects differs primarily in being an assemblage, and thus in not recognising the separation of subject and object which abjection refers to, a difference relevant to feminists who would avoid distinguishing agents from discourses or objects. Alongside becoming-woman and the fold I would take up the concept of assemblage as productive for feminist deployment of Deleuze. Deleuze and Guattari argue that 'Assemblages are necessary for states of force and regimes of signs to intertwine their relations' (1987: 71). That is, an assemblage is simultaneously a way of being and a mode of signification, relevant to feminist recognition of the discursive power of terms like subject and woman. I want to unfold this entwinement of signification and subjectivity a little further in this context with reference to Virginia Woolf.

Jardine describes the feminine figure of modernity (and the postmodern) as 'gynesis':

the putting into discourse of 'woman' as that *process* diagnosed in France as intrinsic to the condition of modernity; indeed, the valorization of the feminine, woman, and her obligatory, that is historical connotations, as somehow intrinsic to new and necessary modes of thinking, writing, speaking. (1985: 25)

Despite the overextension of the phrase *l'écriture féminine*, the concept of 'feminine writing' illustrates the dependence of late modern interpretative models on defining the decentred subject as 'feminine' – a project which continues to underline the masculinity of the subject. It is refusing this subject that distinguishes Deleuze's account of the little girl or the schizo from fragmentations of a still normative subject, and from resembling Kristeva's references to madness. The 'woman' attached to the schizo is not the maternal Other of post/modernism, but becoming-woman, and Deleuze does not propose a decentred subject, but modes of subjectivity which were never centred. As Kristeva's definition of postmodernism exemplifies, the 'postmodern' intervention in modernist aesthetics is inadequate precisely because it fails to address this feminised subversion's continued dependence on the subject, whether as negative or as fragmentation, and I would contend that Kristeva, rather than Deleuze, is postmodern in this regard.

Kristeva distinguishes her understanding of this 'feminine' within language from *l'écriture féminine* (1986: 200), but her critical practice exemplifies this dependence and defines this femininity by the always prior 'maternal'. Her postmodernism is 'a basic realignment in style that can be interpreted as an exploration of the typical imaginary relationship, that to the mother, through the most radical and problematic aspect of their relationship, language' (1980: 139–40). Kristeva argues that this imaginary remains resurgent in language, in writing,

precisely in its return to the space-time previous to the phallic stage – indeed previous even to the identifying or mirror stage – in order to grasp the becoming of the symbolic function as the drive's deferment [*différence*] faced with the absence of the object. (1986: 143)

Kristeva's 'becoming-woman' is a feminine opposition also, in fact more effectively, available to men as authors. That impossible struggle to identify with a paternal order which Kristeva sees as definitive of the girl is doubly difficult for women struggling to be artists, she argues, a struggle she associates with suicide: 'I think of Virginia Woolf' (Kristeva 1986: 157). This is possible precisely because the pre-symbolic is located in a mother centred on the son, and gives force to Deleuze's use of the girl as traversing such orders. It is clearly true, however, that Deleuze's becoming-woman is also, and perhaps more effectively, available to men. The distinction between Deleuze's and Kristeva's appropriations of 'woman' as artistic and revolutionary process lies not in what is available to men, or in the contingent distinction between men and women, but in what is available to women. While Woolf's own work frequently utilises figures of the girl in the late modern sense of a woman in process (*adolescent*) – the daughter, the unmarried woman, the ambivalent young wife – the connection between the girl and Woolf is not about her characters. Both Kristeva and Deleuze refer to Woolf as an exception to a set of normative models understood as psychoanalytic, an exception located in her characterisations but also in her style and in her life. Woolf produces this 'girl' as an escape from Oedipalised territories and, as *Orlando* (1928) exemplifies, from any other fixing of the girl in relation to sexual difference concretised as a binary opposition located in either the body or identity. There is no girl in *Orlando*, only a boy who becomes a woman. While Kristeva would see this as symptomatic of the girl's traumatic struggle with the paternal symbolic, the girl might otherwise be seen, as Deleuze and Guattari infer in *A Thousand Plateaus*, as a name for *Orlando*'s process of becoming-woman.

Like most advocates of an aesthetic definition of 'postmodernism', Kristeva valorises the artist's power to signify the unsignifiable, paradigmatically the late modern avant-garde project (1982: 23). Fredric Jameson argues that such

[A] modernist esthetic [sic] is . . . organically linked to the conception of a unique self and private identity, a unique personality and individuality, which can be expected to generate its own unique vision of the world and to forge its own unique, unmistakable style. (1983: 114)

This suggests that Deleuze would critique either this modernist project or the theory of signification that underlies it. In this context Deleuze and Guattari utilise Woolf to consider forms of subjectivity and signification which might be multiplicitous rather than dualist, as in the proliferating intervals of *Between the Acts*.

The plane of consistency on which such multiplicities occur can be a body – like the production of various characters in connection to Isa or Miss LaTrobe – and a field of signification – like the play or the music – but it is not the unconscious. The play and the music in between the acts, like the possibilities of the little girl, do not produce by activating any unconscious or presignifying self or language, they produce by connection and disconnection, by a process of assemblage, like *A Thousand Plateaus* itself (Deleuze and Guattari 1987: 22). If such assemblage opposes some modernist styles it conforms to others, including, as Rosi Braidotti notes, a vision of modernity as a collapse 'opening way to other forms of representation' (Braidotti 1994b: 100). While often compared to impressionism, Woolf's style might also be described as assemblage, and her theory of subjectivity, while employing terms like essence or soul, is a process of desiring attachments and detachments.

The personal style which Jameson describes as modernist, and Kristeva analyses, is what Woolf criticises in (particular) 'modern' men's writing as the shadow of the certain individual: 'a straight dark bar, a shadow something like the letter "I"' (1972: 98).[8] Woolf's deferral of the unified or even split subject as the basis of writing is evident across the range of her texts: in the personae diffusing the apparently solid I of the speaker in *A Room of One's Own*; or in *Orlando*. Deleuze and Guattari quote:

'This will be childhood, but it must not be my childhood,' writes Virginia Woolf. (*Orlando* already does not operate by memories, but by blocks, blocks of ages, blocks of epochs, blocks of kingdoms of nature, blocks of sexes, forming so many becomings between things, or so many lines of deterritorialization.) (1987: 294)

This is precisely the aspect of Woolf to which de Beauvoir and Kristeva object. De Beauvoir, stating that she read and reread Woolf's 'feminist texts', said of her novels: 'They don't have any center. There isn't any thesis' (Bair 1986: 154). In *A Room of One's Own*, Woolf states that this exclusion is vital to her project of 'breaking the sentence' and imagining a different thinking in common for women, while exactly this positioning of women is disrupted in the same texts. Woolf might indeed agree with de Beauvoir's account of transcendence, an identity not determined by the body but still embodied, but this is too easily referred to Woolf's famous call for 'androgyny'. It is, as Deleuze and Guattari argue,

no more adequate to say that each sex contains the other and must

79

develop the opposite pole in itself. Bisexuality is no better a concept than the separateness of the sexes. It is as deplorable to miniaturize, internalize the binary machine as it is to exacerbate it. (1987: 276)

Woolf does not settle on where androgyny's dualism might be located, claiming simultaneously that distinguishing two sexes is an effort, that two sexes are not sufficient, and that there must be 'two sexes in the mind corresponding to the two sexes in the body' (1972: 96). This is not, as Toril Moi argues, about writing Woolf's 'free play of signifiers' (1985: 9), a process Moi explains as sourced in a Kristevan unconscious (11–15). For Woolf, as for Deleuze, despite her interest in Freud and Freudian theory, woman is an infinitive, a process or event, a speaking position perhaps but not an identity.[9]

Kristeva's references to feminism emphasise its incompatibility with 'healthy' subjectivity and with the productive use of language. If feminised concepts which refuse reference to women link Deleuze's and Kristeva's interrogations of the subject, another striking similarity lies in their representation of feminism. Deleuze and Guattari famously concede the necessity of the feminist project:

It is, of course, indispensable for women to conduct a molar politics, with a view to winning back their own organism, their own history, their own subjectivity: 'we as women . . .' makes its appearance as a subject of enunciation. But it is dangerous to confine oneself to such a subject, which does not function without drying up a spring or stopping a flow. (1987: 276)

This concession resembles Kristeva's history of feminism in 'Women's Time', where she claims 'It follows that a feminist practice can only be negative, at odds with what already exists so that we may say "that's not it" and "that's still not it"' (1986: 137). An interesting parallel is possible between Kristeva's account of universalists, essentialists, and post-gender feminists; Grosz's account of egalitarian, social constructivist and sexual difference theorists; and Deleuze and Guattari's line of becoming-woman, becoming-animal and becoming-imperceptible.[10] Each of these narratives about feminism posits a future movement which transcends the difficulties of previous positions, and yet Woolf, for example, could be assigned to all three terms in each series. Their concession regarding feminist politics leads Deleuze and Guattari directly to a discussion of Woolf's theories about the subject of women's writing, where they bring becoming-woman closer to Kristeva's *Revolution in Poetic Language* (1984):

[W]riting should produce a becoming-woman as atoms of womanhood capable of crossing and impregnating an entire social field, and of contaminating men, of sweeping them up in that becoming. The rise of women in English novel writing has spared no man: even those who pass for the most virile, the most phallocratic, such as Lawrence and Miller, in their turn continually tap into and emit particles that enter the proximity or zone of indiscernibility of women. In writing, they become-women. (Deleuze and Guattari 1987: 276)

If for Kristeva gender and desire are bound together in repro-ducing the symbolic order in language, for Deleuze both gender and major languages are channellings of desire motivated by the maintenance of such orders. Gender entraps desire or, rather, claims to trap desire: a territorialisation shaping desire into a signifying and signifiable field. Becoming-woman is a deterritorialisation of the organised body precisely because it uses gender against that organising signification. This differs from Kristeva's call to go beyond gender principally in being not a manifesto for an unrecog-nisable future but a redirection of how gender and the marginali-sation of women currently work. While Kristeva uses Woolf as representative of the gender order's entrenchment, Deleuze attaches her to the girl's role in slipping through and between signifying orders, including the psychoanalytic subject's dualism. The girl's 'block of becoming' quoted above is 'The only way to get outside the dualisms . . . to be-between, to pass between, the intermezzo – that is what Virginia Woolf lived with all her energies, in all of her work, never ceasing to become' (Deleuze and Guattari 1987: 276–7). Deleuze's account of the event – as with the baroque concert (1993: 80) – resonates richly with Woolf's conception of art, including the play (perhaps *Orlando*) in *Between the Acts*. While Deleuze selects Joyce, among other writers, as producing such a 'chaosmos', Woolf's fiction crystally produces texts in which 'bifur-cations and divergences of series are genuinely borders between incompossible worlds, such that the monads that exist wholly include the compossible world that moves into existence' (Deleuze 1993: 81). Woolf explores relations between the visible and the articulable, paradigmatically in the field of sexual difference, the contingent kind of dualism which Deleuze finds in Foucault as a 'preliminary distribution operating at the heart of a pluralism' (Deleuze 1988: 83). While this might be aligned to the 'polymor-phous perversity' supported by psychoanalysis, this foregoes Deleuze's call for 'thought of the outside': 'a multiplicity of relations between forces, a multiplicity of diffusion which no longer splits into two and is free of any dualizable form' (1988: 83–4).

Kristeva's account of the '*sujet-en-procès*' – the trials and processes of producing the subject in language, especially discernible in disruptions of the symbolic – is an unsettling of the subject which resembles Deleuze's discussion of both desire and signification as proliferations of processes (as multiplicitous), except that this process overlies and is constrained by her structural continuities. What passes for identity in Deleuze is an assemblage, a cluster producing momentary subjectivities at its edge. The assemblages proposed by Deleuze and Guattari are such assembled identities and group-identities as a 'mélange of bodies' (1987: 112). An assemblage, 'in its multiplicity, necessarily acts on semiotic flows, material flows, and social flows simultaneously' (Deleuze and Guattari 1987: 22–3), and the girl is an assemblage which comprises various desires and other actions. If 'The first concrete rule for assemblages is to discover what territoriality they envelop' (Deleuze and Guattari 1987: 503), then to that end the girl encompasses a set of movements outside the Oedipalised family and the model of gendered subjectivity which relies upon it. One of these identificatory movements is across the binary code of gender. Our assignation as gendered does not wholly constitute identities, and assemblage is perhaps a way of appropriating its collaborative formation with other positions. The questions remain: how productive a machine is gender, and in connection to what other machines does it produce other than hierarchically? The ways contemporary cultural theory understands gender often continue to be oppositional – woman's identity/man's identity – a gender machine which may shut feminists down into reactive strategies: not because it does not matter that there are women, but because this forecloses gender's productive fluctuations.

Finally, I would point to Deleuze's use of the nomad, which Braidotti has also linked to Woolf's work in *Three Guineas* (1952). Woolf's theories of identity were both more receptive to and more directly divergent from psychoanalysis than most 'modernist' authors or the general conception of 'modernism' allows, and, as feminist critics often note, her understanding of gender and of the category woman are more critical than is generally attributed to modernism. This does not place her as a precursor to the postmodernism Kristeva describes or Jardine analyses. A Deleuzean critique of Kristeva, towards which both Woolf and Grosz might be employed, does not require 'postmodern feminism' of the kind Braidotti espouses, but rather allows this among many interventions in the dualist conception of identity. Woolf's style is not amorphous and fluid, after the style of Kristeva's maternalising vision of the postmodern, nor simply an internalised contradiction of identification after Braidotti's postmodern woman – rather, it is the different, and less predictable, process of assemblage.

Assemblage is connected in *A Thousand Plateaus* to what Deleuze and Guattari call nomadic culture, another anti-hierarchical way of conceiving of the subject, this time specifically against the State organisation of property and materiality. The centred or decentred subject is presented as similarly sedentary: 'You will be a subject, nailed down as one, a subject of the enunciation of the statement – otherwise you're just a tramp' (Deleuze and Guattari 1987: 159). While Kristeva's analyses founded on original territories are implicated by contrast, nomadism is not a refusal to claim space (Deleuze and Guattari 1987: 380). If girls are institutionally directed from some territories towards others, this exile is also an escape and feminists are also nomads: a movement in relation to a territory, a group identity. If 'the life of the nomad is in the intermezzo' (379) this does not foreclose on territorialising marks like signatures and names: Woolf, woman, or feminist. To close with a quotation from Deleuze and Guattari: 'If one is to free movement from the distortion of consciousness and conceive of it as it is in itself, one must adopt as a model "a state of things which would ceaselessly change, a matter-flow in which no anchoring point or center or reference would be assignable"' (1986: 85). This is not only applicable to traditional figures of femininity and to interrogations of them, but also to a style such as Woolf's, territories in relation to which women continue to assemble.

NOTES

This chapter is indebted to David Bennett, who first gave me *Anti-Oedipus* even though he didn't like it, to Ian Buchanan, and to Deborah Staines's passion for Virginia Woolf.

1. Under 'Deleuze' I am also considering the texts he produced with Félix Guattari, including principally *Anti-Oedipus* (1977) and *A Thousand Plateaus* (1987). Guattari's influence on Deleuze's analyses of psychoanalysis cannot be underestimated, but the collapse in this case serves to underscore connections between Deleuze's work in, for example, *The Logic of Sense* (1990b), *Foucault* (1988) and *The Fold* (1993), and in the *Capitalism and Schizophrenia* texts.
2. This isn't necessarily an unproductive situation, as Deleuze's use of

Lacan recognises. Butler perceptively argues this case in her introduction to *The Psychic Life of Power*, for which 'the subject is the
modality of power that turns on itself; the subject is the effect of
power in recoil' (1997: 6). That is, the subject's conformity to a pattern
that precedes it is not a simple matter. However, Kristeva's accounts
of the difficulty with which women negotiate inevitable dualisms like
the Oedipus complex are not making this interrogation.

3. Kristeva's account of being a woman does not remain phenomenological, as does de Beauvoir's. Psychoanalysis, despite its awareness
of social constructions and compatibility with forms of phenomenology, often remains resolutely non-phenomenological insofar as it
traces effects of pre-existing structures. Even understood as itself a
linguistic construct, the drives refer to a pre-linguistic structure which
exists before experience, whereas for phenomenology 'it is only
through existence that facts are manifested' (Merleau-Ponty quoted
in de Beauvoir 1972: 39). Grosz's positioning of Merleau-Ponty as the
problematic step before her turn from interiority is relevant to this
conflict.

4. Kristeva argues, in *Revolution in Poetic Language*, for example, that
'semiotic functioning . . . will become more complex only after the
break in the symbolic. It is, however, already put in place by a biological set-up and is always already social and therefore historical'
(1984: 118).

5. Meaghan Morris notes that Deleuze and Guattari consistently deploy
non-exclusive dualisms, a process for which 'we can't assume that
lines of flight are necessarily creative, that smooth spaces are always
better than segmented or striated ones' (quoted in Morris 1996: 24).
Jameson (1997) discusses Deleuze's use of dualisms as a redeployment
of Marx but, unlike Morris, finds them ultimately ideological if not
mythical.

6. I have elsewhere discussed the figures of the little girl and the
becoming-woman in Deleuze's work (Driscoll 1997). Considering
Kristeva's work in these terms has necessarily redirected this discussion to a more detailed consideration of the place of the girl in the
Oedipal frame, and the currency of that figure in poststructuralist
feminist theory.

7. In *Kafka*, Deleuze and Guattari argue that: 'A minor literature doesn't
come from a minor language; it is rather that which a minority
constructs within a major language. But the first characteristic of
minor literature in any case is that in it language is affected with a
high coefficient of deterritorialization' (1986: 16). In *Kafka*, Deleuze
and Guattari find young women repeatedly at the edge of flight, a
role which 'ends when she breaks a segment, makes it take flight,
makes it flee the social field in which she is participating, makes it
take flight on the unlimited line in the unlimited direction of desire'

(64). These girls deterritorialise stereotypes, by an assemblage which destabilises the law fixing and evaluating subjectivities or literature, which is not to say that is the only way the girl and comparable assemblages could deterritorialise in literature.

8. Woolf certainly also describes both independence and a 'mature' mind as necessary to a (woman) writer (1972: 104), and for Woolf it is immaturity that women writers must overcome when they have escaped poverty. Woolf may thus be aligned to the popularisations of psychoanalysis prominent around her, but it excessively simplifies her position on questions of subjectivity or writing to equate her with 'Freudianism'. As critics and biographers repeatedly note, Woolf not only met Freud but directly both employed, varied and argued with his theories in her writing.

9. Deleuze's later understanding of becoming draws on his discussion of infinitives in *The Logic of Sense*. Becoming-woman describes a process which reappears in all Deleuze's work without necessarily being referred to women. For Deleuze 'the something is a One, not a pregiven unity, but instead the indefinite article that designates a certain singularity' (Deleuze 1993: 76).

10. This line disappears in *What is Philosophy?* perhaps due to the same 'persistent subjectivist misunderstandings' (Massumi 1992: 82), Massumi claims motivated Deleuze and Guattari to replace the term 'desiring machines' with the term 'assemblages' in *A Thousand Plateaus*. The point of desiring machines, however, as Buchanan argues, is that 'machines are not metaphors' but 'are the site of activation of a certain relation' (1997: 83).

4

Body, Knowledge and Becoming-Woman: Morpho-logic in Deleuze and Irigaray

DOROTHEA OLKOWSKI

It is undoubtedly not easy to make generalisations about contemporary feminist philosophy, particularly with regard to its methods, practices and aims. Given this ungeneralisability, it is all the more instructive to witness the nearly universal caution and hesitancy with which feminist thinkers have encountered the work of both Gilles Deleuze and Luce Irigaray. Not surprisingly, the two names are seldom spoken together and even when they are spoken separately by feminists, it is usually with a certain amount of reserve and even disdain. With respect to the work of Gilles Deleuze, disdain is apparent in the comments of Alice Jardine and Judith Butler in particular. Both are important in this regard since most feminists' initial foray into the work of Gilles Deleuze (along with his sometime collaborator Félix Guattari) has been guided by the assessment of either one or the other of these feminist thinkers. Jardine's critique may be the best known insofar as she explicitly addresses Deleuze in the title of her essay and, she virtually warns feminist theorists against even considering reading Deleuze and Guattari. Jardine claims that there is nothing in Deleuze and Guattari that conforms to feminist interests in the 'putting into discourse' of either 'woman' or 'the feminine', that there is nothing that would allow for the creation of feminine spaces to challenge traditional, masculinist, conceptual boundaries (Jardine 1984: 48). Jardine gives such creation the name *gynesis*; it is the 'valorization

of the feminine, woman, and her obligatory, that is, historical connotations as somehow intrinsic to new and necessary modes of
thinking, writing, speaking' (25). Her dislike appears to be due to
the fact that Deleuze alone or Deleuze and Guattari together fail
to address the familial-psychoanalytic as well as the academic-textual
point of view. Instead, they opt for a cosmic vision of the world,
one involving '[s]ea animals, computers, volcanoes, birds, and
planets' (Jardine 1985: 209). In short, nothing in Deleuze and
Guattari seems to correspond to the immediate focus on textuality,
family, state, or religious power, bodies, gender, psycho-social
repression, or linguistic authority.

For her part, Butler finds even less in Deleuze to appreciate. In
her earliest published book, Butler criticises Deleuze for a naive or
universalising conception of desire that flies in the face of what
she takes to be the inevitable Hegelian subject. She argues that, for
Deleuze (following Nietzsche), 'the Hegelian subject can be understood as a product of slave morality' (Butler 1987: 213) or, as
Deleuze expresses it, the agent of reactive forces. In response to
Hegel, it appears to Butler that Deleuze proposes an emancipatory
model of desire, and that this model is built upon 'the reification
of multiplicitous affect as the invariant, although largely repressed,
ontological structure of desire', an 'insupportable metaphysical
speculation' (214). In Nietzsche's analysis of slave morality, as
Butler also points out, the noble and powerful, the high-minded
call themselves good. In so doing, they create 'good' as a value.
The high-minded and powerful call what is common and lowly
'base', signifying a critique of all that is common. For Nietzsche,
evaluations carried out on the basis of a 'noble' way of life carry
the value 'good' and those arising from a lowly life are valued 'bad'
(Nietzsche 1969: 36). But Deleuze does not concur with Nietzsche's
valuations respecting good and bad; instead, he draws the conclusion that valuations derived from a mode of being, a way of life, are
critical and creative, that is, ethical and aesthetic, and that they are
constituted as difference at the origin, the result of active force.
Most evaluations, however, are not active; most can be traced back
to revenge, thus they are reactive. But for Deleuze, this is not the
result of Hegelian synthesis, repression from the outside, whether
that of Christianity or the coercive force of capitalism and psychoanalysis; it is really a matter of a base way of living.

Thus Butler claims that Deleuze makes desire 'the privileged
locus of human ontology' (Butler 1987: 206), an ontology that
suffers for lack of historicised context. Yet, for Deleuze, desire as

active or reactive force is manifested only as a mode of life, an aesthetic and ethical mode. So, it cannot be exactly right that Deleuze conceives of desire as an 'insupportable metaphysical speculation'. Still, the absence of specific social and historical conditions qualifying Deleuze's conception of desire leads Butler to conclude that desire is an 'ontological invariant', 'a universal ontological truth' that Deleuze has managed to release from an interminable period of suppression. Butler refers to Deleuze's notion of desire as 'emancipatory', 'a precultural eros', 'an originally unrepressed libidinal diversity', and 'an ahistorical absolute' (Butler 1987: 213–15). Such qualifications are damning in Butler's view, since in her estimation, it is principally the willingness to locate desire in purely social and historical terms that elevates the work of Michel Foucault above his (approximate) contemporaries Deleuze, Derrida and Lacan. Given Butler's Hegelianism, only to the degree that historicisation takes place can philosophy effect its break with the Hegelian system that always already accounts for any rupture with itself.

Now, equally arresting are the views of feminist readers with respect to the work of Luce Irigaray. In numerous early encounters, American feminist theoreticians, in particular, committed themselves to describing Irigaray as an essentialist in at least some respects. This reading seems to have arisen, in part, as a response to the masculine or male hegemony thought to have been established by psychoanalytic interpretations of cultural institutions, if not of human life itself. As a critique, this reading of Irigaray faults her for 'the temptation to produce her own positive theory of femininity' (Moi 1985: 139); that is, any attempt to define woman must necessarily be an attempt to determine what is essential to woman. Often, the essentialist critique has been mitigated by an equal emphasis on the social construction of the body, or by the reference to morphology (Schor 1989; Whitford 1991).[1] As such, Irigaray was not taken to be a pure essentialist, but, at most, a strategic essentialist who made use of morphology and/or social constructions to undermine and resist masculine hegemony. Still other feminists have argued that Irigaray deconstructs either the Lacanian phallic economy or logocentric discourse, or mimics such discourses so as to resist their hegemony (Fuss 1989: 55–6; Grosz 1989: 113; Butler 1993: 48). Political theorists have tended to be the most cautious of all for, in spite of Irigaray's critique of Western philosophy's obliteration of gender differences, Irigaray's demystification of the male subject of reason is rejected as not compatible with establishing a female subject who is an autonomous female agent (Benhabib 1995: 22).

A more recent direction in feminist theoretical readings of Irigaray relies on close contextual analysis of both Irigaray's own texts and those in the history of philosophy in terms of which her work arises (Chanter 1995).[2] In many respects, this last approach has served to open up the terms of discourse beyond an indeterminate yet no less prescribed field of interests deemed 'feminist'. The point has been made that the charge of essentialism, and, I suspect, numerous other charges made against the philosophy of Irigaray, 'originate[s] from a well-meaning but outmoded idea of what feminism should be' (Chanter 1995: 5). And I would also endorse the point, made by Tina Chanter, that the attitudes of American feminists towards Irigaray, from caution to outright dismissal, serve to enforce or instantiate the very structure of dichotomies that Irigaray wishes to put into question. But I would go further; I would argue that it is not merely some particular dichotomies (sex/gender, nature/culture, biology/society), but the very existence of a philosophical framework that admits of dichotomies at all, which the philosophy of Irigaray challenges, and which, until the logical and philosophical limitations of a structure that tolerates dichotomy are clarified, her work may never find acceptance among contemporary feminist theorists, or even worse, will be accepted for the wrong reasons. Irigaray herself has commented upon the misunderstandings of her work which may not just be a matter of linguistic mistranslation, but of cultural and philosophical mistranslation (Irigaray 1993a).[3]

So the question that lies before us is: how to read these two philosophies, that of Gilles Deleuze and that of Luce Irigaray? For reasons that will be made clear later, I will resist an analogical reading; rather, what I will suggest is that certain concepts created by Irigaray are compatible with Deleuzean concepts (a problem in itself since there is no 'singular' viewpoint from which to read anything in Deleuze). Furthermore, I would suggest that by folding the two theories together, a creative and original point of view on certain feminist problems or issues may be constructed. Thus, this reading is guided by a philosophical position that Irigaray has in no way embraced, yet which shares her critique of the logical and philosophical structures that produce dichotomy. Although the philosophies of Gilles Deleuze and Luce Irigaray are seldom paired for any positive outcome, I want to suggest that, by folding together their interests in pragmatics and praxis, social activism, literary language and artistic practices, something new may be created, a new philosophical framework, one that embraces multiplicity without producing binaries, and without which no feminist reading of Deleuze or Irigaray can succeed separately or together.

I would like to begin this process with Irigaray's claim that her research 'attempts to suggest to women a morpho-logic that is appropriate to their bodies' (1993a: 58–9). Not simply a morphology, and not simply a logic, but a *morpho-logic* appropriate to the 'bodies' of women. Such a morpho-logic, I would suggest, is not only a function of philosophy, for no simple phenomenology can describe it. It requires thorough immersion in practices that are undergone or carried out among women involved in activist movements working for women's rights. It can also be located in the practices of literature and art, insofar as Irigaray's social critique is 'accompanied by the beginnings of a woman's phenomenological elaboration of the auto-affection and self-representation of her body' (59).[4] While the appropriateness of phenomenology to the creation of morpho-logic is in no way guaranteed and must at some point be examined, I would like to defer that examination for another time and focus here on clarifying the parameters of morpho-logic itself. For example, let me begin by offering a literary practice in terms of which 'morpho-logic' operates, and, in the process, begin to lay out the parameters of that philosophical framework which morpho-logic produces.

A woman, a resident in a Brazilian city, is riding a tram home after her day's shopping in the market. The unexpected but otherwise ordinary sight of a blind man chewing gum jolts her into compassion:

> She had skilfully pacified life; she had taken so much care to avoid upheavals. She had cultivated an atmosphere of serene understanding, separating each person from the others. Her clothes were clearly designed to be practical, and she could choose the evening's film from the newspaper – and everything was done in such a manner that each day should smoothly succeed the previous one. And a blind man chewing gum was destroying all this. (Lispector 1972: 41–2)

Confused, the woman misses her stop and exits the tram unexpectedly at the botanical gardens:

> Now that the blind man had guided her to it, she trembled on the threshold of a dark, fascinating world where monstrous water lilies floated. The small flowers scattered on the grass did not appear to be yellow or pink, but the color of inferior gold and scarlet. Their decay

was profound, perfumed. But all these oppressive things she watched, her head surrounded by a swarm of insects, sent by some more refined life in the world. The breeze penetrated between the flowers. Anna imagined rather than felt its sweetened scent. The garden was so beautiful that she feared hell. (Lispector 1972: 43–4)

Finally, reaching her home, she feels that the 'wholesome life she had led until today seemed morally crazy, yet, '[s]he loved the world, she loved all things created, she loved with loathing. In the same way as she had always been fascinated by oysters, with that vague sentiment of revulsion which the approach of truth provoked, admonishing her.' The danger of everyday living infuses Clarice Lispector's story, a danger which, in Lispector's world, women are most aware of and most subject to. Monstrous flowers, a blind man chewing gum, missing the right tram stop, oysters oozing grey, revulsion: all these things produce joy and fear.

This kind of awareness, as well as this reality, argues Luce Irigaray, belongs to new fertile regions producing 'a new age of thought, art, poetry and language: the creation of a new poetics' (Irigaray 1989: 118). A poetics of 'sexual difference' is a term that is, for Irigaray, the 'burning issue of our age', that which alone preoccupies us, 'our salvation on an intellectual level' (118). Taken literally, as text, as reality, as an elaboration of a process, and not as metaphor or representation, Anna's revulsion and fear imply that the situation is desperate. We are nearly at the end of this modern or postmodern era, and yet, the whole practical matter of women's lives, women's fears, women's sense of the danger in living is seldom acknowledged, even less seldom revered. How can we think about 'a revolution in thought and ethics' that will radically alter not simply the relationships of subject and discourse, subject and world, subject and the cosmic, microcosmic and macrocosmic, as Irigaray suggests (119), but will actually recognise that such relationships do not even exist in the logical and linguistic order of today's philosophy and social practices?

No relationships between the subject and any other thing exist insofar as subjectivity is by definition a rigid, rooted system, precisely the type of system that Irigaray examines, explores and questions. Her persistence, her will to 'poke around' in systems which no one has previously approached in this manner, produces the reality of those philosophical systems. They are, she discovers, systems of thought dominated by the logic and linguistics of male sexual organs. While this appears to have been the chief discovery of psychoanalytic theory, there remains a sense in which, outside of the specific concerns of psychoanalysis, we do not seem to acknowledge the practical aspects of such domination. Perhaps this is because we are so accustomed to it that the potential obscenity of this language and logic escapes us.

Indeed, in and of itself, the predominance of a logic of male sexual organs in our thought amounts to nothing startling or strategic. What makes this predominance a matter for concern is that this logic and its accompanying rhetoric structures systems in which, as Irigaray describes it:

[W]oman [will] always tend towards something else without ever turning to herself as the site of a positive element . . . she remains on the side of the electron, a negative charge always directed toward an opposite positive charge. There is no attraction or support that excludes disintegration or rejection, no double pole of attraction and decomposition. (Irigaray 1989: 121)

This occurs everywhere, for example, under the Freudian regime of repression, a mixture of 'women's own constitution' and 'social custom'; a repression as a result of which, the little girl's 'precocious abilities' are explained away, her early childhood 'leads in development' are reduced to nothing more than 'the effect of her desire to function, herself, as "merchandise,"' in order to appear more attractive (Irigaray 1985b: 24). Thus, '[c]ulturally, socially, economically valorised female characteristics are correlated with maternity and motherhood: with breast-feeding the child, restoring the man. According to this dominant ideology, the little girl can thus have *no value* before puberty' (25).

Otherwise said, no matter who she is, how she feels, what she can think, how she sees, what she can do, how she can articulate what manifests itself to her, society only sees, only wants to see, and only can see in her, the mother, the wife, the nurturer, the caregiver, the support staff; her task in life is to restore the man – both the infant and the adult. Her purpose is to give way to and make possible the dominance of the heterosexual male body: a structure in accordance with which we 'erect' material superstructures, and thereby regimes of power and systems of philosophy; we 'penetrate' foreign arenas; we engineer 'projectiles' for defensive and offensive purposes; we tolerate, even demand, 'phallocratic' systems of government and law; we encourage one another to be 'hard' on the issues; we 'size' up situations; we admire a 'cocky' attitude as well as a 'comer'.

Our language is permeated and structured by the singularly

phallic and heterosexual male body, so much so that, in most cases, it is the blind spot; there is nothing to blush about here. Still, is it any wonder that women who recognise the blind spot wish to challenge it? In the arts, for example, certain contemporary female performance artists wish to manifest their own positivity in this regard. Carolee Schneeman, who often creates performances addressed to the particularity of female sexuality, decries what she calls '[t]he dominance of the sex-negative imagination', that is, a devitalised body, a body that is neither active nor even passive but simply reduced to its genital functioning (Juno and Vale 1991: 73). She states:

[T]he authenticating source of vitality is a distanced, male god. . . . And all the female attributes are completely distorted so you get this demented mythology where the god is born from a Virgin [!] or from a god's forehead or from an underarm . . . *anything* that can *usurp* the female primacy. (Juno and Vale 1991: 73)

The marginal and marginalised work of many contemporary women artists is exemplary of women's confrontation with the denial of women's bodies, a denial that has proceeded by means of what Schneeman calls a 'heroics of *evasion*' (73). As such, we have no standards to account for the kind of work women produce, no principles by means of which it can be judged, not even an acknowledged tradition within which it can be called theatre, or visual art, or poetry. Thus the 'work' (if it is work) is often silenced or it is taken to be a sort of naive and embarrassing emotion-fest, a manifestation of postmodern morbidity, or a romantic celebration of schizophrenia.

When Diamanda Galas or the more infamous Karen Finley smear their bodies with slimy substances, when Annie Sprinkle or Valie Export expose their bodies (especially their breasts and vaginas), when Linda Montano is photographed in a wild array of costumes and 'pornographic' poses, when Suzy Kerr and Dianne Malley respond to Operation Rescue's training manual by visually relating it to the *Malleus Maleficarum*, that they perform these acts in order to separate themselves from the dominant ideology according to which the girl has no value before puberty, is lost on a public that is either openly condemnatory of what they can only interpret as excess, or they are silent. While this body of work could be taken as no more than an assertion of difference, the fact that these acts appear to us to be wild or crazy, bizarre, remote, or meaningless indicates the degree to which there is no symmetry in the system of language and logic, no symmetry that is, except that of the degraded copy.

What it would take, Irigaray argues, is a logic of fluidity and fluid mechanics. This chapter will argue that Irigaray's conceptions of fluidity and morpho-logic are related, that morpho-logic is the logic of fluids that are not forced into solids in order to be scientifically assessed in accordance with the limitations of solid mechanics. In the logic that structures our thought and sets the standards for truth, a system of formalisation that accounts for the fluidity of bodies does not seem to exist. In logic, one finds only hegemonic and rigid hierarchies, which, in turn, demand that language conform to them in order for there to be intelligibility. Thus Irigaray equates propositional logic with solid mechanics, the mechanics of masses that resist changing shape and that offer resistance.

Irigaray supposes, first, that there might be a kind of 'improper' language, a language that expresses multiplicity and, above all, fluidity:

[I]f we examine the properties of fluids, we note that this 'real' may well include, and in a large measure, a *physical reality* that continues to resist adequate symbolisation and/or that signifies the powerlessness of logic to incorporate in its writing all the characteristic features of nature. (Irigaray 1985a: 106)

The resistance of physical reality to linguistic and logical symbolisation is due either to the inadequacy of logical symbols (rigid and hegemonic while this reality is fluid) or to a complete lack of power on the part of logic to 'incorporate' fluid reality. The inadequacy of symbols and the inability to incorporate have necessitated that fluid physical reality be subject to idealisation. The result of idealisation is the creation and maintenance of the relationship between rationality and the mechanics of solids, insofar as solids conform to the normative and universalising judgements of a subject. This is reflected in both the subject–predicate structure of Aristotelian logic, according to which an attribute is said or predicated of a subject, so as to represent a fact in the world, and in the focus of logic on the precise definition of terms.

However, some feminists have pointed to the fact that 'natural language is ambiguous, unsystematic, and uneconomical. Metaphorical expressions combine with a shifting multiplicity of meanings to produce concepts that can never be delineated sharply' (Nye 1990: 129). Even when fluids are made to conform to the demands of a logic of solids whose terms can be precisely defined, the problem has been that the meaning of the concept shifts, and the judgement of the proposition's truth value cannot be made with absolute certainty. No doubt, it is the slippage inherent in the relation between concepts and subjects that has given many feminists the hope that room can be found for multiplicity and diversity within the Aristotelian model. But Irigaray, I would claim, is not content with metaphorical slippage in the concept. For in addition to registering opposition to the 'laws of equivalence' operating in metaphor, she passes up this useful 'flaw' in predicate logic to note that even in logic, there has been a shift from attempting to establish clear definitions of terms to an analysis of the relations between terms, a shift that may hold some hope (1985a: 107).[5]

In *Of Grammatology* Derrida maintains that, by means of writing, language is always already algebraic, thus mathematical (Derrida 1976b: 295–316). Insofar as, in writing, a visible signifier always separates itself from speech and supplants it, it anticipates the absolutely non-phonetic, universal writing of science. As such, it is tantamount to the death of speech, that is, alphabetic writing and mathematical theorems are death at the very origin of language, before and within speech such that the whole metaphysics of presence and the truth supposedly contained in speech are but a trace. This again affirms the slippage in the concept, and the undecidability of language. I want to make it clear that this is also not Irigaray's position and that she seems to be operating within the parameters of an entirely different framework.

What does interest Irigaray is the shift, by some contemporary logicians, from an analysis of terms (subjects or substances and predicates) to an analysis of the relations between terms, a shift that does not need mathematics to be formalised, even though mathematical logic has grasped it as their project (1985a: 107). So what appears to some feminist theory to be a disadvantage – that is, the turn, among logicians, from predicate logic to mathematical functional analysis – might actually hold some advantage for a theory of fluidity, though only because of its treatment of relations, not because it is mathematical nor because it introduces slippage into the concept. Irigaray's disappointment with mathematical logic arises only with the realisation that, at least for Gottlob Frege (1848–1925), the only role for fluidity is in the copula, which does not remain outside and independent of terms, but which is always already appropriated and incorporated into 'the constitution of the discourse of the "subject" in set(s)' (1985a: 109). It is the same with the theoretical fluids of pure mathematics. Mathematical science loses its relationship to the 'reality of bodies' positing movements with up to infinite speeds that are '*physically unacceptable*' (109). A lot depends here on what is meant by 'bodies' and 'the reality of bodies',[6] concepts upon which so much depends, but Irigaray's basic point is that the bodily character or morphology that is related to women is fluid and that a morpho-logic of fluid bodies can be created.

Yet as we know, we do not do this, or we do not do it with any great commitment, for all such practice and thought has already been territorialised as pathology and error. Women, according to Freud, go through the first libidinal stages in the same way – in the same way, that is, as men do (Irigaray 1993b: 28). In the same way as men, when they were little boys, little girls show equal aggression (equal to boys) at the sadistic-anal stage; so equal, in fact, that they are little men. And what is so mystifying, so frightening, for Irigaray, is that in this process of becoming a 'normal' woman, there is never any vulvar 'stage', no vaginal 'stage', nor any uterine 'stage' (Irigaray 1993b: 29).[7] No discussion of what Irigaray calls 'placental economy' has ever emerged as critical to the woman's developmental process (Irigaray 1985b: 41). Such an economy is not only paradoxical, it is a fluid negotiation between the woman and what is clearly other, but within an economy of a difference that again and again produces new forms of life. This logic strikes us as nonsense and it makes us shudder just to hear these words used, as if they had no place in a philosophy that erects laws and principles and thinks in a penetrating manner. In fact, they do not have a place.

The little girl's body, its folds and the secret pleasures it provides her are unknown and unknowable to Freud. He can only think by analogy, a logical mode requiring no distinctions on the material level. One thing is like another, two parallel lines which never meet, between which there is no connection possible: like but separate. The girl must have something like the boy's penis; the girl's body at this stage must be like that of the boy, parallel but not connected. The weakness of analogy is manifested in the weakness of the girl's pleasure in her penis-equivalent, her small-scale organ. But the analogy also becomes a case of social hegemony when the '*change* to femininity' takes place, a change made necessary, not by a change in the girl's own body, but by a change in the boy's behaviour (Irigaray 1985b: 30). He discovers castration, that he has what she does not have, the organ which has been the model for hers all along. How terrifying it would be to Freud, Irigaray suggests, if he 'knew' about the woman's body, not just the maternal body, but her multiple and layered pleasures: there are the two (sets of) lips, the clitoris, the vagina, but more – the layering of her body and its 'specific sensitivities', which, as a cluster, have no analogy to the boy's own organ, thus no way of being 'known'. From this point of view, *'there never is (or will be) a little girl'* (1985b: 48).

Even so, because of the law of analogy, and that of the transcendental signifier/signified, the Law of the Phallus, (s)he is diagnosed as unintelligible and pathological, (s)he remains 'a flaw, a lack, an absence, outside the system of representations and autorepresentations which are man's' (1985b: 50, 52). In her desire to be (like) him (principle of analogy), the 'same' (law of non-contradiction), (s)he suffers envy. Here Irigaray asserts that Freud is completely blind to considering the "disadvantage" mother nature puts you to by providing only one sexual organ' (1985b: 52). Rather, in Freud's schema, 'her' lack, her envy, is what makes his organ valuable. 'Woman's fetishisation of the male organ must indeed be an indispensable support of its price on the sexual market' (1985b: 53).

All this confirms what we suspect about knowledge itself. The philosopher leaves Plato's cave but returns in order to confirm his knowledge and self-identity, to give order to the shadow-images reproduced there in the sensible world that the mother represents (1985b: 342–9). Irigaray writes:

So men have lived in this cave since their childhood. Since time began. They have never left this space, or place, or topography, or topology, of the cave ... The cave is the representation of something always already there, of the original matrix/womb which these men cannot represent since they are held down by chains that prevent them from turning their heads or their genitals toward the daylight. (1985b: 244)

And it goes without saying that only if 'man' is freed from this cave, leaving behind every artifact (those chains), every vestige of the sensible world that he lived in there, only then has he the capacity to think divine thoughts (1985b: 339). But even in the cave, the men are aligned, not, of course, with the mother, not even with the topography of the cave, but in accordance with the transcendental law of the Father. The men are '[e]ternally fixed', '[f]ictive representation of the repetition that leads, and can only lead, to the contemplation of the Idea' (1985b: 249).

Amazingly, the cave cannot be explored; they simply sit. 'Heads forward, eyes front, genitals aligned, fixed in a straight line. A phallic direction, a phallic line, a phallic time, back turned on the origin (*hystera*, the origin that is behind them – daylight)' (1985a: 245). The Platonic origin is light, and it blindly envelops and encircles, produces, facilitates, and permits any and all representation. Even the fire in the cave is not for warmth, but serves merely as the *analogue* to the sun. For the primary function of the cave, notes Irigaray, is, '[o]pening, enlarging, contriving the scene of representation, the world as representation' (1985a: 255). What holds the prisoners, what holds their attention, is the projection on the wall in front of them, the very illusion that evoking the origin (daylight, the sun, the good) is the same as a repetition of that origin itself:

Everything in this circus will sustain the blinding snare. Fetish-objects, wall curtain, screen, veils, eyelids, images, shadows, fantasies are all so many barriers to intercept, filter, sift the all-powerful incandescence, to charm and shield the eyes while at the same time displaying and recalling, even from behind such masks, its own cause and goal. The gaze is ringed by a luminous, infinitely reverberating blindness. By a dazzling orbit. (1985a: 256)

Thus, even in the cave, symmetry, a certain order and framing that constitute good sense are already operating to enforce the necessity of certain effects – effects of the Idea which 'dominates, exceeds, and guarantees discourse' (1985a: 258).

What links the prisoners and their situation to the philosopher (Plato) and his students (us) is the claim that '[t]hey are like ourselves', that they all see the same things, and that if they speak at all, it is to agree that what they see are beings; proof that analogy is governed by the principle of identity. Within the cave, the standard of judgement is a question of 'proportions of a more or less correct relation to the sameness (of the Idea)' (1985a: 262), the proportions of which determine that all images, reflections and reduplications are good copies of the Idea. All this is possible because, as Plato represents it, the cave itself is virgin with respect to origins and mute with respect to voice; that is, the cave/womb is not the origin but merely the reflective surface upon which transcendental origins are projected from behind a man-made wall that encompasses the cave in Platonic division and multiplication, in the silence of a theatre where men hear themselves speak the same.

Nonetheless, when an inhabitant is forced out of the cave into the sunlight of the Father, it becomes clear that everything in the cave was only a projection which must be forgotten in order to remember what is truer. So the gap between the 'earth's attraction and the sun's allure' is never conjoined. Concludes Irigaray:

For Being's domination requires that whatever has been defined – *within the domain of sameness* – as 'more (true, right, clear, reasonable, intelligible, paternal, masculine . . .) should progressively win out over *its* 'other,' its 'different' – its differing – and, when it comes right down to it, over its negative, its 'less' (fantastic, harmful, obscure, 'mad,' sensible, maternal, feminine . . .). Finally the fiction reigns of a simple, indivisible, ideal origin. The fission occurring at the beginning, at the time of the primitive conjunction(s) is eliminated in the unity of concept. (1985a: 275)

Because of the necessity of forgetting her, the forgetting of that womb/matrix (what evades the action of the Idea), except as a projection which is the image of the Sun, woman certainly has no access to the 'sublime circles of sameness' (the law of non-contradiction) or 'intelligible heights' (the transcendental signified/signifier). Still, in order to confirm its value, in her highest moments and, insofar as she is the (lesser) analogue to the male sex, woman still aspires to rise above sensation, the events of the city, or mere opinion (1985a: 342). Yet she cannot. She cannot, because she is judged to be simulacral and so she does not participate in the order of good sense.

Gilles Deleuze has also reflected upon this in his essay 'Plato and the Simulacrum' (Deleuze 1990b). The real purpose of Platonic division in the dialogues, as in the cave, he argues, is to select from among claimants (to the truth), by placing them in a structure of oppositions. The effect is to separate the pure from the impure, authentic from unauthentic, in other words, to test for sameness and likeness, and to exclude what does not meet the test (Deleuze 1990b: 254). Copies are 'authorised by resemblance' to the Idea, so they operate fully within the system of representation. Their claims, by analogy and under the principle of identity, thus as interior and spiritual, correspond to the Idea. Simulacra, on the other hand, are false claimants, 'corrupted by dissemblance' whose claim is sensible, and so it 'is made from below, by means of an aggression, an insinuation, a subversion', 'against the father' and without passing through the Idea (1990b: 256, 257).

Even though the material receptacle can, according to Irigaray, attain beauty, goodness and intelligibility by submitting to the imprints of the form, the Idea, it can do so only very poorly, 'below the self-realisation of the type' (1985a: 343). So we encounter in philosophy and society what appears to be a common problem among women. They are confused, uncertain, unsure of how to proceed with their lives. This occurs because women do not know their definition, representation, or relation with others insofar as they are unstable with regard to the Idea. They are without measure, because they are without limits and proportions which must be referred back to the Idea. In short, as Deleuze expresses it, 'the simulacrum is an image without resemblance' (1990b: 257), and woman, we judge, is such an image.

Everything Deleuze says about the character of the simulacra in Plato's dialogues folds into the analysis of the other, the woman in Irigaray. He writes:

The simulacrum is constructed around a disparity, a difference; it interiorises a dissimilitude. That is why we can no longer even define it with regard to the model at work in copies – the model of the Same from which the resemblance of the copy derives. If the simulacrum still has a model, it is another one, a model of the Other from which follows an interiorised dissimilarity. (1990b: 258)

That the simulacrum implies dimensions, depths and distances that the observer (Father) cannot dominate or master is no surprise. Because of their heterogeneity, their differential element, their sexual difference, their madness, their inclusion of the spectator in the flux, and their limitlessness, simulacra have the same appearance as the work of women artists: pure, unlimited, becoming – they are anomic. 'For the sensible', notes Irigaray, 'will never rise to the perfection of the type [form]' (1985a: 342). If women do not know their definition, if they are without measure and limit, this is not only because the model of sameness will return to the lower regions of 'fakes' only under orders of the Father, but also because of the cut, the gap, whereby the most perfect image is cut free from matter which is itself a 'subversion of the depths, an adept avoidance of the equivalent, the limit, the Same, or the Like: always simultaneously more and less, but never equal' (Deleuze 1990b: 258).

Deleuze's concern is to overthrow Platonism, to raise up simulacra, to assert their rights over icons or copies, to affirm the positive power of the simulacra that negates original and copy, model and reproduction. Intersecting with this, Irigaray concludes that finally, one cannot even invoke a model of the other, for 'woman continues to exist, she continually undoes his work, distinguishing

100

herself from either envelope or thing, and creat[es] an endless interval, game, agitation, or non-limit which destroys the perspectives and limits of this world' (1993b: 122). This is her turning upon herself as a positive element, and it disconcerts the erection of a male subject.

For Deleuze (following Nietzsche), even given the degree to which the cave/matrix has been colonised by the Idea and its projections, there is behind every cave, a still deeper cave, behind every so-called foundation, an abyss in which the Father could no longer recognise himself (Deleuze 1990b: 263), and concerning which he has no myths to speak of which can serve as foundations (Deleuze and Guattari 1987: 237). This still deeper cave is no myth, no analogy; it is real though virtual; Deleuze calls it becoming. Becoming produces nothing other than itself. We fall into a false alternative if we say that you either imitate or you are. What is real, Deleuze argues, is the becoming itself, the block of becoming, not the supposedly fixed term (like woman) through which that which becomes passes. This is the point to clarify, a becoming lacks a subject distinct from itself; but also that it has no term, since its term in turn exists only as taken up in another becoming of which it is the subject and which coexists, forms a block, with the first (Deleuze and Guattari 1987: 268). A thousand tiny subjects, we might say, constitute every global, logical subject.

For Deleuze, becoming is not woman; becoming is not evolution out of the matrix/womb; becoming is not analogy through a series, and it is not the analogy of variables in relation to a structure; it is not a movement from genus to species by means of the determining difference. Becoming is rather, a peopling, a crowd, a pack phenomena, which proceeds by alliances, symbiosis, contagion and 'mucosity' Irigaray sometimes calls it. To 'hear' it, she claims, requires other than attunement to good form(s), a kind of refusal of recognition and of the proper so one can hear:

That it is continuous, compressible, dilatable, viscous, conductible, diffusible . . . That it changes – in volume or in force, for example – according to the degree of heat; that it is in its physical reality determined by . . . movements coming from the quasi contact between two unities hardly definable as such. (1985a: 111)

The key term is 'unities hardly definable as such'. That is, does Irigaray look for a concept such as 'fluidity' to express what is 'physically real' or will she have language collapse into pure bodily fluid diffusion?

In *The Logic of Sense*, Deleuze draws our attention to the logical conception of becoming in Lewis Carroll's children's tale *Alice in Wonderland* (1978). As she eats and drinks various cookies, liquids and even plants, Alice shrinks and grows. She *becomes* larger than she was, but also smaller – that is, at the same stroke, Alice becomes larger than she was but smaller than she will be (Deleuze 1990b: 10). What is characteristic of becoming in this respect is that it evades the present determinable as a discrete 'now', insofar as becoming cannot support distinctions between before and after, past and future, more and less, active and passive, cause and effect. In this notion of becoming, two meanings are affirmed at once so that identity is evaded, an identity which, as Irigaray attests, is fixed by language insofar as language limits and measures, and so fixes qualities such that small *is* 'the small' and large *is* 'the large' because they each receive the action of the Idea (Deleuze 1990b: 10):

Alice herself is led to ponder the situation over and over:

I wonder if I've been changed in the night? Let me think: *was* I the same when I got up this morning? I almost think I can remember feeling a little different. But if I'm not the same, the next question is, 'Who in the world am I?' Ah, *that's* the great puzzle!' And she began thinking over all the children she knew that were of the same age as herself, to see if she could have been changed for any of them. (Carroll 1978: 35–7)[8]

But insofar as there is another language, one which expresses movements and becomings, one which subsists below or behind the Ideas, there is also a language of becoming, that language of the paradox which Alice undergoes. Such a paradox, in Deleuze's analysis, is what destroys good sense as the unique sense, and ultimately destroys common sense as the assignation of fixed identity. And given Alice's role in Deleuze's thought, it is no surprise that becomings-woman have a special introductory power (Deleuze and Guattari 1987: 248).

Irigaray has specifically questioned and apparently rejected Deleuze's concept of 'becoming-woman'. While she is not opposed to the pack or the crowd – that is, the concept of multiplicity which is so critical to Deleuze's notion of becoming – she is concerned that without first rearticulating the difference between the sexes, women's pleasure(s) will be blocked or diminished in the rush towards multiplicity (1985a: 140–1). In other words, what sense does feminism make without making the assertion of sexual difference pre-eminent? Since, as Irigaray argues, the girl has a sexualised body that is different from the boy's body long before the Oedipal stage, this is the body that needs to be articulated for women, and conceptual multiplicity appears to her to be neutral with respect to sexual difference. This seems to be why Irigaray objects to both the notion of the body without organs and the claim that Deleuze and Guattari make, in *A Thousand Plateaus*, that becoming-woman is the key to all other becomings, that it has a special introductory power (1987: 277). For Irigaray the body without organs is no more than the historical condition of women – no singular organ dominates the woman's body, thus no pleasure belongs specifically to her – thus becoming-woman is a presumption, a fantasmatic position for a male subject who, once again, supplements his own pleasure. In other words, she takes becoming-woman to be another appropriation of the woman's body by the male. These are serious criticisms that need to be addressed.

Much has been made (not always positively) of Deleuze and Guattari's acknowledgement that women must continue to 'conduct a molar politics, with a view to winning back their own organism, their own history, their own subjectivity' (Deleuze and Guattari 1987: 276). But little if any notice has been given to the lines that follow: 'But it is *dangerous* to confine oneself to such a subject, which does not function without drying up a spring or stopping a flow' (276). What does this mean? What is dangerous about molar subjectivity? A complete articulation of this claim would exceed the limits of this chapter. However, some preliminary arguments can be laid out here. We have seen that both Irigaray and Deleuze are seeking a logic that passes through the dualisms constructed by language as well as by social and legal institutions. For Deleuze, the way to carry this out is to argue for a conception of relations that are between terms but independent of them: relations that never could be absorbed into the terms they relate and which may change without affecting the terms (Deleuze 1991a).[9] Deleuze insists upon this so as to guarantee that the world is not characterised as a closed totality, but remains what Deleuze calls, an open whole that guarantees transformation, creation and difference.

Irigaray likewise expresses concern over a totalisation that defines all its relations in advance when she notes that, even in logic, the 'all' of the system 'has already prescribed the "not-all" of each particular relation established', thus the role given to the universal quantifier is to contain relations within the 'limits of the identity of (the) form(s) of syntax (1985a: 108). However, Irigaray appears to stop at the concept of an open whole, dismissing it on the grounds that it would rule out in advance any determination of values for terms or relations. Instead of conceptualising relations as independent of terms and instead of conceptualising the world as open and changing, Irigaray retains an essentialist (with respect to relations) and totalising framework, even while insisting on fluidity. This puts a large burden on the notion of fluidity, for it must be in excess with respect to form as well as permanently unstable by nature within the confines of a closed system moving towards entropy.

The difficulty with this approach (aside from the always encroaching charges of sex/gender essentialism, which this position need not and indeed does not entail) could be stated as follows:

> Precisely speaking, it is not enough to create a logic of relations, to recognise the rights of the judgments of relation as an autonomous sphere, distinct from judgments of existence and attribution. For nothing as yet prevents relations as they are detected in conjunctions (NOW, THUS, etc.) from remaining subordinate to the verb to be. (Deleuze and Parnet 1987: 56–7)

This difficulty, stated by Deleuze, is given the same expression by Irigaray, who, as we have seen, argues that fluidity is reduced to the copulative link which is appropriated in advance by the process of formal symbolisation. Thus the difference between the two approaches appears to lie in this philosophical position: is the multiple subordinate to the unity of being, or does multiplicity inhabit each thing, freed from unity, though not reduced to chaos either?

I have noted throughout this chapter how Irigaray reveals that the girl has a sexualised body that is different from the boy's prior to Oedipal intervention. Deleuze and Guattari focus their discussion of becoming-woman on the little girl, the pre-Oedipal girl Alice, precisely to make this point: that the body of the girl is stolen from her and that this takes place 'first':

> Stop behaving like that, you're not a little girl anymore, you're not a tomboy etc. The girl's becoming is stolen first, in order to impose a history, or prehistory, upon her. The boy's turn comes next, but it is by using the girl as an example, by pointing to the girl as the object of his desire, that an opposed organism, a *dominant* history is fabricated for him too. (Deleuze and Guattari 1987: 276, emphasis added)

Oedipus is constructed; the boy is constructed on the basis of construction of the girl. To rearticulate the girl's becoming before her body was stolen from her requires, from Deleuze and Guattari's point of view, the 'anorganism of the body' (the Body Without Organs), the restoration of becomings. Legally and socially, according to Irigaray, the girl must be defined by virginity; it should be guaranteed as a right (1993a: 86). Ontologically, say Deleuze and Guattari, the girl is not defined by virginity, but by a series of relations, by which they mean that the girl or the woman is not an absent presence, since there is no molar term in their logic against which she could be measured (Deleuze and Guattari 1987: 276).

The disagreement cannot be resolved here; it is doubtful that it can be resolved at all. In fact, feminists should be wary of letting go of Irigaray's social politics for the sake of conceptual freedom. Still, it remains the case that, even though there is no logical or analogical order to becomings and transformations, women's practices often provoke women's insight into multiplicity and difference, both of which are needed to evade the determination of an identity that limits, measures, and fixes qualities as essences. On the other hand, as Irigaray especially recognises, the space of the *logos* demands fixed ideas whose relationship with the sensible is wholly theoretical. From this point of view, that is, that of the formalisation of laws laid down by the *logos*, the matrix/womb has no consciousness, memory, or language (Irigaray 1985b: 340). As a result there is no access to the Platonic cave and its wisdom; the *logos* does not set up a space in which the babbling and stuttering of that which remains below the level of the type can be heard.

But 'when our lips speak together', notes Irigaray, it is precisely to question this notion of what is alike and to evade the *logos*. She writes, 'I don't quite understand "alike." Do you? Alike in whose eyes? in what terms? by what standards? with reference to what third?' (1985a: 208). In fact, far from being able to judge that something is like another, Irigaray insists that, literally, a single word can never be uttered. Affirming becoming on the level of language is the affirmation of 'several voices' who do not speak alike, but who speak in 'several ways' so that the words resound endlessly between a you and an I who are also 'several at once' (1985a: 209). In language, everything comes from everywhere and it comes all at once; this is a language that expresses multiplicity, that holds together without submission to the *logos*.

So it seems to me to be very important to follow Irigaray in conceptualising physical reality as not in service to the Oedipal family, religion, or state, and perhaps, not even as bodily, but as the elaboration of several voices, several senses, and several selves; and, to consider the Deleuzean conception of multiplicity: assemblages, arrangements, configurations of speeds and intensities. These distributions consist of bodies' actions and passions, bodies intermingling and reacting to one another, but this is not all. There are also more complex levels of organisation, semiotic regimes of signs that are formalisations of expression that vary in relation to the assemblage they express (Deleuze and Guattari 1987: 104). Thus there are no fixed bodies, fixed like the inhabitants of the cave, but instead voices, senses and selves that are several; intensive lines of flight, intensive vectors that are the assemblages that produce minoritarian groups: the oppressed and prohibited, those in revolt or on the fringe, the anomic, those outside or against the rules. How to conceive of this?

We can begin, perhaps, by separating ourselves from analogy, its principles that determine the series, its structures containing variables. It is clear that Irigaray seeks to release woman from her assigned role as the degraded or pathological element in the mythic structure. In becoming, 'we are fluid, luminous, beings made of fibers' (Deleuze and Guattari 1987: 249). In this sense, becomings are multiple, fluid, fibrous, rhizomatic, luminous – not merely reflecting light – but themselves, filaments. Think, says Deleuze, of how a square is cut out of a circle, a circle cut out of a sphere, a sphere cut out of a five dimensional form, a five dimensional form cut from one of six dimensions (Deleuze and Guattari 1987: 251). Then, think of a plane, a surface cutting across all these dimensions, intersecting all these concrete forms. This plane of consistency is nothing 'like' Plato's serial analogy which begins with the fire in the cave and ends with the sun. It is nothing 'like' the structure constituted by its own variables. This surface is one along which all that differs is expressed univocally, such that univocity is what holds it together. Not substance, form, or Idea, but a univocal open plane cutting across an infinite number of dimensions, an infinity of modifications that are nonetheless part of one another on the plane of life (Deleuze and Guattari 1987: 254).

This is the self. This is the body. These fluid, luminous planes of consistency, becomings-woman, -child, -animal, but also becomings-elementary, -cellular, -molecular, -imperceptible. The world of Anna in Clarice Lispector's tale is evoked by these becomings. Would this not be the 'more refined life of the world'? Refined in the sense of the monstrous, elemental flowers, the oozing, elemental oysters, the molecular revulsion, the imperceptible scattering of yellow in the grass – not fixed bodies, but refined, molecular life – fluid structures. In this sense of becoming-woman, these transformations on the plane of consistency are in no way analogous to woman in phallocratic or heterosexist institutions, whether that of family, religion, or state. To make becoming-woman an analogue would be to (re)present the origin as sun-light, the heterosexist structure of the Father.

Becoming-woman on a plane of consistency of an assemblage is the production of molecules that cross the entire plane so that the body of the woman cannot be stolen from her in order to make it that foundation upon and out of which the male thinks, acts, and lives. Becoming-woman gets fixed, stabilised, territorialised, when, as Irigaray has so clearly seen, the girl becomes the example of castration for the boy, then the body of the girl and the body of the boy are organised around the castrated organ of the girl and the threat of castration for the boy. The becoming-woman of any 'molar' male or female – that is, the culturally inscribed self or body – is then a matter of getting back the body that has already been constituted by castration, and perhaps even of getting on what Deleuze and Guattari call the Body Without Organs, that is, the body *not* organised by castration or its threat.

The Body Without Organs on the plane of consistency is not defined by relations of analogy, nor by the degradations of the myth; it is, rather, a life of movement and rest, speed and slowness in relation to the dimensions it cuts across. In becoming-woman across the plane of consistency, '[s]he is an abstract line', write Deleuze and Guattari, 'or a line of flight' (1987: 276–7). The somewhat dizzying result of this kind of thinking is the multiple and multi-dimensional body, the assemblage of a multiplicity of sexual forces, a multiplicity of behaviours for all the becomings that pass between the powerful, fixed bodies constituted by analogy. Woman as becoming is thus anomic, against and outside the rule, the principle, the structure. Her molecules are a powerful contagion, spread by symbiosis and mucosity. And if we succeed in depathologising everything associated with women by constituting a logic and language of fluidity, all those words that are so distasteful because they express the body of woman – the uteral, the vulvar, the clitoral, the vaginal, the placental, or woman's luminous body itself – may then enter, for the first time ever, into our knowledge.

NOTES

The topic for this chapter arose out of a conference held at Brock University, Ontario, Canada, in November 1992. My thanks to David Goicoechea, conference organiser, for suggesting the topic and for permission to reprint parts of this chapter which appeared in the conference proceedings.

1. Whitford criticises the narrow literalist reading of Irigaray as an essentialist and links Irigaray's morphology to 'the aim of transforming the social contract' (1991: 173).
2. Chanter provides a complex and multifaceted reading that addresses not only the tradition of feminist readings of Irigaray, but also seeks to situate Irigaray's work in terms of the philosophical tradition that Irigaray addresses, in particular, de Beauvoir, Hegel, Nietzsche, Heidegger, Levinas and Derrida.
3. Thus we find Irigaray's irritated response to Alice Jardine's question in *Je, Tu, Nous: Toward a Culture of Difference* (1993a): 'Are you as convinced as you were in 1974, when *Speculum* was published, that the introduction of the female body into the male corpus is an essential strategy?':

   > It makes me wonder how *Speculum* was translated in America for me to hear such misunderstandings of this book . . . But, apart from the translation, I think that there are other reasons for these misunderstandings. I suspect that one of these is the reduction of fact to rumor or opinion on the part of those who haven't actually read the text.
   >
   > Thus, *Speculum* cannot suggest getting the 'female body' to enter into the male corpus, as the female body has always figured in the male corpus . . . Such research attempts to suggest to women a morpho-logic that is appropriate to their bodies. (58–9)

   It is instructive that there seems to have been no attempt to address this matter.
4. Irigaray has discussed the philosophical and political work of social activists like the Milan Women's Bookstore Collective as central to the project of women elaborating the auto-affection and self-representation of women's own bodies. See 'More Women than Men' an interview with Luisa Muraro (Irigaray 1993a: 93–9).
5. In a note, Irigaray reconsiders the status of metaphor and suggests that the laws of equivalence (one thing is like another) operating in metaphor are problematic (1985a: 110).
6. Although the definition of these terms seems to be central to the thesis of this paper, I do not think that it is a simple matter to define them. Certainly, as Judith Butler has shown, Irigaray makes the argument that the feminine has been cast outside of the logical and linguistic system as its 'nonthematizable materiality' (Butler 1993: 42). However,

Irigaray's repeated references to the 'physical reality that continues to resist adequate symbolisation and/or that signifies the powerlessness of logic' (Irigaray 1985a: 106–7) suggests that there is more to Irigaray's conceptualisation of bodies than an unrecognised ground (even one qualified as an absent presence). Irigaray's treatment of Merleau Ponty in *An Ethics of Sexual Difference* (1993b), while condemning the privilege he gives to vision, nonetheless, embraces his call for a return to prediscursive experience. It seems to me that her concept 'fluid physical reality' is tied to such positive gestures.

7. Here I must mention that the very notion of a 'stage' implies a static and fixed economy. It may be necessary to redefine the notion of stages in terms of becoming; as such, a term like process might make more sense here.

8. In addition to Alice's continuous questioning of her identity she finds that certain aspects of the past evade her. Each time she attempts to recite a poem, for example, the words are changed, and she also engages in certain paradoxical readings as when the mouse complains of his 'long and sad tale' and Alice responds that it is a long 'tail' (Carroll 1978: 52–3).

9. In Deleuze's book on Hume, *Empiricism and Subjectivity* (1991a), Deleuze argues for an empiricist conception of relations as external to and independent of their terms because it makes possible both practical and moral activities (32). By denying that relations are derived from terms, Hume also makes it possible to deny a conception of the world as a closed totality. He makes a similar point in *Nietzsche and Philosophy* (1983), by means of the notion of the 'dice throw' (26–7).

5

Is Sexual Difference a Problem?

CLAIRE COLEBROOK

I. HOW DOES THE QUESTION OF SEXUAL DIFFERENCE RELATE TO METAPHYSICS?

Since the 'second wave' and the more recent problematisation of the sex/gender distinction, feminist theory has been concerned with questions that are explicitly metaphysical. While liberal or Marxist feminisms could accept the working philosophy of their 'host' theories and ask the question of women *within* a given paradigm, the question of sexual difference starts to question the character and limits of the theoretical paradigm itself. Perhaps the work of Luce Irigaray has been the most influential in raising the possibility that *philosophy itself* may bear the hallmarks of the (sexed) body. And it is from the work of Luce Irigaray that difference has been launched as other than an intra-philosophical problem. For if philosophy in general were gendered then the task of feminism would entail thinking philosophy's limit, or thinking the feminine as different from the identity of metaphysics. The possible connection between theory and the body put forward by Irigaray is primarily a question of the subject (Irigaray 1993b: 6; 1996: 45). Irigaray's claim that thinking has traditionally been defined as self-representation demands that any challenge to standard notions of thought will concern the self which thinks. Irigaray's reflection on philosophy's history is also, therefore, a reflection on the subject. What *Speculum of the Other Woman* (1985b) reveals is that the identity of the subject and the identity of philosophy are mutually constitutive, and that this constitution occurs through the sublation[1] of difference.

The recent interest in Deleuze by feminist theorists suggests that a new path is being taken, that difference may not, primarily, be a question of the subject (or the subject's body) and that we might do away with the transcendentalist or quasi-transcendentalist questions that motivate the post-phenomenological work of both Derrida and Irigaray: questions which turn back from presence, consciousness or subjectivity to its conditions. For according to even the most sophisticated readings of Derrida and Irigaray, the question of difference still *begins* with the metaphysical project of the condition for difference. For Derrida, any given difference is the effect of a prior difference which is never itself given (and is only perceivable *as prior* through the question of the condition). But the *question* of the condition or origin is still used to problematise the transcendental project. Derrida describes his method, therefore, as 'ultra-transcendental' or 'quasi-transcendental'.[2]

For Irigaray, however, the very logic of conditions suggests a certain comportment of self-origination which occurs through the negation of the maternal ground; here, the subject's condition is always perceived as a modification of the subject (1985b: 136). For Irigaray, sexual difference is not a topic to be introduced into metaphysics, but determines metaphysics as such. To be a true genesis or a more authentic metaphysics – to be other than a repetition of the Same – would demand asking the question of the condition for presence beyond self-representation, in a different relation to the origin and not as self-origination. The metaphysical question of the possibility or condition of thought becomes, with Irigaray, a question of sexual difference. Any transcendental condition or metaphysical ground is also, she argues, a 'folding back' or 'turn' of empirical determination which *then* constitutes itself as transcendental. Sexual difference has been feigned by a single term producing itself as *subjectivity in general*. Irigaray's method is to open the transcendental to its empirical determination and, at the same time, to see any determination or identity of the empirical (such as 'man' or 'woman') as produced through a transcendental logic. According to Irigaray traditional metaphysics is sustained by a gap or break between the sensible and the ideal: 'between empirical and transcendental *a suspense will remain inviolate*' (1985b: 145). Irigaray's task is precisely to violate this suspense and to show that the transcendental is a *sensible* transcendental, that any empirical particularity is given through a general account of what is; but this general grounding is also constituted in the particular. The traditional transcendental closure achieved by effacing the

111

'irreconcilable gap between the sensible and supersensible' attempts to ground all particularity within a meaningful and subjective horizon. Irigaray demonstrates the limits of the transcendental schema by opening this 'gap' to an otherness which cannot be determined *in advance* (1985b: 206). An ethics of sexual difference has as its goal a 'confounding' of 'the opposition between immanence and transcendence' (Irigaray 1993b: 33).

II. DELEUZE'S PHILOSOPHY OF IMMANENCE AND TRANSCENDENTAL EMPIRICISM

The feminist 'turn' to Deleuze may appear at first hand as a departure from these questions of conditions, horizon and difference as the condition for the possibility of the subject. Certainly, the initial reception of Deleuze in feminist theory was critical precisely because Deleuze was seen to collapse the question of sexual difference into difference in general (Braidotti 1991: 108). Furthermore, Deleuze's project of a philosophy of immanence immediately suggests that questions of the character of thought *in general* (and hence the project of a specifically feminist thinking, defined against masculine thought) might need to be abandoned. Given that the question of sexual difference has been, for the past decade at least, a *metaphysical* question, and that this metaphysics has been one of the conditions of the possibility for thought, feminist theory might now question its understanding of the ostensibly necessary connection between feminist ethics and metaphysics. If metaphysics remains an inevitable horizon for feminist questions,[3] it may at least be worth asking *how* we are to understand what metaphysics is. Is feminism a critical inhabitation of metaphysical closure, or the task of thinking a new metaphysics?

Deleuze's work invites us to open again the relation between ethics, gender and metaphysics. In particular, the Deleuzean corpus provides a way of asking whether, as an ethical question, sexual difference demands a metaphysics.

In his book on Hume Deleuze suggests that philosophy presents two possibilities: transcendental philosophy (which asks the question of how the subject relates to the given) and empiricism (which locates the constitution of the subject within the given) (1991a: 87). The question that follows from this is, perhaps: how would we decide or choose between these two forms? Furthermore, could such a decision be philosophical? The question of sexual difference as it has so far been articulated in feminist theory has, on this interpretation, been one of transcendental philosophy. For the recent debate over sexual difference concerns nothing other than the possibility that the gendered subject may not just encounter a world, but that sex occurs as a specific relation to the world. The question of essentialism raises the possibility that subjects might be constituted differently, not just within the world (in terms of gender) but in their comportment as such (in terms of sex). Sexual difference may be ontological rather than ontic (Braidotti 1989; Irigaray 1996: 146). The critique of the sex/gender distinction, on the other hand, has proceeded as a questioning of the simple division between worldly (ontic) difference and the (ontological) ground for such difference (Gatens 1996a: 15–18). Any such posited ground – such as sex, materiality or essence – needs itself to be questioned according to its conditions for possibility and cannot be regarded as a brute given (Butler 1993: 27–55). The possibility of essential difference and the rejection of gender as pure social construction have been raised as ethical questions that are inextricably intertwined with the very origin of meaning and representation. Not surprisingly, Derrida's deconstruction of the positing of any pure origin has been adopted to question the notion of some sexual origin which is *then* rendered meaningful. Sex is, rather, seen as inextricably tied to a meaning production which can itself never be presented as fully meaningful. To this extent both Derrida and Irigaray, and those feminist theorists who explore the implications of the problem of the origin, work with the transcendental programme of the subject's relation to the given, and the genesis of the meaning of the given.

Deleuze's work, on the other hand, is avowedly located within the second (empiricist) possibility. Despite its name, transcendental empiricism is not a transcendentalism. As a philosophy of immanence Deleuze's empiricism tries to avoid any explanandum or transcendence that would function as a condition for *what is*. The question of philosophy, for empiricism, is not to account for the condition or meaning of the given but to respond to the given. Philosophy's response to the given takes the form of concepts (Deleuze and Guattari 1994: 33). But this is one form of response among others and not the condition or ground for the given in general. Philosophy's creation of concepts is not a clarification or formalisation of possible experience, but a form of experience itself. Concepts are not empty formalisms, pale negations, limits or frozen idealities which remain above and beyond the given. Nor are they conditions for the possibility of experience, conditions that would be radically anterior to experience. In this regard the Deleuzean understanding of the concept might best be defined in opposition to the Kantian theory of pure concepts. For Deleuze concepts are *creations within the given* with their own character and existence. Concepts are 'interventions' which answer problems or local situations (Deleuze 1994a: xx). Concepts work, have effect and enable positive connections (Deleuze and Guattari 1994: 21). The implications of this for ethics (including feminist ethics) are at least twofold. First, philosophy is not an omni-relevant horizon. If its domain – that of concepts – is not a general condition or horizon for what is, but a particular response to what is, then philosophy represents one form of response among others. Feminist ethics might take the form of the creation of new concepts, but it might take other forms of response: artistic or scientific. Ethical questions might not necessarily demand a metaphysical response. In fact, metaphysics itself would be an ethical position among others. Second, feminist philosophy's engagement with concepts might not be *critical* – asking the condition of thought, subjectivity or difference – but *inventive*: creating new concepts, new questions and new problems.

Furthermore, the ethic of philosophy as empiricism or immanence is, according to Deleuze and Deleuze and Guattari, not a justification, legitimation or *critique* of existence but an *amor fati* (Deleuze 1990b: 149; Deleuze and Guattari 1994: 159). By opening itself out to what is, philosophy will be both the creation of concepts but also an affirmation of events. Events are neither already meaningful and conceptually determined entities given by the structure of thought, nor are they radically anterior conditions which produce thought's structure. Neither condition nor conditioned, neither genesis nor structure, events are the singularities of existence, moments of sense that exceed already constituted concepts but which open the problems that concepts will answer. By affirming events philosophy will not be a critique of the given – asking how events are possible or meaningful. Rather, the challenge for philosophy as *amor fati* is the creation of concepts that are equal to the event: not as representations or formalisations, but as creations that work within the field of events, enabling new events, new questions and new possibilities.

A philosophy of the event would attempt to affirm, rather than react against, possibility and becoming. The virtuality of the event lies in the relation of positive difference; the virtual is a becoming-different of difference in an event. As a distribution of difference the event is also a performance of *sense*, a connection among a being, an articulation and a movement. The event, as sense, refers to a singularity that is neither a denoted thing, nor a signified meaning, nor an expressed intention. Rather sense is the event that completes and opens the relation between denotation, signification and expression. Described in non-Deleuzean terms we might say that sense fills out the gap between a word, the world, the specific use made of that word and that to which it refers. In an isolated instance of meaning, sense is what makes this particular meaning meaningful on this occasion. It is therefore a unique and singular occurrence. But this very singularity raises the possibility of the *opening* of sense: concepts with no denotation, things with no concepts, or movements of sense among denotation, signification and expression. In all these cases thought is presented with a task, to answer the event of sense, and it may choose to do so in the form of philosophy.

In order to understand the peculiar and dynamic character of sense, we could also look at the way poetry works on language and understanding. When William Blake uses the word 'harlot' in the final stanza of his poem 'London', the sense of the term presents a challenge for new ways of thinking. As the word appears in the poem, it bears all the associations of moral condemnation – used alongside the discourse of 'curse' and 'plagues':

> But most thro' midnight streets I hear
> How the youthful Harlots curse
> Blasts the new-born Infants tear
> And blights with plagues the Marriage hearse.
>
> (Blake 1966)

At the same time it is this very moral usage, its connection with judgement, condemnation and religion, which also shows a certain plague of moralism; we see that the disease or plague is the word 'harlot' itself. The use of 'harlot' alongside 'Marriage hearse' shows the effect of a moralistic vocabulary. The poem places the word in such a way that it is shown as a denial of life: forms of desire are associated with death. In this presentation of the moral lexicon, Blake creates a new sense for 'harlot'. It is now seen for *what it does* and the connections it makes. Rather than claim that all women are *really* innocent – 'they are not harlots' – a claim that would remain within moralism's concepts, Blake presents a new concept. 'Harlot' is used as a symptom that indicates the disease of moralism.

This simple event of sense demands that we think morals differently, and that we reconceptualise a possible ethical vocabulary.

Sense can be thought of as the presentation of problems, the philosophical response to which would be new concepts. Deleuze's examples of concepts in philosophy demonstrate what these new concepts *do*. Eternal return allows us to think of existence as innocent, as not subjected to another (transcendent) order or value. As such, these concepts – such as eternal return, the monad, duration, the rhizome or expression – are also practical and enable new ways of life. For a concept which answers to the event of sense will think differently and operate as a different response to the given. It is in this regard that events are *ideal*: not given as part of the world but as possible responses (Deleuze 1990b: 53). If philosophy creates new concepts it does so in response to the irreducible *difference* of the event, as the possibility of a new question. Because the event of sense prompts new ways of thinking it cannot be located *within* thought, nor seen as thought's anterior condition. On the contrary, the field of sense is an effect of a prepersonal distribution of singularities, different in themselves, and not constituted as *different from* the position of thought. Thinking takes place as movement around this nomadic distribution of singularities; and it is from this prepersonal distribution of difference that concepts and identity are thought.

Difference, here, is not the *effect* of conceptual distinction, nor is it the *condition* for concepts. Difference is, among other things, the *task* of philosophy. If philosophy is *not* opinion it is so only because it *thinks*. One of Deleuze's many endeavours has been the redefinition of thought as a 'heterogenesis' (Deleuze 1994a: xvi; Deleuze and Guattari 1994: 20) which confronts chaos. That is, thought should not be valued according to its correctness or with regard to some model of good sense or common sense. Rather than *recognise* thought, philosophy ought to think differently. To repeat or justify current ways of thinking is to deny the virtual possibilities of sense or events. Reflection, contemplation, critique and the transcendental enquiry into conditions are all forms of *reaction*. By locating the philosophical question in its *difference from* the given, transcendental philosophy sees the actual as something in need of justification. Furthermore, philosophy's posited conditions for the given have always been modified repetitions of the given itself (Deleuze 1990b: 122). The subject as ego is grounded by the transcendental subject. But true genesis cannot be included within consciousness, which is merely one event among others. Philosophy

116

is, as a consequence, presented with two challenges: first, avoiding the *inclusion* of chaos, genesis or difference within the individual or consciousness and, second, avoiding the notion of a general outside or ground which would provide thought with a transcendental limit or ground.

Rather than seeing philosophy as a question of conditions, Deleuze and Guattari's *What is Philosophy?* suggests that we think any such posited conditions as illusions of transcendence (1994: 49). To see all transcendent conditions as illusions generated from within immanence involves recognising that these illusions (such as the subject, God or Being) are effected according to a good image of thought. The idea of a grounding transcendence ensures *in advance* what thought will be. The positing of a general transcendent condition enables thought to continue as self-recognition. In a radical empiricism, however, immanence is no longer *immanent to* something else (Deleuze and Guattari 1994: 47). Immanence is only conceivable as immanence *to* some transcendence if there is a pre-established plane: a general field already understood or determined in a certain way. The realisation that there is this plane is the first challenge of Deleuze's empiricism. The second challenge that we might avoid altogether this transcendent 'Something = x' and think THE plane of immanence (and thereby thought 'without an image') is the less immediately realisable task (Deleuze and Guattari 1994: 59). In *Empiricism and Subjectivity* (1991a) Deleuze sets the problem of immanence in relation to Kant's philosophy of representation. Transcendence, Deleuze argues, is an empirical fact. Only transcendental philosophy takes this fact and places it within the domain of representation such that the given becomes a 'Something = x' (an effect of the subject). The given, here, is seen to depend on the subject's synthesis (Deleuze 1991a: 111). An empiricist philosophy, on the other hand, looks at 'what we are doing' to establish relations within the given (133); in which case, there would be no transcendence in general (Being) but a distribution of different connections, habits, singularities and passions. An immanent philosophy creates its concepts, not according to a pre-established plane, but in an attempt to think new planes.

If we see philosophy, not as an enquiry into the *conditions* of difference but as the challenge to think difference in the absence of conditions for difference (Deleuze 1994a: 28), then philosophy will be a creative rather than a critical procedure. If the 'illusions' of transcendence are inevitably reintroduced (Deleuze and Guattari 1994: 51) this is because concepts, once created, are taken as eternal.

As the creation of new concepts, philosophy *is* the challenge of immanence, the task of thinking a concept as event, and not as a representation of some predetermined transcendence. Philosophy is the challenge of an immanence that would be 'accommodated to itself' (208) and not justified by something other than, or transcendent to, the event of thought. This is why philosophy is not history of philosophy but 'becoming' (59).

But if philosophy is not an explanation of the genesis or possibility of difference but the creation of *different* concepts, what happens to sexual difference – that difference that has functioned as the exemplary instance of difference in theories of ethical difference? Early feminist criticism of Deleuze recognised one thing clearly enough: if difference is no longer an originary condition, and if difference is no longer the difference of the genesis of the subject, then sexual difference is no longer foundational, no longer the difference from which all other (given) differences are effected. Against Deleuze and the collapse of sexual difference into difference in general, feminist ethics in a number of forms has suggested that we remain within the transcendental or quasi-transcendental question, the question of the conditions for determinate differences.[4]

III. DERRIDA AND SEXUAL DIFFERENCE

In *Limited Inc* Derrida defines metaphysics as the question of intentionality: the promise of meaning which is both necessarily inaugurated by any concept but which is also, necessarily, never fulfilled. The question of metaphysics – the 'question of the possibility of the question' (Derrida 1976: 167) – is nothing other than this telos of intentionality which 'opens' any given or determined instance of a concept, and which inscribes a certain 'ethicity' in language (Derrida 1988: 122). The meaning of a concept, for Derrida, always lies above and beyond any factual or contextual determination; for the concept, *as concept*, can always be cited again and opened to new contexts (116). The metaphysical question of the 'in general' – the possibility of meaning beyond any singular instance – opens any specific definition by showing that a concept's promise is never fulfilled. At the same time that the concept is a promise of a future meaning forever deferred, it is also an effect of an anteriority. To this extent concepts are not indeterminate. They may be undecidable – always open to future citation – but they are never absolutely open (148). They possess a promise or opening to future meaning, but they also delimit, mark or trace in order to enable meaning. The concept is a decision, delimitation or determination. But this decision is not the effect of a fully self-present intention, for all intention itself depends upon the differentiation that characterises conceptuality. The decision of any concept, because never fully present, is also the effect of an undecidable anteriority (116). This anteriority is only understood *as anterior* through conceptualisation; it can never be rendered present and its *meaning* is similarly deferred, and effected through deferral.

Ethics is inscribed in this temporality of the concept. Because the meaning of any term is never fully given, all concepts effect a certain telos: we can only have 'justice to come' or 'democracy to come'. But the concept is also the effect of a radically anterior undecidability (something we can never fully decide or conceptualise). The concept is both a future promise and an anterior burden. In speaking, we bear responsibility for the necessary impurity or contamination of the promise, its openness to future meaning and its delimitation. The concept is never the purity of an intent nor the autonomy of a decision. As *meaningful*, concepts are the iterable effects of a singular *différance* that can never be rendered meaningful. The non-conceptual status of this quasi-condition,[5] like the promise of meaning, generates a certain 'ethicity'. For the quasi-transcendental condition precludes the claim to ethical autonomy; with the recognition of the limit of any concept and its anterior debt language bears a certain *responsibility*. We must speak and in so doing we assume responsibility for those concepts that make any ethics both possible (in its promise) and impossible (in its deferral). Ethical judgements are effects of a *différance* which – precisely because it can never be fully comprehended or rendered present – renders us non-autonomous, indebted (Derrida 1995: 261). In speaking, however, we are nevertheless responsible for a concept which is both ours and not ours; a concept's future meaning and anterior conditions always take us beyond ourselves. A concept opens existence to a promise that will always remain to come. At the same time, this promise is always contaminated by the limit it places on the undecidable, pre-promisory possibilities of its genesis (Derrida 1989: 39).

The consequences of this deconstructive ethics of language are clearly and faithfully drawn by Drucilla Cornell. If a law has a certain meaning then this meaning must hold above and beyond any single interpretation. As such the law is never fully instantiated. We must always recognise the futural promise in law, its gesture to a telos forever deferred (Cornell 1992: 111). At the same time, any articulation of the law is effected through a decision and determination which renders us responsible for its necessary exclusion. On the issue of sexual difference, Cornell has used this opening of the law to criticise Lacanian determinations of sexual difference. Lacan's explanation of sexual difference accepts the *determination* of difference. The acceptance of symbolic determinations of 'woman', 'the phallus' and the law of the father fails to recognise the undecidability of these concepts. As a meaningful concept, 'woman' necessarily marks a limit; but it is in the recognition of this limit that ethics is possible. For Cornell 'woman' as the fantasised origin is also capable of gesturing to 'the power of the feminine as the beyond to supposedly omnipresent symbolic' (Cornell 1991: 78). The undecidable difference which is the condition for any concept – including the concept of woman – is also an opening and solicitation of the concept. Even if *différance* here is *quasi-*transcendental, its definition and effects operate according to the critical question of the *conditions* for any given difference. Sexual difference in its accepted binary form would be challenged and opened by asking the question of the *différance* which enabled this difference. In the case of Lacanian sexual difference, the phallus acts as a signifier only because it can never be fulfilled. Furthermore, its ability to act as a transcendental signifier (which orders the gender system) depends upon its difference from any actual body part. As the signification of full presence the phallus must be other than any penis; the fullness of the signifier is, therefore, dependent on its lack at the level of signified. It is therefore neither given in man nor woman. The phallus is both the gender system's centre and its limit. To think the phallus as the condition for the system of gender – masculinity and femininity as having or not having the phallus – is also to think the paradox on which the gender system rests. The system's condition of difference, between the phallus and lack, is also the system's site of incoherence (Cornell 1996). We are never able to locate a pure difference which would answer the question of a general condition; for any such described primary difference is always given *within* a particular system. Nevertheless, the question of difference in general opens the determination of any given difference.

As the general question of the conditions for difference, Derrida's metaphysics shows sexual difference to be a difference among others, a particular determination of *différance*. However, any description of *general* difference is always articulated as a determined difference (Derrida 1983). For Cornell and Derrida, then, a deconstruction of the gender system would lead not to authentic sexual difference, but to a proliferation of differences (Cornell 1991: 198; Derrida 1995: 108).

IV. IRIGARAY AND FEMINIST TRANSCENDENCE

Irigaray's critique of presence, on the other hand, locates sexual difference not as a difference within the given, but as an effect of the difference which enables the given. For a world or presence to be given, a division must be effected between a subject and that which is given. It is this differentiation and its constitution of presence which has, until now, produced sexual difference as a non-difference. The subject, traditionally conceived, is a directedness towards a present and inert object, which the subject presents to himself. In *Speculum of the Other Woman* Irigaray refers to 'the subject. In whose sight everything outside remains forever a condition making possible the image and the reproduction of the self' (1985b: 136). In this constitution of the given *as an object*, the subject produces himself as a representational subject (184). Philosophy so far has been a representationalism in which the subject presents to himself the conditions of his own emergence. Irigaray's 'transcendental sensible' (1993b: 32), however, short-circuits the closure of representationalism by showing that the condition which the subject repeats and refigures as his own ground can never be fully comprehended by the subject, precisely because the subject is nothing other than an *effect* of this repetition (354). In presenting the origin *as object* the subject is produced as a subject. But this repetition of the origin *as presence* can never itself be presented. In order to be fully present to himself the subject must negate his corporeal facticity. According to Irigaray, it is this turn against (and representation of) 'empirical naivety' (1985b: 204) that constitutes metaphysics as such. The subject as pure thought thinking itself must exclude or objectify its corporeality. It must differentiate itself as subject, and in so doing constitute an object as other. The subject's first (constitutive) object is effected through a figuration of the maternal. Metaphysics *is* sexual difference: the production of a self-present subject in opposition to an object-in-general. The sexual difference of metaphysics has therefore been a *difference within* the self-sameness of the subject, an 'apriorism of the same' (1985b: 27). Otherness is never recognised, but determined *in advance* as what can be presented to the subject.

121

Refiguring metaphysics demands refiguring sexual difference. No longer a relation between a subject who can adequately (re)present a transcendent object, an ethics of sexual difference would enable two transcendences or two modes of relation. This would take the form not of representation but of *recognition*. It would no longer be a question of the subject's relation to the given, but of a relation to another mode of transcendence, another mode of givenness. Irigaray's ethics of sexual difference is not just a critique of determined gender differences; it is the production and recognition of two ways in which determination might be given:

> It is evident that male and female corporeal morphology are not the same and it therefore follows that their way of experiencing the sensible and of constructing the spiritual is not the same. Moreover, women and men have different positions in relation to genealogy. (Irigaray 1996: 38)

This ethics is at once transcendental, for it concerns the general relatedness of the subject to transcendence, the subject's relation to otherness. At the same time this ethics is sensible, for such relatedness is always (sexually) embodied. The question of sexual difference is an ethical question – *the* ethical question – because the recognition of the other *as other* demands their distinct identity (1996: 47). And this identity, to be ethical, and to exist in a relation of *recognition* (1996: 144), must be seen as a mode of transcendence or becoming (and not as an object). The philosophical question for Irigaray is still transcendental. The subject is still constituted as an originary relation. And if the refiguration of this relation takes the form of *sexual* difference this is because philosophy has always been founded on the necessary exclusion and negation of the feminine. If ethics, for Derrida, is the opening of the philosophical question, for Irigaray it is something more. Ethics is no longer the question of the limit of the concept but a positive reformulation of the relation to the given, a relation now mediated through the recognition of the other, not an other who will confirm or reflect my own relatedness but an other with a different mode of relatedness.

How we understand sexual difference is a question of how we understand philosophy. If philosophy is, as Derrida argues, a question of the question in general, then no determined difference, such as sexual difference, can fulfil the metaphysical telos. An ethics of the opening of any meaning is, therefore, both 'purely formal' (Derrida 1994) and futural. Sexual difference, like any other difference, is always disrupted or opened by the question of its meaning and condition. Derrida's work operates on a conditional acceptance of a traditional definition of metaphysics. If philosophy is the question of pure truth – the question of the concept in general – then it necessarily affirms both the promise of the concept in the fullness of its meaning (above and beyond the limit of any instance) and the impossibility of this promise (for the purity of the concept is always contaminated by its own anterior conditions of production). Following Derrida's conditional acceptance of philosophy as the project of pure truth, a certain ethics of sexual difference operates around this 'double' strategy of possibility and impossibility, affirmation and critique. The promise of the sexual other is a promise which, as meaningful, always exceeds the specificity or singularity of any concrete other. The other's *identity* is both an effect of the loss of their specificity – insofar as they are identified – and the condition of their specificity, we recognise them as other only through identity. We can only experience the other, *as other*, through meaningful difference, such as sexual difference, but *as meaningful*, this difference will always be located within the Same. The *différance* which effects the *meaning* of the other both promises an otherness beyond the concept and locates the limit of the concept. As a *general* critique and affirmation of identity and difference, deconstruction does not yield an ethics of sexual difference but it can be deployed to that end. But it also suggests that a project of ethics confined to sexual difference, or based upon sexual difference, would have foreclosed an essential ethical opening.

Sexual difference for Irigaray, on the other hand, is necessary for the transfiguration of metaphysics. Irigaray's emphasis on recognition and the production of two modes of transcendence only partially accepts the transcendentalist project of conditions. The subject is still a relatedness-towards, still an intentionality. Unlike Derrida, Irigaray does not locate a quasi-transcendental condition for the sensible; the sensible *as lived* is never fully present, but it is not radically anterior, not a logical or 'purely formal' limit. The sensible is *proximate*. Neither the full presence of experience, nor the radical anteriority of a transcendental condition, the sensible is given in the *other body* whom I recognise as another form of becoming, as a 'concrete universal' (Irigaray 1996). Relatedness or transcendence is no longer towards the given but to another subject. Autonomy is not self-authorship but the sense of the embodied specificity of my identity which is gained through recognition of the (differently) embodied other. Sexual difference, for Irigaray, is not a difference among others but responds to a certain problem: if we think in terms of a certain philosophical plane – that of the subject, and ethics as the recognition of other subjects – then sexual difference provides a way of thinking through possibilities *within this plane.*

V. SEXUAL DIFFERENCE AS A PROBLEM

But what if sexual difference thought itself as a *problem* and effected a new plane accordingly? If philosophy were neither a question of the opening of pure truth, nor a question of recognition, but the confrontation of new problems and concepts, then sexual difference would be a different form of difference. For feminist ethics the overcoming of subjectivism and of the metaphysics of transcendence and intentionality has presented itself as the problem of the body. A response to this problem can take a number of forms. If we consider the body in terms of the psycho-genesis of the subject then the body becomes a body-image: constructed as part of a representational relation to the given (Gatens 1996a). Thought in this way the body is an effect of the subject's emergence in a field of specular-representational relations. Alternatively, the body has been defined as necessarily repressed, as a radical anteriority, or as that which thought must negate to have an image of itself as pure presence. But here the body is conceived as that which pre-cedes the given, as a horizon or posited condition of the subject.

A non-reactive feminist ethics of the body may have to locate the body on a different plane. Not the condition of thought, thought's limit or thought's image, an ethics of the body might locate the body in its effects, forces, modes and circumstance. And such an ethics might have to ask different questions: not 'what does this body mean – what is its intent, condition or genesis?' but 'how does this body work?' Would this be an ethics of sexual difference? No, if this means that sexual difference is an originary difference constitutive of the ethical subject. Yes, if the 'problem' of sexual difference is embraced to produce a new plane. Deciding among these options is not philosophical insofar as from any given defin-ition of philosophy the questions of difference will demand a specific type of response. (The decision is, if you like, pre-philo-sophical.) But the question of sexual difference is ultimately philosophical insofar as the decision as to what philosophy is will determine the status of this difference. If we want sexual differ-ence to be a problem we may have to rethink philosophy.

The decision about what sexual difference means, what the question of sexual difference amounts to, is currently thought in terms of an understanding of the nature of philosophy. If philosophy is the question of the question (Derrida), an ethics of sexual difference would take the form of an enquiry into the condition of difference, difference in general. If philosophy has been a form of auto-representation (Irigaray), then philosophy's transformation will take the form of the recognition of an other: autonomous sexual difference. And if philosophy is an ethics of *amor fati* and the creation of new concepts, then sexual difference will be the task of thinking differently. Could sexual difference be a different sort of problem?

If philosophy is the challenge of *amor fati*, not reacting against existence, then it will set itself the task of empiricism: trying to think within immanence, trying to think without the illusion of transcendence. The body is not the only way in which such immanence might be thought but it presents itself as the possibility for a new plane, a new image of what it means to think.[6] It *might* be a way of not accounting for what is in terms of some other value or condition. Sexual difference might enable us to think the body, not as an explanandum, anteriority or condition but as a form of positive difference.

Sexual difference might open the question of different bodily comportments, different responses to the given within the given. And this opening might lead us beyond the notion of general comportments towards the world or theoretical accounts of the possibility of the given. Drawing upon some of the *problems* of feminist ethics, it might be time to ask how feminism as a question might transform thinking. It might be time to think of the body in its various distributions. This would not mean offering a Deleuzean theory of the body, but would look at the body to think differently. If subjects are constituted by contingent relations within the given, then a general theory of subjectivity, even embodied subjectivity, may no longer be desirable or possible. Feminism has already frequently confronted the question of different problems of different bodies who bear different relations to the given. Accordingly, we might dispense with a notion of 'the given' (or being, or the body) and think of various distributions, various modes of thought.

Mightn't the anorexic body, which posits a radical disjunction between body-image, lived body and empirical body, disrupt the dreamed-of unity of the phenomenological subject? But this would not offer us the 'truth' of the body in general. A pregnant body, on the other hand, would demand thinking a body beyond body-image and body boundaries; for the sense of pregnancy exceeds the visible. The obese body, the injured body, the erotic body, the athletic body or the surgically enhanced body all present different distributions of the way thought relates to one of its events, the corporeal event, the sense of the corporeal. It would not be a question of deciding a correct theory of the body: Lacanian sexual difference, Irigarayan recognition, Derridean questions, phenom-enological lived bodies. For all these accounts of the body in general explore various events of sense, ways in which thought connects and responds. This is why Deleuze argues that philosophy *proceeds from* an image of thought (Deleuze 1994a). And this idea may present feminism with the challenge of taking Deleuze beyond Deleuze. Rather than appeal to the schizo-body or the Body Without Organs, feminism might look to its bodily questions – of eating disorders, abortion, beauty, care, rape, difference – and realise *that a philosophy of the body is less appropriate than a bodily philosophy.*[7] Thought takes place in a body, as a body, and so a theory of the body in general could not be a true response to the problem of the body. This body is *in some instances* a body-image, in others it is a body-thing, and often a body-effect. Any theory of *the* body might follow or accord with a philosophy of sexual difference. However, if sexual difference is not theorised *from* a metaphysics, but is confronted as a problem, then we might take the issues of sexual difference and use them to *think*. One response might not be to think of *the* mind–body relation, but to see as many relations as there are bodily questions.

NOTES

This essay originally appeared in *Social Semiotics*, 7.2 (1997). We gratefully acknowledge permission from the publishers to reprint the essay in this volume.

1. The Hegelianism of this term is intentional. The Hegelian idea that the subject of philosophy is effected through a relation to an other is sustained by Irigaray. However, Irigaray's project for the transforma-tion of metaphysics demands both a *recognition* of the constitutive (and not merely negative) character of the other and, therefore, a *maintenance*, rather than a sublation, of difference.
2. According to Derrida, 'the value of the transcendental arche [*archie*]

must make its necessity felt before letting itself be erased' (Derrida 1976b: 61).

3. According to Irigaray metaphysics is the primary and indispensible ground for feminist enquiry: 'The philosophical order is indeed the one that has to be questioned, and *disturbed*, inasmuch as it covers over sexual difference' (1985a: 159).

4. Drusilla Cornell still sees the quasi-transcendental method as the beginning of feminist ethics (Cornell 1991). Judith Butler's quite different approach, which stresses materiality and embodiment, nevertheless locates the body's sexual 'materiality' at the *limit* of discourse (Butler 1993). Even the recent Deleuzean work of Elizabeth Grosz regards the body as 'the *unacknowledged condition* of the dominant term, reason' (Grosz 1995: 32, emphasis added).

5. Derrida refers to '*différance*', accordingly, as an 'aconceptual concept' (1988: 118).

6. Rosi Braidotti recognised that the body, for Deleuze, held neither a privileged nor explanatory position in Deleuze's metaphysics: 'For Deleuze the body is a surface where forces play ... there is nothing essentialistic or primordial about Deleuzian bodies' (1991: 74).

7. Elizabeth Grosz made this point in relation to Deleuze and architecture: that we might need to *think architecturally* (1995: 125–37).

6

Towards a Feminist Philosophy of Mind

ELEANOR KAUFMAN

One of Gilles Deleuze's philosophical achievements is that he renders the classic mind–body dualism both more complex and ultimately beside the point. He does this by showing over and again how the body and the mind are inseparably linked to each other, how they are part of the same assemblage that is to be regarded in terms of what it can do rather than what it is or is not. It follows, then, that to link Deleuze to a concrete distinction between the mind and the body is treading on risky ground. In the same fashion, recent feminist readings of Deleuze by Rosi Braidotti and Elizabeth Grosz underscore the difficulty of the mind–body distinction and suggest a form of 'thinking through the body' as a way to get beyond this dualism. What I propose is an extension of these analyses that builds on their insights yet returns to the unwanted mind–body split to suggest that there are perhaps some things – and things pertinent to both Deleuze and feminism – that a mind in disjunction from its body can still do. Indeed, I suggest that in certain (and often extreme) cases there is a lived necessity of maintaining such disjunctions. Drawing on the work of Braidotti and Grosz, I will outline a parallel but reconfigured framework that puts greater emphasis on the world of the spirit and the mind. Using Deleuze's study of Spinoza and Pierre Klossowski's study of Nietzsche, I will then suggest ways in which the mind's potential for exceeding the body allows access to new states of health and exuberance.

The most explicit treatment of the intersection of Deleuze and feminism in the work of Rosi Braidotti is to be found in her essay

'Toward a New Nomadism: Feminist Deleuzian Tracks; or Metaphysics and Metabolism' (Braidotti 1994a).[1] Braidotti maps the
work of a series of feminist thinkers of sexual difference – including
Luce Irigaray, Monique Wittig, Judith Butler and Donna Haraway
– onto such Deleuze and Guattarian concepts as the rhizome, the
Body Without Organs, becoming-woman and becoming-minoritarian, and finally nomadic thinking. Without rehearsing the various
linkages Braidotti proposes or attempting an overall synthesis on
the same scale, I wish instead to highlight those specific points in
Braidotti's text where she discusses the mind–body relationship
and the relationship of embodiment to thinking.

Initially, Braidotti casts feminist theory as working to overcome
a history of female disembodiment:

[F]eminist theory...expresses women's...structural need to posit
themselves as female subjects, that is to say, not as disembodied entitics,
but rather as corporeal and consequently sexed beings. Following
Adrienne Rich I believe that the redefinition of the female subject
starts with the revaluation of the bodily roots of subjectivity and the
rejection of the traditional vision of the knowing subject as universal,
neutral, and consequently gender-free. This 'positional' or situated
way of seeing the subject is based on the understanding that the most
important location or situation is the rooting of the subject into the
spatial frame of the body. (1994a: 161)

This passage begins by locating a fundamental disjunction between
'female subjects' and 'disembodied entities'. While these disembodied entities have historically fallen on the side of the 'universal,
neutral, and consequently gender-free' masculine subject, the
question at hand is whether there is anything in these disembodied entities that is redemptive for feminism. Moreover, could the
very disjunction female subject/disembodied entity be in itself a
productive contradiction?

Braidotti concludes this passage with a call for a 'rooting of the
subject into the spatial frame of the body'. While such a rooting is
a necessary corrective to a long-standing disdain for the body, it
also seems that more than one such rooting is possible. An alternate,
though to my mind not incompatible, rooting is one that also – or
on occasion – situates the subject along the lines of tension between
the body and the mind. Indeed, later moments of Braidotti's text
provide the seeds for such an alternate form of embodiment. Such
an alternate form entails a body that does not simply correspond
one to one with the physical frame of the person. Rather, the body
is itself a complex interaction of forces, not all of them clearly

readable as either physical or human. It is in articulating such a notion of the body a few pages later that Braidotti has recourse to Deleuze. I quote at length:

> The embodiment of the subject is for Deleuze a form of bodily materiality, but not of the natural biological kind. He rather takes the body as the complex interplay of highly constructed social and symbolic forces. The body is not an essence, let alone a biological substance. It is a play of forces, a surface of intensities: pure simulacra without originals. Deleuze is therefore of great help to feminists because he deessentializes the body, sexuality, and sexed identities. The embodied subject is a term in a process of intersecting forces (affects), spatiotemporal variables that are characterized by their mobility, changeability, and transitory nature. (1994a: 163)

In thinking the body as an interplay of forces,[2] Braidotti uses Deleuze to portray a body that is populated with things and flows and movements that would belie any static or absolute essence to the body. Furthermore, such a fluid conception of the body reinforces the now standard and certainly somewhat simplified critique of the Cartesian system of the mind–body dualism or split. Such a critique would run as follows: if the body really were a complex system of forces, not a distinct entity in itself but rather a system of overlapping and changing boundaries, how can there be some kind of pure and absolute boundary between it and the mind? Braidotti presents precisely this argument when she writes: 'Clearly for feminist corporeal materialism, the body is not a fixed essence, a natural given. . . . [T]he 'body' as theoretical *topos* is an attempt to overcome the classical mind–body dualism of Cartesian origins, in order to think anew about the structure of the thinking subject. The body is then an interface, a threshold, a field of intersecting material and symbolic forces' (1994a: 169). According to such an analysis, the body is used as a philosophical tool to disrupt the mind–body dualism.

In *Feminism and Geography*, Gillian Rose helpfully explicates this use of the body as an anti-Cartesian tool when, after reviewing several feminist theories of space, she concludes that: 'This sense of space offered by these feminists dissolves the split between the mind and the body by thinking through the body, their bodies' (Rose 1993: 146). What Rose puts forth is a bodily appropriation of a mental capacity: thought. Thus, thought is not just the purview of the mind but is also integrated into the fibre of the body, and in this fashion both mind and body partake of the same mechanism. In other words, thought is not thought without the body to 'plunge' into. This expression is taken from the opening lines of Deleuze's chapter 'Cinema, Body and Brain, Thought' in *Cinema 2*. Here, Deleuze presents a slightly different version of thinking through the body, one in which thought, in order to reach its unthought, must delve into the body. Deleuze writes that 'the body is no longer the obstacle that separates thought from itself, that which it has to overcome to reach thinking. It is on the contrary that which it plunges into or must plunge into, in order to reach the unthought, that is life' (Deleuze 1989: 189). While I am not at odds with either of these analyses of mind–body interdependence, I am struck by the apparent ease with which the body can be 'thought through' or 'plunged into'. My question is how might mind–body relations work differently in those cases where the body actively resists integration with the mind or vice versa? Furthermore, could something interesting be said to happen when, to reverse Deleuze's formulation, thought also reaches itself by working through the body as obstacle? That is, could thought work *both through and against* the body in ways that are not exclusively masculinist or retrograde?

To apprehend such a potentially antagonistic working of thought or mind *against* the body entails looking at thought in a new fashion, looking at thought for what it can do. Deleuze's entire oeuvre might be considered as a manual for precisely this, for articulating what it is that philosophy as thought does. It is in this sense, then, that while not drawing necessarily Deleuzean conclusions, my line of enquiry strives to work within a Deleuzean framework of conceptualising that which is potentially new about thought.

Braidotti describes the newness that Deleuze brings to thought when she writes that 'thinking is for Deleuze not the expression of in-depth interiority, or the enactment of transcendental models; it is a way of establishing connections among a multiplicity of impersonal forces' (1994a: 163). Furthermore, '[T]hinking for Deleuze is instead life lived at the highest possible power – thinking is about finding new images. Thinking is about change and transformation' (165). In holding to the spirit, if not the letter, of a Deleuzean quest for thinking as newness, I will use Deleuze to elaborate what I would term a new form of disembodied thought. In the same chapter of *Cinema 2*, Deleuze compares 'cinema of the brain' to 'cinema of the body' and distinguishes them in terms of attitude and gest: 'There is as much thought in the body as there is shock and violence in the brain. There is an equal amount of feeling in both of them. The brain gives orders to the body which is just an outgrowth of it, but the body also gives orders to the brain which is just a part of it: in both cases, these will not be the same bodily attitudes nor the same cerebral gest' (Deleuze 1989: 205). While the brain and body are presented as parallel and equal, they are nonetheless marked by an important differential. This differential occurs on the level of 'bodily attitude' and 'cerebral gest', which, according to Deleuze, are not the same. To push this line of reasoning further, what if we were to magnify the differential between bodily attitude and cerebral gest so that the space in between becomes a radically disembodied and incorporeal one? And if this is done, how could that space be used productively and stragetically?

It is here that Elizabeth Grosz's account of Deleuze with respect to the mind, the body and the incorporeal is of great importance. Grosz provides a series of frameworks for a new conjunction of Deleuze and feminism, drawing on such feminist theorists as Alice Jardine, Irigaray and Braidotti and on such Deleuzean concepts as rhizomatics, the body without organs and becoming-woman. Like Braidotti, Grosz articulates the conjunction of Deleuze and feminism along the axis of the mind–body duality, and more specifically the displacement of this axis by a foregrounding of the body. Grosz first poses her argument for Deleuzean embodiment as a series of rhetorical questions at the beginning of her chapter on Deleuze in *Volatile Bodies: Towards a Corporeal Feminism* (1994a). This series of questions echoes many of Braidotti's formulations, discussed above.

Can accounts of subjectivity and the psychical interior be adequately explained in terms of the body? Can depths, the interior, the subjective, and the private instead be seen in terms of surfaces, bodies, and material relations? Can the mind/body dualism be overcome using the concepts associated with the devalued term of the binary pair of mind and body, that is, are the body and corporeality the (disavowed) grounds and terms on which the opposition is erected and made possible? What happens to conceptual frameworks if the body stands in place of the mind or displaces it from its privileged position defining humanity against its various others? (Grosz 1994a: 160)

Like Braidotti and Rose, Grosz claims the body as the unacknowledged framework for the mind–body duality. By supplanting the mind, the body will allow feminist access to a new space that is neither masculinist nor humanist. My claim is that such a new space has indeed been charted by thinkers such as Grosz and Braidotti among others and has opened the way for still newer

spaces. A newer space that I would propose is also neither masculinist nor humanist, though in privileging a certain concept of
the mind it might appear to be precisely that which a corporeal
feminism is defined against. Yet, just in the way that the body has
been reclaimed as a site of feminist practice, so too does the realm
of the mind contain the same, albeit difficult, potential. In charting
out a Deleuzean-feminist space of corporeality, Grosz simultaneously provides the navigational tools for a feminist enquiry into the
incorporeal.[3]

In the same fashion as Braidotti, Grosz gives a new definition of
the body which surpasses the restricted physical space of the person.
However, Grosz goes beyond Braidotti in inscribing the incorporeal into this new definition of the body. Following from Deleuze
and Guattari, Grosz specifies how such seemingly disembodied
notions as the incorporeal, the non-human, and the inanimate can
help to form a new definition and practice of the body:

[Deleuze and Guattari's] notion of the body as a discontinuous, non-
totalizable series of processes, organs, flows, energies, corporeal substances and incorporeal events, speeds and durations, may be of great
value to feminists attempting to reconceive bodies outside the binary
oppositions imposed on the body by the mind/body, nature/culture,
subject/object and interior/exterior oppositions. They provide an
altogether different way of understanding the body in its connections
with other bodies, both human and nonhuman, animate and inanimate,
linking organs and biological processes to material objects and social
practices while refusing to subordinate the body to a unity or a homo-
geneity of the kind provided by the body's subordination to consciousness or to biological organization. (Grosz 1994a: 164–5)

If the body combines 'corporeal substances and incorporeal
events', it seems that the act of thinking, or an act of mind, would
also be just such an incorporeal event in conjunction with a corporeal substance. For where exactly lies the disjunction between
mind and matter, thought and body? In his study of Bergson,
Deleuze links the coincidence of mind and matter to a form of
virtual perception. Explicating Bergson, he writes that, '[W]e perceive things where they are, perception puts us at once into matter,
is impersonal, and coincides with the perceived object . . . There
cannot be a difference in kind, but only a difference in degree
between the faculty of the brain and the function of the core,
between the perception of matter and matter itself' (Deleuze
1991b: 25).[4] It is this difference, or disjunction, in degree that will
be taken up in what follows, but first it is useful to examine how

the coincidence of thought with matter pushes thought into a new and virtual realm.[5] The virtuality of thought consists not in its being somehow not real but rather in its proximity to and potential for actualisation in matter. In other words, mind too contains the potential to bring together incorporeal events and corporeal substance.

Such a vision of mind as orchestrating a mind–body conjunction is perhaps closest in the philosophical tradition to Spinoza's view of mind as the idea of the body. By this account, the mind and body are inextricably linked, yet the mind as idea also exceeds the boundaries of a single physical body and takes in or intersects other conjunctures of minds and bodies (Spinoza 1955: 97–9).[6] Deleuze glosses this helpfully in *Expressionism in Philosophy: Spinoza*, where he writes that 'the soul, insofar as it is the idea of an existing body, is itself composed of a great number of ideas which correspond to the body's component parts, and which are extrinsically distinct from one another. The faculties, furthermore, which the soul possesses insofar as it is the idea of an existing body, are genuine extensive parts, which cease to belong to the soul once the body itself ceases to exist (Deleuze 1992: 201–2).[7] On this account, the intricacy of the soul or mind is fundamentally dependent on the body's existence. If the body is no longer living, the mind is no longer the idea of the body. Yet, as Genevieve Lloyd underscores in her reading of *Spinoza*, there is a fundamental ambivalence in the final section of the *Ethics* over this question, where Spinoza at once suggests that 'the mind can only imagine anything, or remember what is past, while the body endures' (Part V, Prop. 21) and that 'the human mind cannot be absolutely destroyed with the body, but there remains of it something which is eternal' (Part V, Prop. 23). While Lloyd does not view this conflict over whether the mind outlives the body or coincides with it as a contradiction – but argues instead that 'the mind resorts to the "fiction" of eternity as a state to be attained' (Lloyd 1996: 125) – I think that Spinoza's philosophy of mind is useful precisely because it enables the mind to simultaneously inhabit seemingly contradictory states.[8] That is, the mind is at once interwoven into the very fibre of the body *and* also seeks to outlive or transcend the body (here in the form of taking on a quality of eternity). It is this oscillation between mind as idea of body (or mind as mind–body) and mind as exceeding body (mind as not mind–body) that is at the heart of the philosophy of mind at issue here.

This oscillation, or disjunction, between mind as coincident with body and mind as somehow apart from it contains a potential energy that, if capitalised on, can have useful practical consequences. Not least of these consequences is a revaluation of the complexity of mind in feminist thought. It seems fair to state that in contemporary feminist philosophical discourse, it is the body and not the mind that holds sway.[9] While the body has been studied with all its attendant complexities, the mind is skirted around with much more caution, and this for good reason. Yet it seems that we have arrived at a time and a place in feminist thinking where to move forward might just mean to welcome back the mind (albeit hesitantly) into the registers of acceptable discourse. These registers would not be the old ones where the mind signalled a cultivated humanism, but rather ones where, according to the logic of oscillation outlined above, thought is mobilised to both heighten the mind–body conjunction and to dismantle it. Grosz expresses this twofold dynamic with respect to the body when she glosses Deleuze and Guattari's anti-human and elemental approach to the body:

Deleuze and Guattari produce a radical antihumanism that renders animals, nature, atoms, even quasars as modes of radical alterity... Deleuze and Guattari imply a clear movement toward imperceptibility that is in many ways similar to the quest of physics for the microscopic structures of matter, the smallest component, the most elementary particle. If it remains materialist at this level, it is a materialism that is far beyond or different from the body, or bodies: their work is like an acidic dissolution of the body, and the subject along with it. (Grosz 1994a: 179)

Grosz highlights the way in which the body is not to be thought of as coincident with the human, or with a particular human being. Rather, it is to be considered on a level that is much more elemental (or even molecular, to use Deleuze and Guattari's terminology). In breaking the body down into its affective components, or its components of movement and work, what results is a body that is no longer a body strictly speaking, and a subject that is no longer a subject. If this is the case for the body, then couldn't this same elemental reading be applied to the mind? It would then follow that the mind would similarly not coincide with the human, nor with the subject. Rather, it too would be a space of dissolution and materialism conceived otherwise. Indeed, an illustration of this is Spinoza's notion of the mind that miraculously outlives the body, taking on, as it were, the materialism not only of the mind–body nexus but of the eternity existing above and beyond that nexus.

Whether this eternity actually exists or not is, as Lloyd argues, somewhat beside the point (Lloyd 1996: 126–7). What matters is that the potential or possibility for the mind to outlive or be radically separate from the body serves a function of inciting the mind to new levels of exuberance.[10]

By way of conclusion, I would like to illustrate this logic of the mind as both coextensive with and excessive of the body with reference to two very different concrete situations. The first directly entails a woman-focused approach to the mind–body assemblage. As a participant in various self-defense and martial arts programs designed for women, I find the attention paid in these classes to mental preparation particularly striking. What is emphasised over and again is that self-defence is never merely a matter of executing physical skills but more importantly a matter of combining those skills with mental concentration and awareness. Clearly, the mental and the physical are entirely bound up with each other, and this is nowhere more true than in the emphasis placed on the voice and its crucial function in linking and enhancing the mind–body conjunction. Indeed, much time is devoted to non-contact self-defence in which the voice (which utters a few select words), in combination with a strong neutral or ready stance, is the sole instrument employed on the would-be assailant. Such a defensive strategy illustrates the way in which mind and body come together as both voice and stance and also as the potential for the unleashing of further – and primarily physical – energy. But here mind and body are conjoined under the auspices of a mental energy that is one of collecting, focusing and concentrating. So far, this example attests to the way in which both mind and body think each other and are ultimately not entirely distinct.

There is, however, a second order of defence which mobilises a more radical separation of mind and body. This is a defence called upon when the first order of defence and other physical resistance has failed and an attack may be already in progress. At this stage what is called for is a momentary but necessary disengagement of mind and body in which the body plays at capitulation and the mental awareness moves away from what is happening to the body and instead focuses on the surprise reversal that is about to be unleashed in the form of a full-body throwing off of the attacker. The execution of this powerful technique rests fundamentally on the disentangling of mind and body so that the mind can function as the strategizing spectator to the body's disempowerment. That this moment of mind–body separation may last only a few seconds in no way minimalises its role as a crucial catalyst for the force that is to be unleashed. In this fashion, martial-arts and self-defense techniques employ, at different moments and sometimes in conjunction, *both* mind–body fusion and mind–body separation, and both at the service of women's empowerment. Furthermore, these two formations are at once contradictory and complementary, and in this sense they reflect a unique form of logic, one that does not collapse oppositions but allows them to constructively coexist side by side.

A second example concerns the relation of mind to body as inflected by bodily sickness. In certain cases of illness, the double process outlined above – that of the mind orchestrating a coterminous relation between body and mind, and, second, a break or cracking between the very same mind and body – might be said to reach its epitome. Nowhere is this process better explicated than in Pierre Klossowski's monumental study of Nietzsche, *Nietzsche and the Vicious Circle*, which takes Nietzsche's physical suffering (his migraines) as the central barometer for reading Nietzsche's work – here, quite literally his corpus, or body of thought. Klossowski gives particular attention to the multiple letters Nietzsche wrote between 1877 and 1881 describing his condition. In what follows, I will read Klossowski's reading of Nietzsche's letters in order to show how mind–body conjuncture and disjuncture are staged with regard to sickness.

First, we see the dissolution of the mind–body boundary, this time in the form of the ravaged body's threat to dissolve both itself and the mind that supports it. Klossowski describes how this threatened dissolution is experienced by the mind:

The agonizing migraines, which Nietzsche experienced periodically as *an aggression that suspended his thought*, were not an external aggression; the root of the evil was in himself, in his own organism: his own physical self was *attacking* in order to *defend* itself against a dissolution. But *what* was being threatened with dissolution? Nietzsche's own brain. Whenever his migraines subsided, Nietzsche would put his state of respite in the service of this dissolution. For the dissolution was judged to be such only by the brain, for whom the physical self and the moral self apparently coincide. But the body provided the perspective of *active forces* which (as organic and therefore subordinate functions) expressed a will to break with this servitude. But they could do so only if this will passed *through the brain*. The brain, on the other hand, could experience this will only as its own subordination to these dissolving forces: it was threatened with the impossibility of *thinking*. (Klossowski 1997: 24)[11]

Already the dynamic between body and mind is one of contradiction and paradox, and this at a stage where the body and mind are largely dissolved into one entity of pain. The attack of the body is so strong that it threatens to dissolve the very distinction between mental and physical. Yet this threat of dissolution is perceived as such by the mind, is experienced only by passing through the mind, and is registered as an attack on the mind. Though the mind and body approach a state of collapse into one another – and total collapse for that matter – the mind remains separate from the body in that it perceives this impending dissolution as an attack on itself. In this fashion, we have a dissolution of the mind–body split from the direction of the mind. However, rather than the mind instigating this dissolution (as in the previous example), this dissolution actively presses against the mind. Moreover, this pressing against the mind is experienced as an aggression, an aggression of the body on the mind, but one which simultaneously prevents the mind's dissolution. Of particular note in this passage is the language of attack and aggression, or what Deleuze discusses as active and reactive forces.[12] Rather than signalling an undesirable dualism, these forces produce a tension that has surprising results.

Klossowski goes on to suggest a new and surprising outcome of the mind's relation to the mind–body dissolution: pleasure, lucidity and joy. Through a process of the mind's experiencing the mind–body dissolution in its fullest thought-shattering intensity, a strange reversal occurs where new and voluptuous thoughts are actually produced: 'Physical suffering would be livable only insofar as it was closely connected to joy, insofar as it developed a voluptuous lucidity: either it would extinguish all possible thought, or it would reach the delirium of thought' (Klossowski 1997: 25). As Klossowski will elaborate, this potential thought-delirium is achieved through an act of mind that entails a 'spiritualizing' mechanism in which the mind not only experiences the threat of dissolution but responds to this threat by revoking it, a revocation which allows the mind access to still higher realms of lucidity and joy.[13]

Yet, the condition of possibility for this separation of mind and body is none other than an extreme coincidence of mind and body, here in the form of bodily sickness, that makes these two entities virtually indistinguishable:

There seems to be a strict correlation between the phenomenon of pain, which is experienced by the organism as the aggression of an invading external power, and the biological process that leads to the formation of the brain. The brain, which concentrates all the reflexes on fighting the aggression, is able to represent the *inflicted* pain as degrees of excitations oscillating between pain and pleasure. The brain can have representations only if it meticulously spiritualizes the elementary excitations into the *danger* of pain or the *good fortune* of pleasure – a discharge that may or may not result in further excitations. (Klossowski 1997: 25)

There are at least two things here that are of crucial importance for this transformation of pain into something other. First is the necessity of meticulous spiritualisation. This spiritualisation entails the mind perceiving the dissolving pain as simultaneously dissolving and enhancing. In other words, the mind produces a distance, if only a minute one, between itself as coming into imminent dissolution and its unique excitement at this impending prospect. It is this excitement, distilled and magnified, that leads to the possibility of unparalleled joy. Second, it is important to underscore the phenomenon of oscillation, here described as an oscillation between pain and pleasure. Previously such an oscillation has been described as that between the two processes of mind–body conjuncture and mind–body disjuncture. Insofar as pain might correspond to the former and pleasure to the latter (as with the example of sickness, but not in the self-defense strategies), then we are dealing with oscillations of a similar order.

Finally, just as the disjunction between mind and body was a brief but crucial one in the self-defence example above, so too is the short durational quality of the sickness-induced suspension of mind and body emphasised in Klossowski. Such brevity also heightens the experience of confronting and surpasssing mind–body boundaries.[14] In the passage that follows, Klossowski describes the relapse as the shortening of duration combined with the heightening of boundary consciousness:

Convalescence was the signal of a new offensive of the 'body' – this rethought body – against the '*thinking Nietzsche self*'. This in turn paved the way for a new relapse. For Nietzsche, each of these relapses, up until the final relapse, heralded a new inquiry and a new investment in the world of the impulses, and in each case he paid the price of an ever-worsening illness. In each case the body liberated itself a little more from its own agent, and in each case *this agent* was weakened a little more. Little by little, the *brain* was forced to approach the *boundaries* that separated it from these somatic forces, in that the reawakening of the self in the brain was brought about *ever more slowly*. And even when it occurred, it was these same forces that seized hold of the functional mechanism. The self was broken down into a *lucidity that was more vast but more brief*. (Klossowski 1997: 30-1)

According to this analysis, the brevity of the mind–body separation is directly proportional to the intensity of the lucidity it brings about. Furthermore, as the separation shortens and the lucidity increases, the boundary between mind and body is approached. One might picture a hyperbola that comes ever closer to the axis it approaches without ever coinciding with it. Such is the experience of mind–body separation at its highest, where the very boundary necessary for the experience of separation is simultaneously at its most tenuous, yet still distinct from a complete dissolution. It is this state of disjunctive equilibrium, momentarily balanced yet about to explode, that, when mobilised, represents one of the most extraordinary states of being.[15] Such a state is in many respects not far from a body-centred exploration of mind–body boundaries. Yet it seems that a body-oriented focus works best in the realm of the positive while a mind-centred one helps precisely at that point – and perhaps it is the briefest of points – where the body is besieged by or under threat of great pain.

NOTES

1. See also Rosi Braidotti (1991, 1994b).
2. For a detailed reading of the body as an interplay of forces, especially as it relates to Nietzsche's active and reactive forces, and Deleuze's reading of this in his study of Nietzsche, see Dorothea Olkowski (1994), especially page 120, where she writes: 'The body is not a medium and does not designate substance: it expresses the relationship between forces. The term 'body' does not simply refer, for Deleuze, to the psychophysiological bodies of human beings. Bodies may be chemical, biological, social, or political, and the distinction between these modes is not ontological.'
3. Here, it is important to note that corporeal and incorporeal, embodiment and disembodiment, are not strictly oppositional. Insofar as both necessarily contain elements of the other, I would signal the difference between these sets of terms as one of gradation and emphasis rather than opposition as such.
4. For a detailed analysis of Deleuze's relation to Bergson and to the virtual, see Boundas (1996).
5. Here again, 'disjunction' and 'coincidence' are not taken as opposites but as themselves differences of degree of the same thing.
6. Spinoza writes, for example, that 'although the external bodies, by which the human body has once been affected, be no longer in existence, the mind will nevertheless regard them as present, as often as this action of the body is repeated', Proposition 17 (p. 99).

7. For helpful analyses of Deleuze's readings of Spinoza, see Hardt (1993: 56–111) and Gatens (1996a: 162–87).

8. Such an expansive vision of Spinoza's notion of mind parallels and complements Moira Gatens's analysis of how Spinoza complicates 'embodiment': 'When the term "embodiment" is used in the context of Spinoza's thought it should be understood to refer not simply to an individual body but to the *total* affective context of that body' (Gatens 1996a: 131). In the same fashion, mind would also refer to the total affective context.

9. Exemplary of this is the work of Judith Butler, who, like Braidotti and Grosz, also charts out the dense field of relations that comprise the mind–body duality (Butler 1993). I have not given more attention to Butler's work here because, unlike Braidotti and Grosz, her work is more in conversation with Derrida, Foucault, and Hegel than with Deleuze.

10. A cautionary note is in order, as this radical potential for mind–body disjunction is not without its pitfalls. In *Technologies of the Gendered Body: Reading Cyborg Women* (1996), Anne Balsamo illustrates how the potential for body alteration or disembodiment contained in the cyborg or in virtual reality often works to reinscribe the most traditional of gender, racial and sexual norms. As Balsamo writes, '[T]here is plenty of evidence to suggest that a reconstructed body does not guarantee a reconstructed cultural identity. Nor does "freedom from the body," imply that people will exercise the "freedom to be" any other kind of body than the one they already enjoy or desire' (128). This critique notwithstanding, I feel there are positive disembodiment examples to be found, and I take up two of them in my conclusion. The critical difference between my examples and the cyborg/virtual reality ones is that the latter project disembodiment on to a generically ideal body, while the ones I will take up do not project disembodiment on to an ideal but negotiate it within the contours of the limited body at hand.

11. I have discussed this same phenomenon of sickness and its relation to the mind in a reading of different passages in Klossowski's study of Nietzsche in 'Klossowski or Thoughts-Becoming' (Kaufman 1999).

12. Deleuze takes up the importance of sickness in Nietzsche, but to a more limited extent than Klossowksi. In *Nietzsche and Philosophy* (1983), he analyses sickness in terms of power of reactive forces. I quote at length:

> What Nietzsche calls an active force is one which goes to the limit of its consequences. An active force separated from what it can do by reactive force thus becomes reactive. But does not this reactive force, in its own way, go to the limit of what it can do? . . . A reactive force can certainly be considered from different points of view. Illness, for example, separates me from what I can do, as reactive

force it makes me reactive, it narrows my possibilities and condemns me to a diminished milieu to which I can do no more than adapt myself. But in another way, it reveals to me a new capacity, it endows me with a new will that I can make my own, going to the limit of a strange power . . . Here we can recognise an ambivalence important to Nietzsche: all the forces whose reactive character he exposes are, a few lines or pages later, admitted to fascinate him, to be sublime because of the perspective they open up for us and because of the disturbing will to power to which they bear witness. (Deleuze 1983: 66)

In this passage, Deleuze overturns the hierarchy between active and reactive forces, arguing with Nietzsche that the reactive force of sickness can be its own form of activity and can inaugurate new and interesting states of being. Such a pronouncement is all the more interesting in light of Deleuze's own and subsequent period of long convalescence and sickness before his death in 1995. One need only cite one of his latter works, such as *Critique et clinique*, as a testament to the lucidity of thought produced under conditions of extreme physical hardship.

13. It is not insignificant that Deleuze is one of the finest readers of Klossowski, and it is Deleuze to whom Klossowski dedicates his book on Nietzsche. It is Deleuze who describes the Klossowskian logic of opposition as a 'disjunctive syntheses' and who cites Klossowski's *Nietzsche and the Vicious Circle* extensively in *Anti-Oedipus*. Above all, in his appendix to *The Logic of Sense* (Deleuze 1990b), 'Klossowski or Bodies-Language', Deleuze underscores the positive aspects of revocation. He refers to another context in which the mind and body work in disjunction, that of the pure body coupled with an impure mind and the superior disjunction of an impure body coupled with a pure mind:

Does Klossowski simply mean that speaking prevents us from thinking about nasty things? No; the pure language which produces an impure silence is a *provocation* of the mind by the body; similarly, the impure language which produces a pure silence is a *revocation* of the body by the mind . . . More precisely, what is revoked in the body? Klossowski's answer is that it is the integrity of the body, and that because of this the identity of the person is somewhat suspended and volatized (291).

14. This boundary-surpassing might take different forms when the mind–body disjunction occurs over an extended period of time, and also when it is consciously imposed. An example would be various practices associated with intake of food. In 'The Problem of the Body in Deleuze and Guattari, Or, What Can a Body Do?' (1997), Ian Buchanan analyses anorexia as an interplay of forces or relations

between food and the body. Although he discusses it in somewhat different terms than the mind–body disjunction, he describes an intensified state of being that results from a reactive relation to food: 'If we are to relieve ourselves of the sometimes intolerable pressure that food places on us, we must confront food differently. But, since we cannot change what food does to us, we must change ourselves. This demands that we somehow find a new way of being, which effectively means a new way of becoming' (78–9). While Buchanan is careful to point out the negative effects of such an anorexic-becoming, his analysis of the process underscores the delicacy and complexity of this grey zone of mind–body disjunction. While I have underscored the positive side of such a zone, it is clearly one of those liminal spaces that, with a slight twist, collapses into the negative and the destructive. This is not to say that positivities cannot be found even in this negative realm, but discussing them would entail a differently positioned and more nuanced analysis.

15. Such a state is, I think, captured by such films as *The Living End*, directed by Gregg Araki (1992), which depicts living with AIDS as the exuberant intensity of living with imminent sickness and mortality and more recently *Sick: The Life and Death of Bob Flanagan, Supermasochist*, directed by Kirby Dick (1997), which depicts the quest for extreme S&M experience alongside the succumbing to fatal cystic fibrosis.

7

Deleuze and Feminisms: Involuntary Regulators and Affective Inhibitors

NICOLE SHUKIN

PART ONE: 'THESE ARE A FEW OF MY FAVOURITE THINGS'

Gilles Deleuze was interviewed on film by Claire Parnet in 1988. Although originally to be released posthumously, Deleuze relented and gave permission for the dialogues to be broadcast on television a year before his death, in 1996. The eight-hour series of interviews, entitled 'L'Abécédaire de Gilles Deleuze, avec Claire Parnet', moves through a charming, almost childlike, string of key words beginning with each letter of the alphabet. Each letter, of course, accommodates fascinating digressions. Under 'M for Malady, or Illness', for instance, Parnet recalls Deleuze's relationship with food: Parnet points out that he has a special relationship to food since he doesn't like eating. Deleuze says it's true. For him, eating is the most boring thing in the world. Drinking is something extraordinarily interesting, but eating bores him to death. Having said this, Deleuze continues, he certainly has things he enjoys immensely that are rather special. Continuing, Deleuze imagines that someone might ask him what his favourite meal might be, an utterly crazy undertaking, he says, but he always comes back to three things that he always found sublime, but that are quite properly disgusting: tongue, brains and marrow (Deleuze and Parnet 1987).

There are many points at which one could enter into a discussion of the affinities or non-affinities between the thinking of Gilles

144

Deleuze and contemporary feminisms. One could, for starters, clarify from which feminism the discussion was being broached. I will forestall solidifying the 'school' of feminist thought that I carry into dialogue with Deleuze's work, however, in order to follow instead the anomalous lure of the above scene. The anecdotal opening of the interview allows me to steal into a crease between the spontaneous and the premeditated terms chosen by Deleuze and to read the above scene as an intertext to *A Thousand Plateaus: Capitalism and Schizophrenia* (Deleuze and Guattari 1987). The interview – perhaps because of its conviviality mixed with a still naive perception that conversation, even filmed conversation, dissipates in a way that text does not – makes Deleuze vulnerable, tempts feminisms to enlarge upon an almost negligible remark: 'eating bores him to death'.

Choosing to engage with Deleuze via an autobiographical remark in itself implies a perverse feminist return, since historically it has been women's texts which have been refracted through autobiographica, magnified through glass buttons she did or did not leave unfastened and through her crystalline or clouded propriety. The autobiographical genre is in this case a flourish, however, introducing an anecdote which begs to be read as a lush metonym for how Deleuze, with Félix Guattari, poses sexual difference in *A Thousand Plateaus: Capitalism and Schizophrenia*. Deleuze's remark is an unsuspected site hording dense and blood-red affects that can possibly be released only through a feminist reading of his work.

When Deleuze exposes an exclusive taste for brain, tongue and marrow, he aligns his physical appetite with a philosophical appetite for forces, manifested variously in his work as the concept, as the desiring, war, or criminal machine, as nomadic movements, lines of flight, rhizomatic fissurings, and becomings. In the work of Deleuze, 'thought is what confronts us from the outside, unexpectedly', as Elizabeth Grosz writes (1995: 129). 'Thought is active force, positive desire, thought which makes a difference' (129). Brain, tongue and marrow occupy a pivotal contradiction in terms of the thinking body: they are involuntary regulators. At one and the same time they respond to an essential organism and hint at the nervous possibility of drumming, throbbing their way out of the cavities that contain them. I see the involuntary as corresponding to 'pure relations of speed and slowness between particles' and as occupying a vital role in the 'enterprise of desubjectification' dramatised in *A Thousand Plateaus* (270).

Deleuze's 'pragmatism', his preference for becomings generated on surfaces, leads him to favour sites of extreme potency, or, in machinic parlance, motor power. His affirmation of creative force is reflected in a culinary fetish: of food that secretes power and prowess, metonyms for the 'liberated elements' in what Deleuze and Guattari call 'the body without organs' (1987: 260). Deleuze's favourite things, furthermore, connote a virility of force and a blood-lust for becomings that are peculiarly male gendered. Unverifiably, but arguably, brain, tongue and marrow emit a muscular and raw masculinity. Considering Deleuze's philosophical renovation of the self as an assemblage that scatters and reconvenes, a composition ever on the move, it is indeed hard to imagine him nurturing a taste for duck or fish, for meals consisting of whole organisms. Indirectly linked with the richness of his favourite foods is an emphasis on intensity as a valid ontology and the belief that molecular units of potency, or 'kinematic entities' (Deleuze and Guattari 1987: 255), are capable of disrupting systems of control and capture, state and family apparatuses.

This aspect of the thinking of Deleuze verges upon a romanticisation of the involuntary that threatens to exclude embodied women. One can trace the notion of the involuntary to *Proust and Signs*, where Deleuze links it to what he calls 'the virtual': 'Proust asks the question: how shall we save the past as it is in itself? It is to this question that involuntary Memory offers its answer... This ideal reality, this virtuality, is essence, which is realized or incarnated in involuntary memory' (Deleuze 1972: 60). In *A Thousand Plateaus*, to my mind, the involuntary turns into a relatively submerged quality associated with everything that resists regulatory apparatuses. Yet it is not at the site of the involuntary so much as at its unexpected conciliation with the regulatory implied by his virile tastes that feminisms need to be on the alert.

Deleuze's investment in the involuntary contains ethnographic overtones that are significant to a critical feminist reading. From what can be gleaned from his interviews with Parnet, Deleuze distinctly favours the raw over the cooked. Deleuze disagreed strongly with the structural anthropology of Claude Levi-Strauss and his 'institution of the totem' (Deleuze and Guattari 1987: 237). Yet the text of *A Thousand Plateaus* continuously invokes phenomena that evade domestication – or cooking – by Western culture: 'nomad thought', 'primitive societies', 'the East', war machines, music, packs, swarms, tribes, anomalies, becoming-woman, becoming-child, becoming-animal, -vegetable, -mineral, -molecular, sadomasochism, drugs, and so on. For this reason it is not amiss to resort to the very

146

interpretations that Deleuze took issue with to explore a contrast Deleuze and Guattari stage between 'nonvoluntary transmutation' and domestication (Deleuze and Guattari 1987: 269).

It is because Levi-Strauss reduced different myths to the single structural paradigm, of the raw and the cooked, that Deleuze disagreed with his methodology, just as he disagreed with Freud's absorption of a multiplicity of experiences into the Oedipal triangle. As Levi-Strauss writes:

I propose to show that M1 (the key myth) belongs to a set of myths that explain the origin of the cooking of food . . . that cooking is conceived of in native thought as a form of mediation; and finally, that this particular aspect remains concealed in the Bororo myth, because the latter is in fact an inversion, or a reversal, of myths originating in neighbouring communities which view culinary operations as mediatory activities between heaven and earth, life and death, nature and society. (Levi Strauss 1969: 64–5)

Fire and cooking, Levi-Strauss continues, are 'the origin of man's mortality' (164); cooking instigates not just the nature/culture divide, but also the loss of an innate or immanent power of immortality retained by raw food. Also of importance to my purposes here is the connection Levi-Strauss finds in the myths between women and food: '[I]t is worthy of note that in the myths just discussed the sexual code should be apparent only in its masculine references . . . When the references are feminine, the sexual code becomes latent and is concealed beneath the alimentary code' (269).

It is my contention that the thinking of Deleuze contains a mythological or affective component that can be read according to the interpretations of Levi-Strauss. Deleuze seeks a power of immanence and 'the movement of the infinite' in becomings and machinic assemblages which are largely cast as involuntary (281). A broad division is set up in *A Thousand Plateaus* between an intense 'nomadology' (the raw) and domestic, regulatory structures (the cooked), a distinction that is unexpectedly reminiscent of nature/culture binaries. Finally, Deleuze and Guattari never address the overdetermined historical, mythological, or affective associations between the female gender and domesticity, between women and cooked food. For this reason, gender remains to a great extent latent in *A Thousand Plateaus*.

A Thousand Plateaus contains a critique of the domestication of bodies and their sustenance which deprives us of what Novalis (1973) in his Encyclopaedia calls 'an animating intercourse with the absolutely alive' (11). The only food that can touch or move Deleuze, it seems, is food that carries a trace of the wild, food invested with exotic powers from which he hopes to contract anomaly, difference, exteriority, mutiny, immortality. It is a penchant for the raw that leads to the *ennui* Deleuze feels towards processed food in a general sense and towards the historical and cultural conditions of that food. Deleuze expresses boredom with eating because he can take it for granted; the labour of women who (historically) prepare it is precisely not involuntary, and therefore devoid of interest. Yet Deleuze himself occupies the place of 'the Oedipal family animal' and 'mere poodle' (Deleuze and Guattari 1987: 250) that he abhors, able to shun food because it is so readily available to his domestic scene. Involuntary regulators, enjoying all of the certainties and protections of regulation, Deleuze hankers to be transported out of his organism by brain, tongue and marrow.

In pursuing my elaboration of his favourite things, let me suggest that the involuntary acts as medium, and the regulator as content, so that allegorically speaking, brain, tongue and marrow realise the potent fusion of content and medium, of virile force and 'line of flight'. Or the involuntary could equally correspond to the possible, and the regulator to the actual configurations of a subject. Deleuze, it is well known, refuses to make such distinctions in his work. But because *A Thousand Plateaus* could be said to fetishise 'becoming-woman' (and girls) in tandem with the way Deleuze fetishises foods with raw potency, and because it simultaneously dismisses women who are entangled in 'majoritarian histories' or domesticity, the text itself effects a split: the feminine as involuntary is retained, the feminine as regulatory is not. *A Thousand Plateaus* requires a feminine that performs an involuntary function and promises sheer potential, not drudge domestics. Women's actual, embroiled lives are sacrificed in the text.

It is the ethnographer in Deleuze that feminists must watch. The cultivated man with access to the veal, connoisseur of mad disruption who approximates disruption through a decadent menu, the involuntary regulator who inhabits, but scorns, cooked culture. For Deleuze's philosophy of becoming-Other is highlighted with the poignant eroticism of an ethnographer who invests in the exotic Other all of the possibilities and powers of transformation his culture denies him. Philosophy even lightly brushed with an ethnographic zeal is liable to find women of interest only in their capacity to quicken the blood: carriers of strange winds and estrangement that provide Western man with the conduit he needs to abdicate himself. Estranged woman may seem a step forward from Familiar, Oedipal woman, but not if she is after all added to a collection of Others, one of many rare and authentic means of transport into rites of male becoming.

While the pure vector of the girl-idea (white-hot as the driven snow) qualifies to make an appearance in *A Thousand Plateaus*, 'real' female bodies negotiating a more nuanced and complex corporeality – bodies simultaneously territorialised and deterritorialising – are only cursorily acknowledged. It is because girls have not yet been 'cooked', or domesticated, that they inhabit a privileged place within the becomings described by Deleuze and Guattari: 'becoming-woman, more than any other becoming, possesses a special introductory power' (1987: 248). According to the text: 'becoming-woman, or the molecular woman is the girl herself . . . she is defined by a relation of movement and rest, speed and slowness, by a combination of atoms, an emission of particles: haecceity. She never ceases to roam upon a body without organs. She is an abstract line, or a line of flight' (Deleuze and Guattari 1987: 276–7). If it is taken at face value, the text tells us that neither women nor girls exactly equal becoming-woman, which Deleuze and Guattari claim is an 'in-between', a state of transit between 'molar' (organic) entities. It is exceedingly difficult, however, to maintain a distinction between girls and becoming-woman, especially with so many cultural productions compounding the identification between young girls and enticing possibility. Particularly when the text dares to propose that 'Sexuality, any sexuality, is a becoming-woman, in other words, a girl' (Deleuze and Guattari 1987: 277).

Within the terms with which Deleuze pursues molecular rather than 'molar', or representational, identity politics, labour is a function of the State that vanishes when bodies veer off after temptation or are drawn up a flue. Effort is antithetical to the involuntary. Girls, as figures of the involuntary and of an apparently effortless surplus of alternate speeds and slownesses, are to labouring women as marrow is to bone. 'We know nothing about a body', write Deleuze and Guattari, 'until we know what it can do, in other words, what its affects are, how they can or cannot enter into composition with other affects, with the affects of another body, either to destroy that body or to be destroyed by it, either to exchange actions and passions with it or to join with it in composing a more powerful body' (1987: 257). For Deleuze and Guattari, doing is seldom connected with voluntary effort, since a body is defined in terms of its virtuality rather than its actuality. So the accumulated labour, the uncounted, unpaid body hours of women, insofar as they have sedimented a majoritarian history and reinforced domesticity, are inconsequential compared with the pure possibility that idles within a girl. When its material actualities can be bracketed, the feminine provides a perfectly exotic minoritarian medium. This is a jagged little pill, to use the words of the Canadian singer Alanis Morrissette, but one that marks a site where feminists have to be both most receptive and most careful of Deleuze's hunger for the virtual. Deleuze may incline too far towards the involuntary, neglecting nuances of actual women for the sake of a feminine infinitely in potentia, but it would certainly be no better to place excessive weight on the actual and foreclose what is possible for women. Somehow a balance needs to be struck.

Despite the indifference to actual women communicated on an affective level in parts of *A Thousand Plateaus*, an indifference analogous to the boredom Deleuze expresses in his interviews towards 'cooked' food, the text nevertheless produces many formulations that are vital for feminists to ponder. *A Thousand Plateaus* contains resources to help feminists map bodily practices that evade the pitfalls of humanist, masculinist notions of the self, resources that I suggest require circumspection due to – but that certainly aren't cancelled by – affective inhibitors. So while the following lines can no longer be read innocently (as if their acknowledgement were consistent with affective auras emitted elsewhere around discussions of becoming-woman) they nevertheless deserve to be read again and again: 'It is, of course, indispensable for women to conduct a molar politics, with a view to winning back their own organism, their own history, their own subjectivity... But it is dangerous to confine oneself to such a subject, which does not function without drying up a spring or stopping a flow.... It is thus necessary to conceive of a molecular women's politics that slips into molar confrontations, and passes under or through them' (Deleuze and Guattari 1987: 276).

PART TWO: THE WEIGHT OF HIS INTERTEXTS

If in part one I seemed overly critical of the benefit of the thinking of Deleuze, it is because many strong feminist amalgamations of his thought have emerged in the last few years to illustrate the value of his work for feminist projects. Anti-essentialists such as Elizabeth Grosz were among the first feminists to incorporate elements of Deleuze's radical micropolitics into a volatile corporeal feminism challenging women to explore 'virtualities' rather than limitations of female bodies. In a more recent book edited by Elizabeth Grosz and Elspeth Probyn, *Sexy Bodies: The Strange Carnalities of Feminism* (1995), the thought of Deleuze is invoked numerous times in essays configuring lesbian desire and challenging masculinist psychoanalytic (depth) models of selfhood. Grosz writes: 'Deleuze's work unsettles the presumptions of what it is to be a stable subject and thus also problematizes any assumption that sex is in some way the centre, the secret, the truth of the subject. This unsettling may or may not have positive effects for feminist and queer theory. This will depend on what it enables us to do, to change' (214).

For anti-essentialist feminists, the Deleuze of assemblages and desiring machines is appealing because he promises a turn from what women are to what they may become. In 'Love in a Cold Climate: Queer Belongings in Quebec' Elspeth Probyn draws upon Deleuze to affirm the immanence and performability of desire, as opposed to its portrayal as a lack: 'The body hence as surface' (Grosz and Probyn 1995: 19). There is a real possibility that women can eat the brains, tongue and marrow of Deleuzean force, tap ideas that like Ginseng and Tiger's claw induce super potency for becoming anything. Why shouldn't they? Yet perhaps it is timely to interject, into feminist projects embracing cyborgs and limitless plasticity with an increasing bravado, a warning against mythologising women, as Deleuze and Guattari are want to do, as figures of virtuality. Not all women are in a position to entertain the cyborgian jubilance that suggests, as Rey Chow puts it, 'not only the subversiveness of woman, but also the more familiar, oppressive discursive prowess of the "First World"' (Chow 1993: 111). While the importance of a shift away from discourses of victimhood and oppression to discourses of power and possibility cannot be overstated, heroicising women as dauntlessly mutable could make actual women who wrestle with an admixture of possibility and constraint look pale in comparison.

In the first part of this chapter I contrived to read an autobiographical comment made by Deleuze into *A Thousand Plateaus*. At this point I would like to bring to bear other intertexts that seem to me to exert affective influence over the treatment of sexual difference in the same text. My purpose is not so much to subdue as it is to complicate any hasty adoption of the text in support of feminist virtualities. Deleuze may claim that bodies without organs compose themselves on cartographies unhampered by history, but I hope to show that inherited cultural texts are harder to divest. Women, especially, may trip upon intertexts loaded with sexism that spring for female readers and sleep for men.

Throughout *A Thousand Plateaus*, Deleuze and Guattari indirectly summon up philosophical and social texts with foreboding investments, such as the colonial anticipation of a free playing field in the new world, Plato's allegory of the cave, or mass-produced eroticisations of girls in Western culture. Accompanying Deleuze and Guattari's notion of becoming-woman without being explicitly acknowledged are accumulated texts of patriarchy, imperialism and colonialism: men revelling in the limitless possibilities of geography, men charting geography in terms of the female body, the dark continent, the Bermuda triangle or King Solomon's Mines, as both the unsignifying, unassembled body and the enigmatic seductress capable of casting spells over men.

Are Deleuze and Guattari able to control the historical associations that are evoked with becoming-woman, with the preference for geography over history and the 'plane of consistency' (Deleuze and Guattari 1987: 270) where anything is possible and rules don't apply? The notion of becoming-woman cannot help but resonate in particular with the wholesale sexualisation of girls in the twentieth century – with the media promise that on little girls grown men can play out their wildest dreams and that little girls are outside of the law, outside of humanity, and outside of the keeping of accounts. Hopefully readers of *A Thousand Plateaus* remember to think of becoming-woman as a potential and an in-between rather than as the actual girl next door.

Colonial discourses which elide distinctions between racial others, women, children, animals, flora, fauna and the feral (Tiger Lily's name says it all), also hover around becoming-woman. As with discourses of race, the systematic association of women with everything not human helped to justify women's domination by men. Deleuze and Guattari likewise perceive women (girls) as sites where human, animal, plant, molecule are want to collapse into dynamic assemblages, or 'interkingdoms' (Deleuze and Guattari 1987: 242). The intention, of course, could not be more at odds with colonial projects: they are seeking paths of original potency rather than establishment power (which is in fact without real force: 'power centres are defined much more by what escapes them or by their impotence than by their zone of power', Deleuze and Guattari 1987: 217). Yet insofar as desire performed in the name

152

of the involuntary is seen as outside of jurisdictions and assumes the innocence of the uncategorisable, it should cause some alarm for women. Are Deleuze and Guattari's formulations able to sustain the innocence that they claim when they identify woman with becomings, specifically with sexual becomings? Do they really imagine that they can avoid summoning up exploitative discourses of animalisation and sexualisation that directly oppose the desubjectification they describe as initiated by becoming-woman? More pointedly, how does the crowd of these inexplicit allusions affect the ability of the text to involve women?

Despite Deleuze and Guattari's assertion in *A Thousand Plateaus* that 'we must guard against [thinking] that there is a kind of logical order to this string, these crossings or transformations' and that 'it is already going too far to postulate an order descending from the animal to the vegetable, then to molecules, to particles' (250), the spectre of hierarchy is never quite abolished from their notion of becomings. In his interview with Parnet, Deleuze claims that brain, marrow and tongue 'constitute a kind of trinity', with the brain signifying God, marrow the son, and tongue the holy spirit. After a slight pause, Deleuze re-poses the trinity as God being concept, marrow being affect, and tongue, percept. The potency desired in his thinking is never so blatantly associated with divine powers of creation as it is here. Deleuze not only hints at the possibility of reading for hierarchies of force in a philosophical corpus that seemed hell bent to collapse organisations into plateaus and flat surfaces, he also invokes one of the most virulent intertexts for feminisms in Western culture: the Christian trinity. Deleuze believes, perhaps, that his own iconoclasm is enough to redirect the force of these allusions to subliminally power his own purposes, appropriating momentum from the very texts he means to undo. I would suggest, however, that while Deleuze does manage to siphon enormous affective energy off intertexts that are evoked without being raised, an inexorable weight of allusions pressures his thinking into old molds – particularly when it comes to sexual difference.

The concept, as God, is highest order. Likewise, becoming-woman, as prioritised, recalls another hierarchy, the Renaissance chain or ladder of being. Soon after refuting any logical order to becomings, Deleuze and Guattari write: 'A kind of order or apparent progression can be established for the segments of becoming in which we find ourselves; becoming-woman, becoming-child; becoming-animal, -vegetable, -mineral; becomings-molecular of all kinds, becomings-particles' (Deleuze and Guattari 1987: 272).

Although they claim that becomings do not proceed by resemblance or imitation, becomings nevertheless seem to progress 'down' the ladder of being, away from the man and into the next closest thing, into the women and children who resemble the 'man-standard' but whose proximity to other species makes them a conduit to the next outer ring.

If Deleuze and Guattari retain hints of a ladder of being in their progression of becomings, it is, as with the other allusions noted above, repetition with a difference. While in classical thinking those farthest away from the perfect Form diminished in value, Deleuze and Guattari confer instead the most value on that which has veered out of orbit of the man-standard. Yet girls and women get stuck midway in both the classical scheme and its iconoclastic re-evaluation. If in the former women are always one down from men, in the latter the fact that they border men makes them both the first and the least among becomings. Women remain in *A Thousand Plateaus* a sort of threshold or medium; men travel through women on to ever increasing plateaus of indiscernibility.

Never explicitly raised in the text, but also affectively working to repossess the otherwise liberating notion of becoming-woman, is the last intertext I will discuss. The distinction between content and medium has implanted itself in Western epistemology like a virus since Plato's famous allegory of the cave in his *Republic*. Feminists, starting with Luce Irigaray (1985b) and carrying on with Judith Butler (1993) and Elizabeth Grosz (1995), have revisited the cave allegory to demonstrate how the feminine principle is identified with the *chora* – the receptacle, basket, or passage through which Platonic forms pass into actuality. For feminists, Plato's allegory is read as founding the structuring of sexual difference as a division between content and medium: the masculine, manifesting content and the indiscernible, servicing feminine casement; 'a fascinated self' (Deleuze and Guattari 1987: 245) travelling towards its dissolution along 'an abstract line' (277).

Women as *chora*, woman as bone around the marrow, cavity for the brain, palette for the tongue: do Deleuze and Guattari really outmanoeuvre gendered roles that the history of philosophy has harboured at least since Plato? Are women affectively empowered to perform their own becomings, their own force fields and micropolitics? Or is gender as latent in *A Thousand Plateaus* as it is in the cave allegory, are women still captives of the involuntary? Are they stalled in 'the universal girl' (277) who is expected to mar the infinite playing field of male becomings with no traits or actualisations?

Most dramatic in *A Thousand Plateaus*, but apparent in his other texts as well, is Deleuze's passion for a generative force, an outside that like a blood infusion can spark new compositions, new thought. His creative principle, however, remains affectively virile, a faint tone which is compounded by the host of unacknowledged intertexts evoked by his terms. Affect is one of Deleuze's most valuable contributions to contemporary thought. For women to undermine the affective import of Deleuze's precise appetite and his weighty allusions would not only be foolish, it could be 'a mental health hazard', in the words of Nicole Brossard (1990). Perhaps it is most apt to close this chapter with a quotation from Brossard which speaks to the intensities and affects that I have suggested somewhat constrict the opening that Deleuze otherwise provides feminists:

What I call the cultural field of language is made of male sexual and psychic energies transformed through centuries of written fiction into a standard for imagination, a frame of references, patterns of analysis, networks of meaning, rhetoric of body and soul. Digging in that field can be for a creative woman a mental health hazard. (Brossard 1990: 9)

8

Teratologies

ROSI BRAIDOTTI

I. MONSTROUS TECHNOSCAPES

Imagine, if you will, a lesbian cross-dresser who pumps iron, looks like Chiquita Banana, thinks like Ruth Bader Ginsburg, talks like Dorothy Parker, has the courage of Anita Hill, the political acumen of Hillary Clinton and is as pissed off as Valerie Solanis, and you really have something to worry about. (Tucker 1994: 28)

Late postmodernity is in the grip of a teratological imaginary. The monstrous, the grotesque, the mutant and the downright freakish have gained widespread currency in urban post-industrial cultures. In his classic analysis, Lesley Fiedler (1979) points out that since the 1960s a youth culture has evolved that entertains a strong, albeit ironic and parodic, relationship to freaks. Feminist theory is no exception.

Freaks, the geek, the androgyne and the hermaphrodite crowd the space of multiple Rocky horror shows. Drugs, mysticism, satanism, various brands of insanity are also on the catalogue. Cannibalism, made visible by Romero in *Night of the Living Dead* in the 1960s, became eroticised by Greenaway in the 1980s and made it into the mainstream by the 1990s, with *Silence of the Lambs*. The analysis of the current fascination with the freakish half-human/half-animal or beast-figure alone would fill a page. We may think, as an example, of comic strips (the Ninja Turtles); TV classic series like *Star Trek*; the covers of records and LPs; video-games and CD roms; video clips and the computer-generated images of the inter-net and virtual reality as further evidence of the same trend. They are connected to the drug culture, as much as to its spin-offs in music, video and computer cultures. A great deal of this culture is flirting with sexual indeterminacy, which has been rampant since David Bowie's path-breaking *Ziggy Stardust*.

Quite significant is also the contemporary trend for borderline figures, especially replicants, zombies and vampires, including lesbian vampires and other queer mutants, who seem to enjoy special favour in these post-AIDS days. This is not only the case as far as 'low' popular culture genres are concerned, but is equally true of relatively 'high' literary genres. Authors like Angela Carter, Kathy Acker, Martin Amis and Fay Weldon – as well as the established success of genres such as horror, crime stories, science fiction and cyberpunk – are a new 'post-human' techno-teratological phenomenon that privileges the deviant or the mutant over the more conventional versions of the human.

There is a distinct teratological flair in contemporary cyber space, with a proliferation of new monsters which often merely transpose into outer space very classical iconographic representations of monstrous others. Whether utopian (*Close Encounters*) or dystopian (*Independence Day*), messianic (*E.T.*) or diabolical (*Alien*), the inter-galactic monstrous other is firmly settled in the imaginary of today's media and of the electronic frontier. As Susan Sontag (1966) argued, science-fiction films are not about science, but about disaster. The freakish being descending from outer space allows for a cathartic display of belligerency, panic and cruelty, and thus for the enjoyment of both.

Contemporary culture has shifted the issue of genetic mutations from the high-tech laboratories into popular culture. Hence the relevance of the new monsters of science fiction and cyberpunk, which raise metamorphosis to the status of a cultural icon. 'Altered states' are trendsetters: video drugs now compete with the pharmaceutical ones. This cyber-teratology gives a new twist to the century-old connection between the feminine and the monstrous.

The monstrous or teratological imaginary expresses the social, cultural and symbolic mutations that are taking place around the phenomenon of techno-culture (Penley and Ross 1991). Visual regimes of representation are at the heart of it. From the Panoptical eye explored by Michel Foucault in his theory of 'bio-power', to the ubiquitous presence of television, surveillance video and computer screens, it is the visual dimension of contemporary technology that defines its all-pervading power. With the ongoing electronic revolution reaching a peak, it is becoming quite clear that this dis-embodied gaze constitutes a collision of virtual spaces with which we coexist in increasing degrees of intimacy. In this context, feminist analysis has alerted us to the pleasures but also the dangers of 'visual politics' (Vance 1990), and the politics of visualisation, especially in the field of biotechnology (Franklin et al. 1991).

Whereas the emphasis on the visualisation encourages some of the theoretical masters of nihilistic postmodern aesthetics (Kroker and Kroker 1987; Baudrillard 1995). To reduce the bodily self to a mere surface of representation and to launch a sort of euphoric celebration of virtual embodiments, the feminist response has been more cautious and ambivalent. It consists in stressing both the liberating and the potentially one-sided application of the new technologies (Haraway 1991; Sofoulis 1992). They argue for the need to develop figurations of contemporary female subjectivities that would do justice to the complexities and the contradictions of our technological universe. I will return to this.

The fascination for the monstrous in the cultural imagination can be linked with the 'post-nuclear sensibility' (*Diacritics* 1984), often referred to as the 'posthuman' predicament. The historical fact that marks this shift is that science and technology – far from being the leading principles in a teleological process aimed at the perfectibility of the human – have 'spilled over', turning into sources of permanent anxiety over our present and future. The thinkability of nuclear disaster makes for an almost trivialised popularity of horror. An imaginary world filled with images of mutation marks much more than the definitive loss of the naturalistic paradigm: it also brings to the fore the previously unspeakable fact that our culture is historically condemned to the contemplation of its extinction. By reaction, it triggers in the humans an advanced state of machine-envy and the desire to imitate the inorganic or the non-human.

II. ENFLESHED COMPLEXITIES

I think that working through these issues with Gilles Deleuze can help us to think through the kind of techno-teratological universe we are inhabiting. Rethinking the embodied structure of human subjectivity after Foucault, I would recommend that we take as the starting-point the paradox of the simultaneous overexposure and disappearance of the body in the age of postmodernity. In other words, social constructivism and its corollary – anti-essentialism – result in a proliferation of discourses about, and practices of knowledge over, the body. Bio-power constructs the body as a multilayered entity that is situated over a multiple and potentially contradictory set of variables.

For Deleuze, the genealogy of the embodied nature of the subject can be ironically rendered as: Descartes' nightmare, Spinoza's hope, Nietzsche's complaint, Freud's obsession, Lacan's favourite fantasy, Marx's omission. A piece of meat activated by electric waves of desire, a text written by the unfolding of genetic encoding. Neither a sacralised inner *sanctum*, nor a pure socially shaped entity, the enfleshed Deleuzean subject is rather an 'in-between': it is a folding-in of external influences and a simultaneous unfolding outwards of affects. A mobile entity, an enfleshed type of memory that repeats and is capable of lasting through sets of discontinuous variations, while remaining faithful to itself. The Deleuzean body is ultimately an embodied memory.

This 'faithfulness to itself' is not to be understood in the mode of the psychological or sentimental attachment to an 'identity' that often is little more than a social security number. Nor is it a mark of authenticity for a self that expresses a mostly pathetic sense of importance of one's ego, one's petty likes and dislikes and one's pets. It is rather the faithfulness of duration, of the repetition of the expression of one's continuing and structuring adherence to certain dynamic spatio-temporal coordinates.

A Deleuzean body is an assemblage of forces or passions that solidify (in space) and consolidate (in time) within the singular configuration commonly known as an 'individual'. This intensive and dynamic entity is not, however, the emanation of an inner essence, nor is it merely the effect of biology. The Deleuzean body is rather a portion of forces that is stable enough – spatio-temporally speaking – to sustain them and to undergo constant, though necessarily contained, fluxes of transformation. It is a field of transformative effects whose availability for changes of intensity depends, first, on its ability to sustain and, second, to encounter the impact of other forces or affects.

In Deleuze's radical philosophy of temporally inscribed immanence, subjects come in different mileage, temperatures and beats. One can change gears and move across these coordinates, but it cannot claim all of them, all of the time. This is extremely important to prevent nihilism and self-destruction. Thus, to suggest that the subject for Deleuze is a process of becoming in active processes of transformation does not make it limitless: that would be the expression of a delirium of megalomania and regression. The containment of the intensities, their duration, is a crucial pre-requisite to allow them to do their job, which consists in shooting through the field of the subject, exploding its frame. In other words, the dosage or threshold of intensity is crucial to the Deleuzean process of becoming.

Deleuze's enfleshed, vitalistic but not essentialist vision of the subject is a self-sustainable one, which in some ways owes a lot to the ecology of the self. The rhythm, speed and sequencing of the affects and the selection of the constitutive elements are crucial to the whole process. It is the pattern of re-occurrence of these changes that marks the successive steps in the process of becoming, thus allowing for the actualisation of a field of forces that is apt to frame and thus to express the singularity of the subject.

This is a way of containing the excessive edges of the post-modernist discourse about the body, notably the denial of the materiality of the bodily self. Deleuze proposes instead a form of neo-materialism and a blend of vitalism that is attuned to the technological era. Thinking through the body, and not in a flight away from it, means confronting boundaries and limitations.

These claims also constitute the basis of Deleuze's critique of Lacanian psychoanalysis. Special emphasis is placed on the criticism of the sacralisation of the sexual self by Lacan as well as the teleological structure of identity formation in psychoanalytic theory, which shows its Hegelian legacy. Not the least of this concerns the definition of desire as lack, to which Deleuze never ceases to oppose the positivity of desire. More on this later.

On an everyday sociological level, as Camilla Griggers (1997) points out, the body is striking back, with a vengeance. An estimated two million American women have silicon breast implants most of which leak, bounce off during bumpy airplane flights or cause undesirable side-effects. Millions of women throughout the advanced world are on Prozac or other 'mood-enhancement' drugs. The hidden epidemic of anorexia–bulimia continues to strike one third of the younger women of the opulent world, as Princess Diana so clearly illustrated. Killer diseases today do not include only the great exterminators, like cancer and AIDS, but also the return of traditional diseases which we thought we had conquered, like tuberculosis and malaria. The human immunity system has adapted to the anti-bodies and we are vulnerable again.

In such a historical, bio-political and geo-political context, there is no question that what, even and especially in feminism, we go on calling, quite nostalgically, 'our bodies, ourselves' are abstract technological constructs fully immersed in advanced psycho-pharmacological industry, bio-science and the new media. This does not make them any less embodied, or less ourselves, it just complicates considerably the task of representing to ourselves the experience of inhabiting them.

What is equally clear is that a culture that is in the grip of a techno-teratological imaginary is in need of Deleuze's philosophy. The techno-hype needs to be kept in check by a sustainable under-standing of the self: we need to assess more lucidly the price we are prepared to pay for our high technological environments. We got our prosthetic promises of perfectability, now we need to hand over our pound of flesh. In this discussion that in some way juxtaposes the rhetoric of 'the desire to be wired' to a more radical sense of materialism, there is no doubt that Deleuze's philosophy lends precious help to those – including the feminists of sexual difference – who remain 'proud to be flesh!'

Like Irigaray, Deleuze is in fact a philosopher of radical imma-nence who takes temporality seriously. Both argue that we need to think the deep, dense materiality of bodies-in-time, so as to dis-engage them from the liberal bourgeois definition of the self. As utterly singular but collectively constituted enfleshed complexity, or embodied genealogy, the Deleuzean subject is sustainable: that is, limited, while having firmly departed from any reference to the 'natural' order.

Significantly, both Irigaray and Deleuze are post-Lacanians, though in dissymetrical ways. However critical Irigaray has been of Lacan's psychic essentialism and of his rejection of any possibility of transformation of the structures of the unconscious and the positioning of Woman in it, she remains faithful to the conceptual structure of Lacan's reading of the unconscious. For instance, the symbolic system remains Irigaray's point of reference, although in her reading it is more porous to the influence of historical changes and thus more affected by the workings of the imaginary. Irigaray's radical feminism rests precisely on the investment on the power of the feminine to redefine the symbolic.

Deleuze goes much further in rejecting the Lacanian conceptual scheme of the unconscious altogether. Dismissing the metaphysics of the self, Deleuze redefines the unconscious as a productive, forward-propelling force of flows or intensities. This rests to a large degree on Deleuze's philosophy of time: his Bergsonian read-ing of a continuous present can be opposed to the tyranny of the

161

past in the psychoanalytic reading of memory, repetition or the process of repression and retrieval of the repressed material.

Deleuze's 'minoritarian' definition of memory as a nomadic or deterritorialising force runs against the established definitions of memory as a centralised data bank of frozen information. As a vector of deterritorialisation, memory for Deleuze destabilises identity by stringing together virtual possibilities. Re-membering in this mode requires careful lay-outs of empowering conditions which allow for the actualisation to take place. Like a choreography of flows or intensities that require adequate framing in order to compose into a form, memories require empathy and cohesion between the constitutive elements. It is like a constant reshuffling that yearns for the moment of sustainable balance or expression, before they dissolve again and move on. And on it goes, never equal to itself, but close enough not to lose sight of the structure altogether.

As I have argued elsewhere (Braidotti 1994b), in the short term Deleuze's radical reconceptualisation erodes the foundations of a specific feminist epistemology and of a theory of feminine subjectivity insofar as it rejects the masculine/feminine dichotomy altogether. In the longer run, however, the radically projective concept of the intensive Deleuzean subject opens the door to possible configurations of a variety of subject-positions that are post-metaphysics of gender, or beyond sexual difference.

III. THE FEMINISED OR MONSTROUS OTHER

In the contemporary imaginary, the monstrous refers to the play of representation and discourses that surround the body of late postmodernity. It is the expression of a deep anxiety about the bodily roots of subjectivity.

I tend to view this as the counterpart and the counterpoint to the emphasis that dominant post-industrial culture has placed on the construction of clean, healthy, fit, white, decent, law-abiding, heterosexual and forever young bodies. The techniques aimed at perfecting the bodily self and at correcting the traces of mortality of the corporeal self – plastic surgery, dieting, the fitness craze and other techniques for disciplining the body – also simultaneously help it to supersede its 'natural' state. What we witness in popular culture is an almost a Bakhtinian ritual of transgression. The fascination for the monstrous, the freaky body-double, is directly proportional to the suppression of images of both ugliness and disease in contemporary post-industrial culture. It is as if what we are chasing out the front door – the spectacle of the poor, fat, homeless, homosexual, black, dying, ageing, decaying, leaky body – were actually creeping in through the back window. The monstrous marks the 'return of the repressed' of techno-culture, and as such it is intrinsic to it.

The monstrous body fulfils the magical or symptomatic function of indicator of the register of difference: which is why the monster has never been able to avoid a blind date with women. In the post-nuclear cybernetic era, however, the encounter between the maternal body and the technological apparatus is so intense that it calls for new frames of analysis. Contemporary 'monstrous others', as I argued earlier, blur the dividing line between the organic and the inorganic, thus rendering superfluous also the political divide between technophobia and technophilia. In an age where, as Haraway (1991) astutely observes, the machines are so restless while the humans are so inert, the issue becomes how to redefine the techno-body in such a way as to preserve a sense of singularity, without falling into a nostalgic reappraisal of an essential self. The issue of the boundaries of identity raises its monstrous head.

The specific historicity of this situation may also help to explain the peculiarly reassuring function that the representation of freaky bodies fulfils in the anxiety-ridden contemporary imagination. As Diana Arbus (1972) suggests, freaks have already been through it and have come out at the other end. If not quite survivors, they are at least resilient in their capacity to metamorphose and thus survive and cope. Many late twentieth-century humans may instead have serious doubts about their capacity to cope, let alone survive. Contemporary horror and science-fiction literature and films show an exacerbated version of anxiety in the form of the 'otherness within': the monster dwells in your embodied self and it may burst out any minute into unexpected and definitely unwanted mutations. The monster is in your embodied self, ready to unfold, as in David Cronenberg's remake of *The Fly*. The monstrous growths spreading within one's organism, as Jackie Stacey (1997) reminds us, in the form of cancer or other post-nuclear diseases, are also variations on the theme of the 'enemy within'.

The monstrous, decadent or mutant body is 'feminised' as being abject (Kristeva 1982; Creed 1993). Marina Warner (1994) argues that the image of the destructive monstrous female is especially current in the ways in which contemporary culture portrays feminism. The monstrous female has turned into the monstrous feminist, whom the conservatives hold responsible for all the evils of today's society. Especially targeted for criticism is the single mother. As Warner rightly points out, this is not only a prominent 'problem' for the enemies of the welfare state, but also a general threat to masculine authority. Reproduction without men triggers a deep malaise in the patriarchal imaginary, that moves fast in the direction of resurrecting the century-old myth of gynocracy (Atwood 1985). Women's bodies today are in the same position monstrous bodies were over a century ago: testing-ground for various brands of mechanised reproduction. Are Corea's (1985) nightmare world of 'gender-cide' or Atwood's (1985) dystopia of the techno-brothel likely scenarios?

Much feminist ink has been spilled in the attempt to analyse the link between the monstrous and the proliferation of discourses about 'the feminine' in late postmodernity. This discursive inflation concerns mostly male philosophers, artists, cultural and media activists. With the investment into this kind of 'feminine' as the site of a virile display of crisis, the topos of the monstrous female has proportionally gained in currency. I think it emerges as the expression of the fantasy of dangers that threaten postmodern, or 'soft' patriarchy.

Moreover, both the feminine and the monstrous are signs of an embodied negative difference that makes them ideal targets for the 'metaphysical cannibalism' of a subject which feeds upon what it excludes. Pejorative otherness, or 'monstrous others', helps to illuminate the paradoxical and dissymetrical power relations within Western theories of subjectivity. The freak, not unlike the feminine and the ethnic 'others', signifies devalued difference. By virtue of its structural inter-connection with the dominant subject position, it also helps to define sameness or normalcy among some types. Normality is the zero degree of monstrosity (Canguilhem 1966).

If the monstrous feminist haunts the imagination of the operators of the backlash, a less destructive reappraisal of the monstrous other has been undertaken by feminists needing to redefine 'difference' positively. Multiculturalism and the critique of orientalism and racism have also contributed to rethink the cultural and scientific practices around monstrous bodies. The need has emerged for a new epistemology to deal with difference in non-pejorative terms. In this case, the freak/monstrous other becomes emblematic of the vast political and theoretical efforts aimed at redefining human subjectivity away from the persistently logocentric and racist ways of thinking that used to characterise it in Western culture.

Confronted with such a discursive inflation of monstrous images, I refuse the nostalgic position that tends to read them as signs of the cultural decadence of our times, also known as the decline of 'master narratives', or the loss of the great canon of 'high culture'. I think that the proliferation of a monstrous social imaginary calls instead for adequate forms of analysis. More particularly it calls for a form of philosophical teratology which Deleuze is in a unique position to provide.

I want to argue that a culture, both mainstream and feminist, where the imaginary is so monstrous and deviant, especially in its cybernetic variants, can profit greatly from Deleuze's philosophical teratology. Deleuze's emphasis on the project of reconfiguring the positivity of difference, his philosophy of becoming and the emphasis he places on thinking about changes and the speed of transformation are a very illuminating way to approach the complexities of our age. There is a profound sense of *adequacy* in both the political and aesthetic sensibility of Deleuze, as if he were indeed attuned to the most problematic questions of the day.

From a more cultural angle, Deleuze's intensive approach to contemporary cultural production – be it conceptual, scientific or artistic – casts a most significant light upon some of the most unprecedented aspects of advanced post-industrial cultures. Among them I would list: the desegregation of humanistic subject-positions and values, the ubiquitous presence of narcotic practices and of cultural artifacts derived from the drug culture, the all-pervasive political violence, and the intermingling of the enfleshed and the technological. These features, which are often referred to as the 'post-human' universe, can be read in an altogether more positive light if they are approached from the angle of Deleuze's philosophy of radical immanence, his multiple patterns of becoming and the overthrowing of the humanistic parameters of representation, while avoiding relativism by grounding his practice into a tight spatio-temporal framework.

IV. THE METAMORPHIC DIMENSION

On this score, feminism has much to learn from Deleuze. Contemporary feminist culture is just as 'freakified' as other aspects of cultural practice in late post-industrial societies.

Sexual indeterminacy, rather than 1970s-style lesbianism, has entered mainstream culture. 'Queer' is no longer the noun that marks an identity they taught us to despise, but it has become a verb that destabilises any claim to identity. The heroine chic of Calvin Klein's advertising campaign and the success of waif-like supermodels such as Kate Moss have fashioned the body in the direction of the abject, as hybrid mutant bodies seem to be the trend. A colder, more ironic sensibility with a flair for sadomasochism is the contemporary version of 'no more nice girls'. Mae West has replaced Rebecca West as feminist mother, as Madonna claims in her *Sex* album. Bad girls are in and bad girls carry a teratological imaginary. As Warner puts it: 'in rock music, in films, in fiction, even in pornography, women are grasping the she-beast of demonology for themselves. The bad girl is the heroine of our times, and transgression a staple entertainment' (1994: 11).

Let me analyse some of the reasons why feminist culture is teratological. I want to argue that the reason why the monstrous is a dominant part of the feminist imaginary is that it offers privileged mirror-images. We identify with them, out of fear or of fascination. The monsters are 'metamorphic' creatures who fulfil a kaleidoscopic mirror function and make us aware of the mutation that we are living through in these post-nuclear/industrial/modern/human days.

The structural analogy between 'the monstrous' and 'the feminine', which has become a topos of post-war science-fiction films, has a much older pedigree. Fielder's (1979) analysis of the typology of contemporary monsters classifies them in terms of lack, of excess and of displacement of organs. This facilitates the analogy with the feminine. As psychoanalytic feminism has successfully argued (Wright 1992), the feminine also bears a privileged relation to lack, excess and displacement. By being posited as eccentric vis-à-vis the dominant mode, or as constantly off-centre, the feminine marks the threshold between the human and its 'outside'. This outside is a multilayered framework that both distinguishes the human from (as it also connects it to) the animal, the vegetable, the mineral and also the divine. As an in-between link between the sacred and the abject, the feminine is paradoxical in its monstrosity. In other words, it functions by displacement and its ubiquity as a social or philosophical 'problem' is equal to the awe and the horror it inspires.

Metamorphic creatures are uncomfortable 'body-doubles' or simulacra that simultaneously attract and repel, comfort and unsettle: they are objects of adoration and aberration. In her account of science-fiction texts written by women, Sarah Lefanu (1988) argues that these texts tend to depict women in a bond of empathy with monstrous and alien others. A sort of deep complicity runs between the other of the male of the species and the other of the species as a whole.

Psychoanalytic feminist theory has also cast an interesting light on this aspect of the monstrous imaginary. First, women who are caught in the phallogocentric gaze tend to have a negative self-image and to dread what they see when they look in the mirror. One is reminded of Virginia Woolf and Silvia Plath who saw monsters emerging from the depth of their mirrors. Difference is often experienced as negative by women and represented in their cultural production in terms of aberration or monstrosity. The Gothic genre can be read as female projection of an inner sense of inadequacy. In this perspective, the monster fulfils primarily a specular function, thereby playing a major role in the definition of female self-identity. *Frankenstein* – the product of the daughter of a historic feminist – is also the portrait of a deep lack of self-confidence and even deeper sense of displacement. Not only does Mary Shelley side with the monstrous creature, accusing its creator of avoiding his responsibilities, but also she presents Frankenstein's monster as her abject body-double, which allows her to express self-loathing with staggering lucidity.

The metamorphic dimension fulfils another function. I argued earlier that the monstrous as a borderline figure blurs the boundaries between hierarchically established distinctions (between human/non-human; Western/non-Western, and so on) and also between horizontal or adjacent differences. In other words, the monstrous triggers the recognition of a sense of multiplicity contained within the same entity. It is an entity whose multiple parts are neither totally merged nor totally separate from the human observer. Thus, the monstrous signifies the difficulty in keeping manageable margins of differentiation of the boundaries between self and other.

This problem with boundaries and differentiation is at the core of the mother–daughter question, following the analyses of Luce Irigaray (1985a) and Nancy Chodorow (1978). Any daughter, that is, any woman, has a self that is not completely individuated but rather is constitutively connected to another woman – her mother. The term mother is already quite tangled and complex, being the site of a symbiotic mix-up, which – according to Lacan – requires the ordering power of the Law of the Father in order to restore the boundaries. This is also the line pursued by Barbara Johnson in *My Monster/Myself* (1982), in a title that alludes to to Nancy Friday's popular *My Mother/My Self*. Who is the monster? The mother or the self? Or does the monstrosity lie in the undecidability of what goes on in-between? The inability to answer that question has to do with the difficulty of negotiating stable and positive boundaries with one's mother. The monstrous feminine is precisely the sign-post of that structural and highly significant difficulty.

What is important to note here is that in the 1980s feminist theory celebrated both the ambiguities and the intensity of the mother/daughter bond in positive terms – '*écriture féminine*' and Irigaray's paradigm of 'labial politics' being somewhat the epitome of this trend. By the late 1990s, however, the maternalist/feminine paradigm was well under attack, if not discarded. This shift away from gyno-centric psychoanalytic feminism towards a definitely bad attitude to the mother coincides, as often is the case in feminism, with a generation gap. Kolbowski (1995) argues that Melanie Klein's 'bad' mother has replaced the Lacanian-inspired 'vanilla sex' representation of the M/other as object of desire. Accordingly, parodic politics has replaced strategic essentialism and other forms of affirmative mimesis in feminist theories of difference.

Nixon (1995) reads the anti-Lacanian climate of the 1990s, best illustrated by the revival of interest in Melanie Klein's theory of the aggressive drives: 'in part as a critique of psychoanalytic feminist work of the 70's and 80's, privileging pleasure and desire over hatred and aggression' (72). I would like to situate the new alliance that is currently being negotiated between feminists and Deleuze in this context of historical decline of Lacan's theory of desire as lack and the revival of Klein's theory of the drives. A colder and more aggressive political sensibility has been dominant in the 1990s.

V. IMAGINARY FIGURATIONS

Technological culture expresses a colder and more depersonalised kind of sensibility. In order to illustrate the paradox of the biotechnological era, also known as the era of the information technologies, let us consider the World Wide Web: a huge and practically uncontrollable social space which confronts us with a paradox: on the one hand a cheerful cacophony of clashing bits and bytes of the most diverse information and, on the other hand, with the threat of monoculture and the largest concentration of military-industrial monopolies in the world. I could not think of a better image for the paradox of globalisation and concentration, uniformity and fragmentation which characterises the transnational economy. The theoretical appraisal of this specific historical moment is very varied, ranging from the euphoric promises of the electronic democracy (Kroker and Kroher 1987) to prophecies of doom (Unibomber). Only a few sober scholars like Castells (1996) and Haraway (1991) can actually articulate a theoretical framework that is up to the challenges of our day. For such scholars, the crisis of representation, values and agency that is engendered by the new world disorder is not necessarily a negative mark of decline, but it rather opens up new perspectives for critical thought.

The arena where this discussion is being deployed is the social imaginary, which is a highly contested social space where the techno-teratological imaginary, supported and promoted by post-industrial societies, is rampant. Whether we like it or not, and most of us do not, we are made to desire the interface human/machine. I want to argue consequently that, given the importance of both the social imaginary and the role of technology in coding it, we need to develop both forms of representation and of resistance that are *adequate*.

Adequate representations are the heart of the matter. As I have often argued, Deleuze shares with a great deal of feminists the need for a renewal of our imaginary repertoires. Conceptual creativity is called for, new figurations are needed to help us to think through the maze of techno-teratological culture.

Let me clarify one important point here. I have been referring to the 'imaginary' as a set of socially mediated practices which function as the anchoring point – albeit unstable and contingent – for identifications and therefore for identity formation. These practices act like interactive structures where desire as a subjective yearning and agency in a broader socio-political sense are mutually shaped by one another. Neither 'pure' imagination – locked in its classical opposition to reason – nor fantasy in the Freudian sense, the imaginary for me marks a space of transitions and transactions. Nomadic, in a Deleuzean sense, it flows like symbolic glue between the social and the self, the outside – 'constitutive outside', as Stuart Hall would say, quoting Derrida – and the subject: the material and the ethereal. It flows, but it is sticky: it catches on as it goes. It possesses fluidity, but it distinctly lacks transparency, let alone purity. I have used the term 'desire' – in keeping with my post-structuralist training – to connote the subject's own investment, or enmeshment, in this sticky network of inter-related social and discursive effects. This network constitutes the social field as a libidinal – or affective – landscape, as well as a normative – or disciplinary – framework.

Considering the structure of the imaginary, one cannot claim it possesses any unitary or generalised meaning, nor can any philosopher easily promise an immediate Nietzschean transmutation of values. It is rather the case that the task of decoding and accounting for the imaginary has been a critical concern for social and cultural critics since the 1960s. It has provided the arena in which different and often conflicting critiques of representation have clashed, fuelling the discourse of the crisis of representation. I think this crisis needs to be read in the context of the decline of Europe as a world power (West 1994). It is also intrinsic to the post-nuclear predicament of an advanced world whose social realities become virtual – or dematerialised – because they are changing at such a fast rate under the pressure and the acceleration of a digitally-clad economy.

This state of crisis had engendered a positive and highly stimulating response in the conceptual teratology proposed by Deleuze. Deleuze innovates on the notion of the 'cartographic diagramme' proposed by Foucault in his attempt to provide a materially-based practice of representation of the fast-shifting social landscape of post-industrial societies. The 'diagramme' is a cartographic device that enables the tracking of an intersecting network of power-effects that simultaneously enable and constrain the subjects. It also functions as a point of support for the task of redesigning a framework for subjectivity.

The imagination plays a major role in this process of conceptual creativity. For Deleuze – following Bergson and Nietzsche – the imagination is a transformative force that propels multiple, heterogeneous 'becomings', or repositioning of the subject. The process of becoming is collectively driven, that is to say relational and external; it is also framed by affectivity or desire, and is thus excentric to rational control. The notion of 'figurations' – in contrast to the representational function of 'metaphors' – emerges as crucial to Deleuze's notion of a conceptually charged use of the imagination. Deleuze, not unlike Haraway or, for that matter, the performance artist Laurie Anderson, thinks by inventing unconventional and even disturbing conceptual personae. These mark different steps in the process of 'becoming-minoritarian', that is of undoing power relations in the very structures of one's subject position. Figurations of these multiple becomings are: the rhizome, the nomad, the bodies-without-organs, the cyborg, the onco-mouse and acoustic masks of all electronic kinds.

Terms like 'figuration' or 'fabulation' are often used to describe this politically charged practice of alternative representation (Barr

1993). It is a way of bringing into representation the unthinkable, insofar as it requires awareness of the limitations as well as the specificity of one's locations. Figurations thus act as the spotlight that illuminates aspects of one's practice which were blind spots before. A conceptual persona is no metaphor, but a materially embodied stage of metamorphosis of a dominant subject towards all that the phallogocentric system does *not* want it to become. Massumi (1992) refers to this process as the actualisation of monstrosity.

The process of conceptual creativity in Deleuze and the transformative repossession of knowledge in feminism amount to a common quest for alternative figurations of subjects-in-becoming.

Feminist theories of 'politics of location' (Rich 1987) or 'situated knowledges' (Haraway 1991) also stress the material basis of alternative forms of representation, as well as their transgressive and transformative potential. In feminism, these ideas are coupled with that of epistemological and political accountability (Harding 1991), that is, the practice that consists in unveiling the power locations which one inevitably inhabits as the site of one's identity. The practice of accountability (for one's embodied and embedded locations) as a relational, collective activity of undoing power differentials is linked to two crucial notions: memory and narratives. They activate the process of putting into words, that is to say bringing into symbolic representation, that which by definition escapes consciousness, insofar as it is relational – that is interactive and retrospective, that is memory-driven and invested by a yearning or desire for change, and that is outside-oriented. Feminists knew this well before Deleuze theorised it in his rhizomatic philosophy, that there is a hiatus between the new subject-positions women have begun to develop and the forms of representation of their subjectivity which their culture makes available to them.

In the post-nuclear context of the second millennium a feminist quest for a new imaginary representation has exploded. Myths, metaphors, or alternative figurations have merged feminist theory with fictions. It is precisely this mixture of the techno-scientific with the fictional or fantastic that also triggers the contemporary fascination with the monstrous, both among feminists and in mainstream culture. The monstrous refers to the potentially explosive social subjects for whom contemporary cultural and social theory has no adequate schemes of representation. It expresses a positive potential of the 'crisis' of the humanist subject, which is the *leitmotif* of modernity.

171

VI. CONCLUSION

A new alliance between feminism and Deleuze is being negotiated in the new anti-Lacanian and 'anti-maternalist' colder political sensibilities in the 1990s. This tends to get expressed in a cyber-teratological imaginary that may appear disturbing, even in its parodic manifestations. I have argued that there is a nostalgic or negative appropriation of the monstrous imaginary for the purpose of the conservative backlash or of a crisis of masculinity. There is also however a positive appropriation of it by feminists for the purpose of legitimating alternative representations of subject-positions that are made possible by the crisis of the dominant subject. Feminist figurations are an eminent example of the creative and transformative use of the monstrous imaginary. This profound dissymmetry in the approach to the crisis has to do with power differentials in the locations or places of enunciation.

As Deleuze's philosophical teratology – his valorisation of the positivity of difference – shows, a shift of paradigm is in course, towards the teratological or the abnormal/anomalous/deviant. This does *not* automatically or directly translate into moral, political or cultural decadence. This associative link that connects the pathological or abnormal to the morally deficient or the politically bankrupt is a nineteenth-century topos that strikes me as utterly inadequate as a framework of analysis for the cultural realities of post-nuclear societies.

The challenge that the monstrous throws in our direction is a dissociation of the sensibility we have inherited from the previous end of century. We need to learn to think of the anomalous, the monstrously different not as a sign of pejoration but as the unfolding of virtual possibilities that point to positive alternatives for us all. As Deleuze would put it: the pattern of becoming cuts across the experiential field of all that phallogocentrism did *not* programme us to become. In that sense, the fantasmagoric diversity of monstrous beings points the way to the kind of line of becoming which our crisis-afflicted culture badly needs. I tend to think of this as the last-to-date episode in the de-centring of Western thought: the human is now displaced in the direction of a glittering range of post-human variables, however painful this may be to the collective hubris we – including Western feminists – have inherited from centuries of codified Western humanism.

9

Goodbye America
(The Bride is Walking . . .)

CAMILLA BENOLIRAO GRIGGERS

In this chapter, I attempt to give face to Filipina-becoming in the twentieth century by mobilising, from a feminist ground, the Deleuzean materialism which the philosopher developed in his later collaborations with Félix Guattari. To do so requires a remapping of the Filipina's mediated face as she appears and reappears in various incarnations as war sacrifice, military bride, plantation bride, red-district worker, bride of overseas contract workers (OCWs) and later OCW herself, screen bride, and 'international personal ads' bride. In the process of this remapping, I will identify the Deleuzean concepts I am mobilising.

CONCEPT 1: PLATEAU

'A plateau is always in the middle, not at the beginning or at the end.' (Deleuze and Guattari 1987: 21)

Plateau 1: 24 November 1992 – Screening the Military (Bride)

Amid the heat and drought and fires of el niño in late August 1997, a movie opened in Manila – a Filipino production with an international cast and a budget of US$2 million. *Goodbye America*, directed by Thierry Notz, is a biracial love story set against the backdrop of the closing of the last US military base in the Philippines in 1992: Subic Bay naval base. In the film, a young and beautiful ex-bar girl, played by Alma Concepcion, dreams of marrying the US serviceman

173

with whom she has fallen in love. The American, played by Alexis Arquette, hesitates, worrying over how his dark Filipina beauty will be perceived by his white friends and relatives at home, particularly his career-officer father. Wouldn't a ship-in-port fling be a better relation for him in the long run, his compatriot asks? The American seems true of heart, but in the end he dies a violent death at the hands of a militant American soldier, leaving his would-be bride abandoned and heartbroken in spite of his good intentions.

Producer Michael Sellers had high ambitions for the *Goodbye* project, aiming for Hollywood-style production values while banking on the cheap labour of an entirely Filipino production crew to reduce the cost of the film. On the World Wide Web, Sellers marketed *Goodbye America* as the 'first major step in the globalization of the Filipino movie industry'. Following on the heels of MTV Asia, globalisation had indeed hit the troubled Filipino film industry, which had been taking a beating not only from Hollywood but also from SkyCable. To the extent that Sellers was successful – the film was the only Filipino production to be exhibited at Cannes '97 – his claims about globalisation were accurate. While technically a Filipino production, *Goodbye America* was actually an American production produced in the Philippines. And in this sense, *Goodbye America* really was representative of the globalisation (i.e., Americanisation) of the Filipino movie industry. And as this particular film made clear, not only was the integrity of the Filipino film industry at stake in the globalisation process, but also the public (i.e., international) remembering of key events in the history of Philippine–US relations.

A Filipino-based American, Sellers had formerly been a foreign service officer for the US Department of State, had served as a political officer in Manila, and was intimately involved in negotiations for the closing of Subic Bay naval base. The expulsion of the US military was mandated by the Philippine Congress in response to heated public protest in the post-Marcos years, culminating finally in a Congressional vote against renewal of the longstanding Military Base Agreement with the US. A prophetic volcanic blast from Mt Pinatubo aided the process of departure, and on 24 November 1992, after *ninety-four years* of US military presence in the Philippines, the *Americanos* were finally out. Or at least they seemed to be.

To his credit, Sellers recognised the closing of Subic naval base as the historic event it was – the end to a century-long epoch in the colonial history of the two countries. But his personal investment with the *Goodbye* project was undeniably slanted by his State Department experience. Perhaps this is why, though the film had international sales to two dozen countries, it made only a moderate showing at the national Filipino box office. It was not a *hit*, as they say. The film played one week in Manila theatres, then headed for the provinces, where Alma Concepcion's star appeal would draw more audiences than the film's historical topic.

Not surprisingly, in the heat of the opening days of the worst economic crisis in the country since the assassination of Ninoy Aquino in 1983, Manila audiences were not thronging to see a love story about the closing of Subic naval base. In a country that prefers the melodrama of Thalia's telenovelas imported from Mexico and dubbed into Tagalog, *Goodbye America* was too realistic in its focus on the historic departure of the US military from the Philippines, too tragic in its violent ending in which the girl does *not* get the man of her dreams, and at the same time too nostalgic towards American-Pacific imperialism to be palatable to even mainstream urban Filipino viewers. Emma Salazar, the ex-bar girl in *Goodbye America*, gets nothing in the end, unlike Thalia who played an honest nursemaid who gets the marriage she desires at the end of *Maria del La Barrio* – the final episode of which played in metro Manila on 11 July, the very day the peso took its first ominous plunge in what would become the worst economic crash in Asia since the Second World War. In *Goodbye America*, however, the Filipina's narrative is not the one that is romanticised. The American's military narrative is, on the other hand, and this is where Sellers' film missed the boat, so to speak, on the popular box-office draw. Popular melodramatic sentiment is always for the poor local girl who would-be bride, never for the colonising male character who represents foreign domination – no matter how altruistic his character portrayal. Attempting romance, *Goodbye America* succeeded instead in creating a romanticised nostalgia for the US military presence in the Philippines. In Manila, the film failed to capitalise on its nostalgia because it valorised the perpetrator in an old, old story of betrayal and military domination, and tried to sell this foreign nostalgia to Filipino audiences who weren't buying a past they had turned away from with so much conviction. Yet this new face of 'globalised' imperialist nostalgia, expressed in Alma Concepcion's Filipina glamour, was dangerously seductive. In fact, *Goodbye America* almost seemed prophetic in retrospect, because by 1998 the Americans were back, pressuring

Figure 9.1: Promotional images from the World Wide Web for the global marketing of *Goodbye America* (1997), starring Alma Concepcion. (*http://www.abs-cbn.com/starcinema/images/bnr goodbye.jpg,* Monday 3 August 1998)

the Philippine Congress during a time of extreme economic crisis to accept a 'Visiting Forces Agreement' that would re-establish a US military presence in the Philippines.

Whatever the financial pressures that have always determined colonial and semi-colonial Philippine politics, in spirit and effort Filipinos couldn't say goodbye to America fast enough. In spite of the 1997 meltdown of South-east Asian currencies, including the peso, the Philippines successfully paid off its International Monetary Fund (IMF) debt (read in Asia as US hegemony) in March 1998 for monies borrowed in 1983, 1988 and 1989, when the country nearly went bankrupt from Marcos's twenty-year regime of corruption – a regime backed by the US as long as Marcos continued to sign off on the military-base agreement. Debt repayment came at a high cost in the post-Marcos recovery years. As one researcher summed up the situation, 'By 1988 the Philippines owed money to over 400 private banks and foreign government agencies as well as multilateral institutions, and its total debt had climbed to US$29 billion' (Chant and McIlwaine 1995: 54). The payback was painful and costly in human terms, requiring the country in 1990 to channel 37 per cent of the national budget to debt servicing while cutting health-care services to a miserable 3.2 per cent – with 50 per cent of the population living at or below the poverty line (Chant and McIlwaine: 57). For these reasons, the Freedom from Debt Coalition founded in 1988 called for the Aquino administration to declare a moratorium on foreign-debt service payments until recovery of the Philippine economy. The coalition also recommended repudiation of loans involving fraud or related to private-sector borrowing, and capping annual foreign-debt service to 10 per cent of export earnings (Chant and McIlwaine 1995: 59). Solita Collas-Monsod, Aquino's Secretary of Economic Planning, resigned over this issue when Aquino decided to pursue further loans on the rationale that any break in debt servicing would damage future foreign investment in the Philippines. Aquino was right in the sense that foreign investment capital continued to enter the Philippines after the agreement. However, continued reliance on foreign investment capital for export-led and fast-growth real estate development, not only in the Philippines but in all of Asia, paved the way for the regional investment banking collapse that followed only eight years later.

The 'Letter of Intent' that Aquino signed to the IMF in 1989 in order to secure an additional US$2.8 billion for 1990 to assure the Philippines' ability to uphold its debt repayments required a series of stringent policies that fell hardest on the poor. The IMF agreement, similar to the 'austerity' programmes administered in the early months of 1998 in Indonesia and South Korea in exchange for US$43 billion and US$66 billion in aid packages respectively, required fixing artificially low wages and opening the country to direct foreign investment in key development industries such as the garment industry and subcontracted electrical components – industries which relied on Filipina women for cheap labour to turn profits that increasingly did not return to the Filipino domestic economy (Chant and McIlwaine 1995: 58–62).

Another IMF bailout, if it came to that, would constitute more than just another failed goodbye. The collapse of Asian currencies and threat of new IMF debt fell on the very eve of the centennial of Philippine Independence from 300 years of Spanish colonial rule on 12 June 1898, and, more pointedly, on the centennial of the Philippine–American War that quickly followed that brief independence on 4 February 1899. Understandably then, amid the financial heat of the Asian currency and international banking crash, Filipino audiences preferred the hopeful melodramas of Thalia imported from Mexico, or the dark New York City satire of *Men in Black*, or they stayed home to channel surf SkyCable as the peso devalued from 26 pesos to the US dollar in early July 1997 to a low of 47 pesos to the dollar by early January of 1998.

In the United States, the closing of US military bases in the Philippines was hardly a hot topic for mass consumption. The film wasn't released in the USA. North Americans, it seems, were not really interested in how the Philippines said goodbye to America, or that they wanted to, or why. And they were certainly not interested in watching a film about the history of US imperialism in South-east Asia, or about the sordid gender politics of US overseas military bases in the Pacific – no matter how romanticised.

Sonia Sanchez's realistic documentary on the life of a bar girl named Rose in *Olongapo Rose* (1989) makes a sharp contrast to *Goodbye America*'s nostalgic representation of military-base life and its effect on local communities. Sanchez's candid interviews with US servicemen and Filipina bar girls exposed the gendered power relations that resulted from a military-base economy. Currency exchange rates favourable to US servicemen and a thriving entertainment industry surrounding US bases produced an economic situation in which local Filipinas could earn more money dancing for or prostituting themselves to American military personnel in sordid red-light districts than doing manual work in the provincial villages where they grew up. Entire provincial families could be supported by a dancer's earnings, forcing families to pressure daughters to move to base environs, where life moved forward with the rhythms of military paydays, time-off, and the hope of true

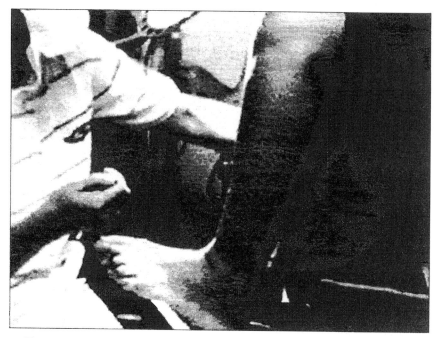

Figures 9.2, 9.3 and 9.4: Filipina bar girls on their way to work, dancing, and getting mandatory gynaecological exams. From Sonia Sanchez's *Olongapo Rose*.

romance and a marriage proposal to lift a girl, and perhaps her family back home, out of a life of poverty. It should be noted that the 'entertainment' industry did not disappear with the closing of Clark and Subic bases. It simply reterritorialised places like Cebu City in the Viscayas, where Filipina entertainment workers who do *not* sell themselves for sex typically earned the equivalent of US$4 per day *before* the 1997 devaluation of the peso (Chant and McIlwaine 1995: 230–7). Cebu's status as an international sex-tourist centre has been facilitated not only by the closings of US military bases in Luzon, but also by international airlinks to Cebu City – expressing another face of the 'globalisation' of the Filipina workforce (Chant and McIlwaine 1995: 212).

If by chance US servicemen had wanted a dutiful, obedient and devoted foreign bride rather than a good time on the town, they could get that too, and could even have the US military provide their Filipina bride with training on how to be a good military wife in the Commander US Naval Forces Philippines Bride School programme. Here, Sanchez's camera documents new brides being taught how to use American kitchen appliances, how to budget for

Figure 9.5: An instructor at the US Naval Forces Philippines Bride School teaches Filipina brides of US servicemen how to operate the washing machine. From *Olongapo Rose*.

household expenses without taking too much away from their husbands' entertainment expenses, and how to avoid domestic squabbles with their military spouses. Sanchez's local documentary challenges Sellers' 'global' representation of the US military presence in the Philippines.

CONCEPT 2: RHIZOME

'A rhizome is made of plateaus.' (Deleuze and Guattari 21)

Plateau 2: 4 February 1899 – The Philippine–American War and the Birth of Cinema

It is the year 1900. President McKinley is running for re-election in the USA, and the war his administration launched in the Philippines on 4 February of the previous year could cost him the election. For a variety of economic, political and ideological reasons, hardly any of them purely altruistic, many Americans opposed the military occupation of the Philippines. The Anti-Imperialist League, a well-funded opposition group whose members included

Mark Twain and Andrew Carnegie, was loudly challenging McKinley's expansionist foreign policy in public forums.

In New Jersey, a small audience sits in the dark waiting for the light of a film projector to illuminate and animate their imaginations. Lights flicker. Suddenly a tall American officer in dark field dress stands up on screen and removes his field coat. He's on the front line of a battle. He appears fearless. A body of water stands between his white torso, in the foreground, and a dozen dark-faced 'enemy' troops dressed in cotton uniforms in the background, along the other bank. The dark men scamper wildly as shots are fired at them by the officer's troops. The officer bravely marches into the water, swimming towards the enemy as if he is going to personally vanquish each one by hand. The dark men flee as the American officer single-handedly pulls a raft of US soldiers across the Baglag River . . .

Meet Colonel Funston. US screen fantasy.

Colonel Funstan [sic] *on the Baglag River* was one of a series of short films produced and directed by Thomas Edison in 1899, and now archived as part of the paper film series in the US National Archive. Shooting on location in the woods of New Jersey, Edison cast African-Americans as the Filipinos who fought against occupying US troops in the Philippines. The racial substitution is

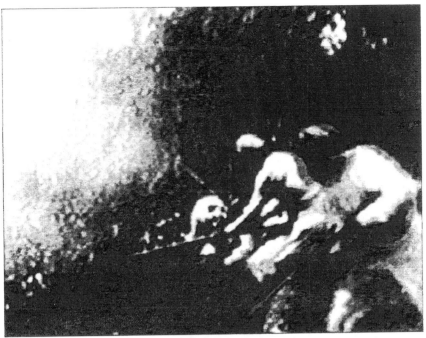

Figures 9.6, 9.7 and 9.8: Stills from Thomas Edison's *Rout of the Filipinos*, shot in New Jersey, showing US troops attacking African-Americans cast as Filipinos. Note the mis-naming of the war as the 'Spanish–American War', which ended in 1898, not 1899. US National Archives.

uncanny in that classic Freudian sense in which something looks strange to one precisely because it is so *familiar*. Black is black, black is brown, black is other – the dark one who is the enemy, the insurgent, the vanquished – but never the hero in these representations of war. Never the victor. And never the innocent victim. Edison's short film, like a hysterical symptom, visually manifests the racism at the heart of the violent military conquest of the Philippines.

As it turns out, the US film industry has a long record of producing American representations of Filipino history. Many of Edison's films about the war bear the date '1899' and the subtitle 'The Spanish–American War'. This conflation of signs is telling, because Filipino nationalists won independence from Spain on 12 June 1898, and formed the First Republic of the Philippines in that year. For 1899 was not the year of the Spanish–American War then, but rather of the Philippine–American War, which began 'officially' on 4 February 1899, only eight months after the independence of the Philippines from 300 years of Spanish colonial rule. The fact is that US military build-up in preparation for the military occupation of the Philippines continued at a heated pace from the time of Spain's surrender until the firing of the 'first shot' against the Filipinos in early February – just two days before the US Senate's ratification of the Treaty of Paris on 6 February 1899 by a narrow margin of one vote, and by which Spain 'ceded' the Philippines to the USA for $20 million. During the months preceding the war, dozens of US military transport ships made the journey across the Pacific to Manila Bay before that first shot was ever fired, bearing 20,000 troops with ammunition, artillery, supplies, horses and telegraph equipment. Eventually, 70,000 US troops would make the journey across the Pacific. Filipinos themselves, however, were excluded from any of the formal negotiations culminating in the Treaty of Paris – a contract proceeding that would set the course of history for the next century for the Philippine Islands, and one that would determine the *value* of Filipino labour, including women's labour, raw materials and finished goods on the world market.

In reality, Funston, the man idolised and idealised in Edison's film, was a ruthless officer whose Kansas volunteers were known during the Philippine–American War to be some of the most brutal and ruthless of US troops. Yet Funston was depicted as a hero by the US press because in 1901 he captured, by ruse, the President of the First Republic of the Philippines, Emilio Aguinaldo.

Around this event McKinley's administration could finally declare to the American public that the war in the Philippines was officially '*over*'. On 4 July 1902 President Roosevelt would make the same declaration (Zwick 1992: 168).

But the war did not end. Executions of Filipino resistance leaders continued until 1912, when the popular religious leader Felipe Salvador was hanged for 'sedition'[1] (Ileto 1997: 249). Combat went on until 1913, the date of the Battle of Bagsak where US troops took the lives of over five hundred Muslim Filipinos, including women and children, in Mindanao (Hurley 1936: 226–30).

The Bagsak massacre was not the worst atrocity of the war, however. In 1906, four years after the war's 'official' end, 800 US troops under the direction of General Wood massacred over one thousand Moro men, women and children in the volcanic crater of Bud Dajo in Jolo. The Jolo Moros had openly refused US rule, and the American occupation military responded with an advanced State-appropriated war machine – one that would set a precedent for twentieth-century warfare in the form of direct violence against citizens. Resisting Moros fortified themselves in the volcanic crater at the very top of the mountain, armed with krises, spears and a

Figure 9.9: The massacre at Bud Dajo, Mindanao, Philippines, in 1906. Eight hundred US troops killed over one thousand Filipino men, women and children in one day. From Oswald Garrison Villard, *Fighting Years: Memoirs of a Liberal Editor* (Harcourt Brace, 1939).

handful of rifles (Hurley 1936: 179–87). Women and children as well as the men positioned themselves inside simple fortifications within the crater. This practice was completely anachronistic to the kind of technical warfare that US troops were about to launch.

When the massacre was over, officials reported many of the dead to have as many as fifty wounds. There were no survivors of over one thousand Moro men, women and children. Not a single child or woman lived through the siege. US troops had mobilised the latest in war weaponry against civilian resistors who were labelled 'insurgents'. Not only were quick-firing repeating guns used, but heavy artillery was shelled into the crater from such a distance that villagers could neither respond nor flee, but were trapped inside. For those who survived the heavy shelling, Gatling guns, rifle grenades and sharp-shooting rifles were utilised next. Even a light gunboat was mobilised in the massacre of Bud Dajo. Popular 'resistance' would have to take on a whole new form and substance of expression in the face of such an imperialist war machine.[2]

Rapid-firing guns, however, were not the only weapons mobilised in the war for the Philippines. Subjection through technical advances in the media was as devastating as heavy shelling – and had an even longer range than the latest artillery weapons. As Paul Virilio in *War and Cinema* (1989) has argued, technologies of remote perception are a key component to military logistics, which is, by definition, also a logistics of perception in which the media has always played a crucial role (2). According to Virilio's reading, the media *is* the battlefield: 'Since the battlefield has always been a field of perception, the war machine appears to the military commander as an instrument of representation' (20). War is a politics of vision and perception as much as a logistics of weapons and tactics. Against Edison's heroic representation of Funston, Mark Twain depicted a scoundrel, a man of dubious means and ethics who used base treachery to capture Aguinaldo in his satiric essay 'A Defence of General Funston', first published in the *North American Review* in 1902. While his essay did help to pressure President Roosevelt to order an investigation of the use of the 'water cure'[3] and other war atrocities in the Philippines, the ageing Twain and his literary pen were unable to compete with the power of the yellow press and its captivating photographic images, or later with the seductive screen illusions produced by the moving images of the cinema – images heralded by Edison's idealised representations of US imperialist expansion in South-east Asia.

Controlling representations of violence is part of violence. Psychological mystification is a kind of weaponry in itself. Consider, for example, the common public perception in both the USA and the Philippines of General Douglas MacArthur (the son of General Arthur MacArthur) as a Second World War hero in the Philippines. General Douglas MacArthur promised to return and liberate the Philippines after Japanese forces drove out US troops. As the popular narrative goes, the younger MacArthur proved true to his word, returning in force to vanquish Japanese troops and liberate the Filipinos, as he had promised. But the 'liberation' of the Philippines came at a great cost – wreaking the utter destruction of Manila, including the historical district of Intramuros. In the end, the war-torn city suffered more destruction from American shelling than from the Japanese. Thus, while the symbolic implication of MacArthur's return was to signify that the USA did *not* abandon the Philippines during the Second World War, but rather stood loyally behind the country in the face of a hostile invasion from enemy forces, the reality of MacArthur's stance in the Pacific front was to sacrifice Filipino citizens and their cultural heritage for the strategic and tactical needs of maintaining US military positions in South-east Asia. Historically, we have to ask the hard, stark question: would the Japanese have invaded the Philippines at all if the US military bases weren't there? If the USA had granted independence to the Philippines in the 1930s say, or even during the 1920s, as many Filipinos had expected, and removed the US naval bases, would war have come to the Philippines at all?[4]

CONCEPT 3: WAR MACHINE

'What we call a military institution, or army, is not at all the war machine in itself, but the form under which it is appropriated by the State.' (Deleuze and Guattari 1987: 418)

Plateau 3: Balangiga, 28 September 1901 –
The Sacrificial Bride

In spite of McKinley's re-election campaign promises, the war in the Philippines did not end in 1900. After the election, the war dragged on. In a letter home, a US cavalry soldier described a scene he witnessed on 28 September 1901, the day of the Balangiga massacre authorised by General Jake Smith's order to 'make Samar a howling wilderness' (Agoncillo 1990: 229).

187

On this day, there is a bride accompanied by her wedding party. She is walking. It's morning. The sun is shining through the trees along the road to the church. The bridesmaids are chattering. The bride is smiling.

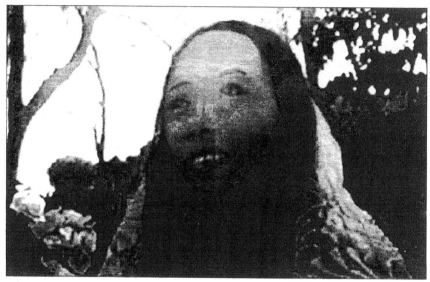

Figure 9.10: The Sacrificial Bride – a reenactment of war violence recounted by a US soldier in a letter home in 1901. Shot on location in the Philippines for *Memories of a Forgotten War* (1999). Co-directed by Camilla Benolirao Griggers and Sari Lluch Dalena.

Figure 9.11: Death of the Bride. From *Memories of a Forgotten War*.

The soldier's company is part of a contingent of forces sent to Samar in retaliation after local bolomen ambushed a troop of US soldiers who had been burning food supplies and killing farm animals. On that morning, the soldier's troop surprises the bride's wedding party on its way to church. The bride is shot (Agoncillo 1990: 229).[5]

By the end of the last Samar slash-and-burn campaign in 1905, five villages had entirely disappeared off the face of the island.

War is war.

In another letter home, a different US soldier described a similar scene.

It was on the 27th of December, the anniversary of my birth, and I shall never forget the scenes I witnessed that day. As we approached the town the word passed along the line that there would be no prisoners taken. It meant we were to shoot every living thing in sight – man, woman or child.

The first shot was fired by the then 1st Sergeant of our company. His target was a mere boy, who was coming down the mountain path into town astride of a carabao. The boy was not struck by the bullet, but that was not the Sergeant's fault. The little Filipino boy slid from the back of his carabao and fled in terror up the mountain side. Half a dozen shots were fired after him.

The shooting now had attracted the villagers, who came out of their homes in alarm, wondering what it all meant. They offered no offense, did not display a weapon, made no hostile movement whatsoever, but they were ruthlessly shot down in cold blood, men, women, and children. The poor natives huddled together or fled in terror. Many were pursued and killed on the spot. Two old men, bearing a white flag and clasping hands like two brothers, approached the lines. Their hair was white. They fairly tottered, they were so feeble under the weight of years. To my horror and that of the other men in the command, the order was given to fire and the two old men were shot down in their tracks. We entered the village. A man who had been on a sickbed appeared at the doorway of his home. He received a bullet in the abdomen and fell dead in the doorway. Dum dum bullets were used in the massacre, but we were not told the name of the bullets. We didn't have to be told. We knew what they were. In another part of the village a mother with a babe at her breast and two young children at her side pleaded for mercy. She feared to leave her home which had just been fired – accidently, I believe. She faced the flames with her children, and not a hand was raised to save her or the little ones. They perished miserably. It was sure death if she left the house – it was death if she remained. She feared the American soldiers, however, worse than the devouring flames. (Cpl. Richard O'Brien, printed in the US Congressional Record, 57:1, 15 May 1902, 5500.) (Cited by Francisco and Fast: 313.)

The entire inhabitants of Samar, estimated at a total population of 266,000, were ordered to 'detention' camps – beds of infectious diseases, starvation and exposure where villagers died in droves. Anyone found outside the camps could be shot on the spot 'no questions asked'. The campaign in Samar was an extermination policy, and it was hardly an exception to the rule. In the same year, General Smith invaded Iloilo, where his troops left behind them a strip of scorched earth sixty miles wide all the way across the island of Panay. The campaign in Batangas that followed Samar was just as brutal (Francisco and Fast 1985: 311–12).

Major General Bell's troops carried out open warfare against 'guerillas' and the peasants who supported them in Batangas, Tayabas, Laguna and Cavite. According to US government officials, 100,000 people died in Batangas as a result of scorched-earth policies. By the next census, one-third of the total population of Batangas had disappeared (Francisco and Fast 1985: 315).

At the turn of the last century, Asia was America's new frontier. And the Filipinos were the 'savages' and 'niggers' of the new empire. After the American Civil War and after the American Indian wars, militarised aggression reached outwards beyond the nation's borders, helping to stabilise national security within by taking racist aggression abroad. 'Hope you will make some "Good Indians" in the hills'; 'Hope you kill some goo-goos'; 'Hope you get some niggers' – American soldiers in the Philippines wrote to one another in the field (Scott 1986: 26). General Samuel Young ordered his men to 'drive these outlaws out or kill them and settle the savages before letting up' (Scott 1986: 26). Even Theodore Roosevelt drew analogies to Native Americans in the growing public debate with anti-imperialists over Pacific expansion: '[If whites were] morally bound to abandon the Philippines, we were also morally bound to abandon Arizona to the Apaches' (Breitbart 1997: 43). While American aggression against Filipinos was represented as democratising and 'civilised', however, Filipino resistance to American aggression was represented as 'uncivilised' and 'barbarous'.

Representing Filipinos as savages was a component of military tactics. Imaging Filipinos as uncivilised would influence debates over the future of the Philippines as a US possession. As in Edison's films, representations in the United States of Filipinos

Figure 9.12: Bontoc Igorot woman on display at the 1904 St Louis World's Fair. Anthropological photographs of semi-nude Filipina tribeswomen manifested the colonial power relations at work in representations of Filipina bodies. US National Archives photo no. 350-p-bb-3-6.6

focused on images that seemed to verify the dark, savage and primitive state of Filipino culture, which in turn rationalised racialised violence against Filipinos. Semi-nude Igorot women in tribal garb were featured at the St Louis World's Fair in 1904, for example, helping to disseminate the perception that Filipinos were primitives. Photos of tribesmen labelled 'headhunters' circulated through the photobooks published during the heyday of travelling journalism and photo-documentation, such as *Harper's History of the War in the Philippines* (Wilcox 1900).

But the reality was that the White Man who carried the 'burden' of his darker brothers was quite capable of his own barbarous violence. Not only was his code of war imperialistic, but often he violated that code. Take the case of the wounded Lieutenant Isabelo Abaya, taken prisoner in Ilocos, as recounted by an American soldier:

I saw one of our non-commissioned officers having a lengthy talk with our officer, and then saw him stop and let the column pass, meanwhile working with his gun as if to clear the magazine. As the stretcher holding Abaya came abreast the non-com, I saw Abaya glance at the non-com and immediately cross himself, for he knew as well as we did that we did not dare to take him in alive. At the same instant the non-com pretended to stumble and fired, immediately killing Abaya. (Scott 1986: 56)

In a landscape in which all resistance was 'insurgency' and insurgency was punishable by death, the best and the brightest of a generation of Filipino men and women were exiled, excommunicated, imprisoned, tortured, hanged, shot, starved and blown up with artillery (Scott 1986: 43). This process of overcoming native resistance by force was called 'pacification'. In an action of classic guerilla warfare foreshadowing Vietnam, villages were burned to the ground, civilian food supplies destroyed, carabao killed, and local economies shut down so that villagers could not supply resources to a general population who might all be potential resisters. Better to burn 25 tons of rice than to let resisters eat. Better to 'shoot all natives who may be found on the road between dark and daybreak' around American telegraph lines and 'cause all houses in the vicinity to be burned to the ground' than to risk the sabotage of communication lines by local villagers night after night (31). Better to hang as spies and traitors those who fed resistance fighters a hot meal, or who transported medical supplies, or who carried a message, or who rang the church bell upon the arrival of troops than to recognise that the entire culture might be resistant to American occupation. The other face of American Manifest Destiny was colonial violence, something that was little recognised or represented at the time, and something that remains remarkably forgotten now in the American cultural psyche.

This failure of memory renders the US schizophrenic in relation to its own foreign policy in the Pacific. The schism comes not in the tactical and strategic implementation of US foreign policy, because military men would never make any bones about their goal in South-east Asia at the beginning of the twentieth century. Their goal was simple and clear: to secure a trade route to China and Japan by positioning US naval bases in Guam, Hawaii and the Philippines. Rather, the schism comes from a failure of memory in terms of how Americans represented their foreign policy to themselves, and out of which they constructed a collective national identity, not as colonisers but as democratisers, not as oppressors but as liberators, not as racist but as universal saviours.

The discourse of insurgency was crucial in the production of this successful anti-memory, carrying out a signifying and subjectivising function for the State-appropriated war machine. 'Insurgent' was a technical term defined by the US military in its code of war during the American Civil War, and was designed to dissuade civilians from resisting military operations. Uniformed members of a defeated army were defined as 'prisoners of war' and guaranteed humane treatment, but other persons who resisted were either 'spies', 'war rebels', 'traitors', or 'insurgents', and were all liable to death by hanging (Scott 1986: 28). When applied in the Native American Wars and in the Philippines, this code launched a practice of guerilla warfare that continued through Vietnam. The code by definition rendered a tactical advantage to US troops. Resistance by a weak people against a powerful army requires

Figure 9.13: Photograph of US soldiers with Filipina women during the Philippine–American War. Courtesy of the American Historical Collection of the Rizal Library, Ateneo de Manila University.

soldiers dressed like farmers, farmers who leave their fields to fight when necessary and who return to them when necessary, civilians who provide food and supplies, and mountain warfare, *guerra de montaña* appropriate for the weak against the powerful. Under such an official State code of war, all options for local resistance available to a minoritarian people without a large standing army was predetermined to be beyond the war 'code', and thus provided legal justification for unveiled violence against resistant civilians. This is the definition of total war, and within this space we find the Filipina as sacrificial bride and mother as she is described in the US soldiers' letters home – the Filipina as civilian war victim in a violent colonial conquest. The public representation of this face of Filipina femininity is of course highly regulated, and would not be found in any of Edison's idealised representations of the war.

On the relation of total war to State capitalism, Deleuze and Guattari state, 'In short, it is at one and the same time that the State apparatus appropriates a war machine, that the war machine takes war as its object, and that war becomes subordinated to the aims of the State' (1987: 418). The distinction here is between the striated, sedentary space of the State and the smooth space of nomadic war machines, whose purpose is 'to destroy the State-form and city-form with which it collides' (418). Once appropriated by the State, the war machine is turned against the nomad and all anti-State factions. The issue is the appropriation of the war machine to the political aims of the State. The emergence of total war can be located here. From their neo-materialist perspective, Deleuze and Guattari assert:

The factors that make State war total war are closely connected to capitalism: it has to do with the investment of constant capital in equipment, industry, and the war economy, and the investment of variable capital in the population in its physical and mental aspects (both as warmaker and as victim of war). Total war is not only a war of annihilation but arises when annihilation takes as its 'center' not only the enemy army, or the enemy State, but the entire population and its economy. The fact that this double investment can be made only under prior conditions of limited war illustrates the irresistible character of the capitalist tendency to develop total war. It is therefore true that total war remains subordinated to State political aims and merely realizes the maximal conditions of the appropriation of the war machine by the State apparatus. (421)

As in all military occupations in which the majority of the population resists, the US colonial war in the Philippines at the end of the nineteenth century was against the people themselves. As in Vietnam, it was a depopulation campaign. People were removed from their villages and subjected to starvation and diseases, non-combatants were terrorised and killed in an attempt to break – in the crudest and most violent forms possible – the actual and natural bonds between local resistance leaders and the people.

US soldiers took few prisoners, and they kept fewer records. By the time the fighting was over in 1913, 1.5 million Filipinos had died of a total population of 6 million.

North Americans like to believe that they haven't a colonial history. Or if they do, that it's somehow better than most. That's what *Goodbye America* was about in the end – about upholding that belief. And that was what Edison's *Colonel Funston on the Baglag River* was about too. It's significant that in both accounts, the sign of that belief is made precisely in the place where such a belief could be the most contested.

CONCEPT 4: MACHINIC ASSEMBLAGE

'The relation between human and machine is based on internal, mutual communication, and no longer on usage or action.' (Deleuze and Guattari 1987: 458)

Plateau 4: 30 June 1997 – Hong Kong 'Turnover'
Plateau 5: 4 June 1989 – Tiananmen Square Massacre

Goodbye America's 1997 release helped to locate the public recollection of the US military withdrawal from the Philippines in simultaneity with another colonial departure of epic dimension – that of the British from Hong Kong on 30 June 1997 – just eleven days before the collapse of the Philippine peso, along with almost every other currency in South-east Asia, on 11 July. Asia of the twenty-first century would be drastically different from the Asia that knew a century of US military domination anchored in military bases in the Philippines, and 156 years of British colonial rule off the coast of mainland China in the island port of Hong Kong.

From its lowly colonial roots as a land base taken by force of arms for British merchants to conduct the illegal import of opium to China, Hong Kong became a hub for Western finance, investment and development in the post-Second World War reconstruction years. No doubt Hong Kong's spectacular rise as an international financial and banking centre in the postwar period was a material effect of the total war that literally flattened two other competing financial centres – Tokyo and Manila. Both cities suffered the utter destruction of new technologies of warfare ironically delivered, in both cases, from US weapons.[7] Tokyo was burned to the ground by US incendiary bombs, while Manila suffered more damage from heavy artillery shelling in MacArthur's aggressive all-or-nothing campaign than any other city in the war except Warsaw. Hong Kong, on the other hand, survived the Pacific front unscathed, quickly transmuting into a capital city for the flow of foreign capital in and out of Asia.

If many in the international banking community wanted to imagine not much would change in Hong Kong after the June 1997 'turnover', however, the June ghosts of Tiananmen Square made them know otherwise. British departure from Hong Kong really began on 4 June 1989, when China's authoritarian police State reacted with force of arms against the million people in the streets blocking the progress of tanks and troops into Tiananmen Square, Beijing, with the world media broadcasting the event globally.[8] After such a brutal display of authoritarian State power, it was clear that the departure of the British from Hong Kong would not just be symbolic. After the globally mediated Tiananmen Square event, prominent members of the Hong Kong banking community began preparations for departure. With the American naval bases withdrawn from the Philippines and the British counting down the clock on its major commercial post in Asia, it seemed Western capital would soon be in retreat, but not without the strategies and tactics of reterritorialisation.

With these two colonial departures occurring in the context of over a decade of consistently high growth among the Asian 'Tiger' economies, the 'global' stage seemed set for Asian countries to redirect the history of the Pacific Rim at the end of the millennium, pursuing development along Asian rather than Western trajectories and interests. Instead, what the Western press labelled a 'contagion' of collapsing currency and stock values seized South-east Asia by mid-1997, causing currencies to devalue overnight in exchange with the US dollar, leaving countries in the morning with two or three times the foreign-debt service of the previous day, or more (Indonesia's rupiah fell 350 per cent by the early months of 1998). The tigers of Asia could be reined in easily on the expandable value of their foreign debt – debt used to fuel rapid and uneven urban development.[9] By the servicing of foreign debt, foreign capital could reterritorialise the entire Asian region, and profit from ever cheaper labour and also gain ownership of local industries through direct foreign-investment initiatives mandated as terms of agreement for IMF bailouts that would not relieve debt, but rather would only help to ensure no immediate discontinuity in debt service.

Like 19 October 1987 crash when the Dow Jones Industrial plunged 508 points, or 23 per cent, causing some $500 billion in losses, the 1997 meltdown in Asian currency and securities values distinguished itself from the 1929 crash that preceded the Great Depression in its electronic speed and global effect. Through computerised networks, the 1987 crash spread internationally to every stock market in the world within 24 hours[10] (Socialist Workers' Party Resolution 1994: 101). The crash of 1987 was a foreshadowing of the global instability that would emerge ten years later, quickly sweeping over South-east Asia and collapsing currency values and markets from Hong Kong to Brazil to Russia, including monumental economies like Japan's, where stocks dropped in value by $242 billion in one week alone (*The New York Times*, 29 August 1998: A1). Eventually, this systemic instability would come home to the USA to ripple the Dow with 500 point drops in value by late August of 1998. By the last week of September Long Term Capital Management collapsed, one of the largest US speculative hedge funds, following the failure of the Russian bailout. Under the leadership of Alan Greenspan, the Chairman of the US Federal Reserve, a consortium of 14 international banks and brokerage firms injected $3.6 billion to keep Long Term Capital from bankruptcy (Morgenson 1998). Two weeks later, with Europeans challenging the supremacy of US domination of the IMF, the US successfully challenged and defeated Japan's proposal to establish a $100 billion Asian Monetary Fund (Wyatt 1998). In the generation of the 'Japan That Can Say No' movement articulated by popular Japanese politician Shintaro Ishihara in 1989, a Japanese-led regional monetary fund would overtly threaten US domination in the Pacific.[11] With the Chinese in Hong Kong, and Asian currencies and stocks collapsing, the US military went back to the Philippines with a Visiting Forces Agreement. The Agreement was signed on 10 February 1999 and put before the Philippine Congress for ratification under severe economic pressure to accept, with the peso only recovered from 44:1 to 38:1 compared to 26:1 before the 1997 crash. (At the end of May 1999, the VFA was ratified.) After only seven brief years since their departure, American aircraft and sea vessels were returning to the Philippines. And the Dow Jones

Industrials and Nasdaq Composite Index began a bull run that would set astonishing records throughout 1999, with the Dow breaking the 11,000 mark even as the US military carried out NATO bombing missions in Yugoslavia, testing new defence weapons against Russian-made anti-aircraft, and sending a strong message to China that the USA was not relinquishing military domination.

In the US press, however, the collapse of South-east Asian currencies and stock markets was represented as either a 'natural' and healthy response of global capital to Asian mismanagement stemming from resistances to free market principles, or as a mutant, viral 'contagion' that, like the deadly Hong Kong chicken flu, had to be properly contained and quarantined – a viral devaluation. Both models obfuscated the role the IMF itself played, and foreign capital in general, in the production of the transregional economic collapse. The IMF did produce a confidential internal report that identified its own policies as exacerbating if not causing the second devasting wave of currency and stock devaluations in Indonesia.[12] But the Western media for the most part traded in headlines about a regional 'pandemic', archaic Asian management styles, cronyism, and payback for Asian pride and protectionist trade policies, for which blame was placed on Asia – not foreign capital investment practices – for the currency and banking collapse.[13] The cover of the 31 May 1998 *New York Times Magazine*, for example, featured the huge heading 'GOING OUT OF BUSINESS SALE!' accompanied by a small globe showing Asia and South-east Asia, followed by the subheading: 'Asian Industries Humbled! Looking for US Investors! Will Acquiesce to American-Style Capitalism!'[14]

With these two 'turnovers', as the Western media named them, British and American colonial reign in the Pacific would have to take new forms and substance of expression – not just a turnover of State, from one State to another, but an enunciative and functional turnover, a transformation from an imperial military machine to a technical subjection machine. America was not about to say goodbye to South-east Asian domination so easily, nor would Britain. The speed of telecommunicated buying and selling of international *values* – demarcated as currencies, stocks, or properties – fed a voracious Western demand for exhorbitant rates of investment return. The technical machine of global banking both created deregulated 'emerging' markets and crashed them in the (dis)organised flow of international capital towards pure profit value.

At the heart of Deleuze and Guattari's concept of machinism in all its technological, social, semiotic and axiological avatars lies the phenomenon of autoproduction, autopoiesis – techne tied to a 'processual opening' (Guattari 1995: 34). This conception of machinism focuses on the 'functional ensemble which associates it with man', on the machine's 'singular power of enunciation', and on the assemblage of multiple components (34). The totality of the machine's components comprises a 'machinic assemblage' (35). The value of the machinic assemblage comes from its autoproductive capacity (39). In such a theory of material production, it is important to distinguish signification (as common currencies of social groups who work with machines) and the a-signifying semiotics of the machinic assemblage itself, which produces 'non-human' expressions, such as equations and diagrammatic plans, functional charts and algorithms and so on (36).

One of the key postulates of Deleuze and Guattari's neo-materialism is the assertion that social formations are defined by machinic processes, and not modes of production (1987: 435). Rather, modes of production depend upon machinic processes. Within this materialist theory, processes of social subjectivisation occur in the *communication* between the human and the machinic. Therefore, it would be an error to consider machinic effects only in terms of human usages. Machinic assemblages produce effects of their own, beyond the human usages designed for them. The role of electronic communications technologies in the Asian economic collapse, for example, cannot be reduced to one of simple human usage within a machine-tool model. The 'tool' here is a complex assemblage of functions and events articulating (autoproducing) effects and events of its own on a machinic ('global') scale.

It is this concept of machinic assemblage that I want to apply to the current condition of women in the Philippines, by which we can see how the Filipina is embedded within a regional machinic enunciation.[15] Filipinas are enmeshed in a machinic assemblage that includes labour, raw materials, real estate, and energy on one level, IMF and Asian Development Bank country charts and development banking algorithms on another level, stock markets, currencies and media images (of political stability/instability for example) on yet another level, along with various investments of desire that constitute different invested subjectivities within this complex, autoproductive landscape. These subjectivities range from international investment houses using computer programs to buy and sell stocks to individual US investors who want a retirement

Figure 9.14: The return of the repressed of local values under 'global' investment practices. A Filipina girl trashpicker. Smoky Mountain garbage dump, Manila. Photograph by Bill Cardoni. Courtesy Bill Cardoni.

home, vacation trips to exotic landscapes, and college educations for their children (to be paid from the high rates of return of a decade of bullish 'emerging markets' investment banking in South-east Asia, South America and Russia), to the impoverished worker in a garment factory in Cebu who struggles to feed and clothe her children and ageing parents.

It is obvious that this machinic assemblage – call it global capital investment – is an imperialist one, preying on developing countries' impoverishment to provide cheaper and cheaper labour for the production of more and more North American value, enunciated in the spectacular rise of the US dollar over all South-east Asian currencies, including the Hong Kong dollar and Japanese yen. Filipinas are caught within this trajectory.

It's important to clarify the assemblage aspect of these economies in order to understand the geo-politics of Filipinas' local relations to the transnational flows of capital. It would be a mistake to confuse machinic effects for individual agencies, both on the side of Filipinas who are victimised and on the side of Americans who perpetrate. Let me start on the side of the perpetrator to clarify this point, and later return to the instance of Filipinas who 'participate' in their own commodification through 'international personal ads' services.[16] The concept of machinic assemblage in this regard suggests Deleuze and Guattari's negation of bourgeois individualism.

The debate over US financier and speculator George Soros' individual role in the devaluation of local Asian values provides an opportunity to distinguish machinic effects from individual domains of agency. From a rhizomatic perspective, Malaysian Prime Minister Mahathir Mohamad's attack on Soros as the cause of the Asian currency devaluation at the time of the 51st annual meeting of the World Bank and IMF in Hong Kong in September 1997 can only be seen as Mahathir Mohamad's nostalgia for a modern notion of individual agency in a milieu of machinic effects of multinational dimension. The belief that one man, even one as powerful as George Soros, could control such a field of machinically orchestrated complexities is highly problematic. This is not to say that Soros had not learned to profit from anticipating the machinic enunciations of global banking practices, or that currency speculators did not contribute their singular role to the assemblage of events that resulted in the development banking collapse of 1997–8, which affected not only the entire Asian region but also South American emerging markets, including Brazil, and later Russia. Soros himself publicly aired his views on the predatory and destabilising mechanisms of laissez-faire ideology when applied to market values in an article entitled, 'The Capitalist Threat', published in *The Atlantic Monthly* in February 1997 – just months before the Asian currency collapse.

Laissez-faire ideology denies the instability and opposes any form of government intervention aimed at preserving stability. [It uses an argument] that goes like this: since regulations are faulty, unregulated markets are perfect. (50)

In the absence of perfect knowledge, however, both free markets and regulations are flawed. Stability can be preserved only if a deliberate effort is made to preserve it. (Soros 1997: 51)

Soros' views are in line with, and probably influenced by, those of Joseph Stiglitz, former chairman of President Clinton's Council of Economic Advisors and currently chief economist and senior vice president at the World Bank. Stiglitz has become perhaps the most prominent vocal critic of free-market economic policies in Asia. His criticism, recounted in an article on the front page of *The New York Times* 'Money and Business' section, is based on the simple premise that unregulated 'free' markets are inefficient because the information available to market participants is imperfect. By this logic, government intervention is not only justified but necessary

(*The New York Times*, 31 May 1998, Sections 3–12). Applying his theory to the current situation in Asia, Stiglitz has openly criticised the IMF's 'austerity' measures on the rationale that higher interest rates do not restore confidence but rather discourage foreign investors and lenders who do not have enough information to distinguish risky from sound investments, while government-spending cutbacks and price increases multiply the damage on local and regional economies, where Filipinas struggle under 'global' systems of value that reterritorialise their local values as cheap labour, entertainment for international tourists, or as commodities for export. This export-based economy maps over the local values of women's labour and social relations, not through a colonial system of slavery but through a technical regime of subjection to electronic capital where the buying and selling of values happens in the accelerated time of milliseconds.

Soros would be the first to admit that global market values 'undermine traditional [i.e., local] values' (1997: 52). On the reality of reflexive feedback mechanisms, Soros stated matter of factly, 'the fiction that people act on the basis of a given set of non-market values has become progressively more difficult to explain' (52). Even the basic laissez-faire principle of supply and demand could no longer be assumed as a given. The crisis in emerging markets and development banking practices in South-east Asia called into question the status of value itself as an economic concept. The currency devaluations were not only region-wide (even Hong Kong succumbed to the 'October attack' on its dollar, and by the centennial of Philippine Independence from Spain on 12 June 1998, the Japanese yen had fallen), but crossed regional boundaries to emerging markets in Brazil and Russia. The 'contagion' was a contagion of signs and values in emerging-market investment banking practices – practices reified by laissez-faire economic principles that rationalised predatory market mechanisms as empirical 'data' and that took (profit) value as a given. The deregulation of Asian markets – in order to open Asia, and by extension Asian women, to the flows of international capital, technology, information and trade – meant opening Asia to predatory investment systems incorporating imperialist ideologies disguised as 'free-trade' development. The system was not driven by market value or by supply and demand and certainly not by local values; it was driven by rate of profit for foreign investors at the expense of internal stability.

terests. "I am friendly, honest, & caring. Seek a person who is loving, friendly, & responsible, age 19 to 34. Please include 1 or 2 nice, good quality photos of yourself."

"Likes: loving, caring, and responsible. Dislikes: irresponsible and dishonest. Ideal man: tall, handsome, understanding, and most of all, honest."

conservative. Typically homebody, nature lover, hospitable. Hobbies: reading, novels, viewing movies & TV programs, strolling." (Same address as RW356.)

compassionate, understanding, loving. He must not drink and smoke, independent, business-minded. Age in a man: 30 to 40 years old."

vider, responsible, who doesn't smoke & drink. He must be a passionate man. I dream to have...a house & car & raise a family." (Same address as RW354).

RW358 Lezlie (27) Tangub City, Philippines/ Lezlie is 5'0 tall, single, & a teacher. She is friendly, frank, understanding, loving & God-fearing. She is seeking a frank person, respectful, humble, loyal, religious, honest in words & deeds. He should be at least 30. "I dislike selfish, self-centered, conceited, alcoholic & dishonest."

RW359 Erika (24) Tagum, Philippines/ Erika is 5'4 & 114 lbs., a saleswoman whose hobbies are cooking, dancing, singing & writing. "I'm a humble type, loving, cheerful. I'm also open-minded about myself. I'm must be 30-45, humble, loving, helpful, open-minded. They told me that foreign people is very nice & gentleman."

RW360 Marilou (26) Bataan, Philippines/ Marilou is 5'1 & 100 pounds. She is a high school graduate who bowls & plays volleyball. "I want to meet a man from overseas to be my future lifetime partner. He must be understanding, loving, caring, at least 30 years old and above. I promise to answer all letters that I will receive."

RW361 Mae (22) Cebu City, Philippines/ Mae works in a bank. She is 5'0 & 96 lbs., a university graduate with a major in accounting. She likes reading, listening to music & playing the piano & organ. "Seek a mature, kind, loving, honest male with good sense of humour, preferably with stable job and nonsmoker, single and Catholic."

RW362 Shelalaine (19) Cebu, Philippines/ Shelalaine is a 5'3, 110 lb., college student. Her interests are reading, singing, hanging-out, & watching movies. "I wish to hear men whose age bracket belongs to 25-40. He should be a Catholic, loving, patient, understanding, never been married, stable and physically fit."

Figure 9.15: RW357–361, *Cherry Blossoms Catalog*, Sept/Oct 1997. Courtesy of Cherry Blossoms.

CONCEPT 5: TECHNICAL MACHINE

'One is not enslaved by the technical machine but rather subjected to it.' (Deleuze and Guattari 457)
'The technical machine is the medium between two subjects.' (458)

Plateau 6: 1974, Cherry Blossoms Catalog founded – The New Global Bride

Within this 'global' system of exchanges, technologies of communication and flows of (imperfect) information manifest a technical machine in which Filipinas' becomings materialise in the international marketplace. Values within this 'global' system are no longer determined by production, but rather by the movements and exchanges of paper capital. Because value is no longer determined by production, workers have little control over the stability of the economies in which they participate. Instead, abstract machinic functions, such as cost–benefit analyses, perform valuations and significations which materialise on the bodies of Filipinas and place them in transnational zones of exchange. In 'Bodies, Letters, Catalogs' (1996), cultural critic Roland Tolentino identifies some of the mechanisms at work in this process.

Beginning with multinationalism, export-processing zones (EPZs) were established by the International Monetary Fund and World Bank (IMF-WB) prescription for Third World industrialization that sought to induce foreign investments. Through the EPZs, the IMF-WB has positioned the

Third World and Third World women in their places, perpetuating its function to oversee their 'development' by marking off the Third World and Third World women in terms of cost-benefit analysis of natural and labor resources. These cost-benefit analyses foreground the direction of multinational capital that collapses national boundaries and homogenizes women's bodies. (1996: 54)

In a milieu in which Filipinas have little control over the international enunciation and circulation of their signs and values, local women are subjected to material transformations of their public and private becomings as their values and signs and bodies enter Western dominated systems of exchange. The public faces of Filipinas – their public enunciations and 'global' identities as that which can be seen on the international market of their histories and experiences and values – emerge materially through an imperialist history of exchanges in which Filipinas are the violent sacrifice, the war prize, the cheap labour and the commodity in an international marketplace.

Immense debt burden and export-oriented development provide the situation of deflated values that drive Filipinas into international migration. Whereas prior to the mid-1980s, most Filipino overseas contract workers (OCWs) were men, since that time about half of all Filipino OCWs are women, seeking their value on the open international market as domestic servants, nurses, entertainment workers, prostitutes and mail-order brides (Chant and McIlwaine 1995: 34, 310). The latest form and substance of expression of reterritorialised Filipina bodies within this technical machine is the internet-order bride. The internet bride business mobilises electronic international marketing and a commodification not only of Filipinas' exoticised gender signs but also of foreign women's domestic labour within the institution of traditional marriage – even as traditional marriages in the USA are on the decline.

Filipinos have a long history of migration to the USA, but the forms of that migration are constantly transmuting. In 1907, when Japanese immigration to the USA was restricted, Hawaiian sugar planters turned to the new colony in the Philippines for cheap labour. Between 1909 and 1931, more than 113,000 Filipinos went to Hawaii, comprising 70 per cent of the plantation workforce by 1932 (Arnett and Matthaei 1996: 236). Women were excluded. The policy of plantation owners was to recruit young, single men, preferably illiterate and rural. The Hawaiian Commissioner of Labor in 1916 bluntly stated the plantation owners' policy,

'Plantations have to view laborers primarily as instruments of production. Their business interests require cheap, not too intelligent, docile unmarried men' (236). Because Filipino men without wives and families were seen as more manageable workers, Filipinas did not fit in the economy of the sugar plantation.[17] The sex ratio in Hawaii in 1910, for example, was ten to one. This policy was true on the mainland as well, where Filipinos were needed for the cheap and manageable labour they provided, while their wives remained at home. In California, only 1,300 of the 24,000 Filipinos who entered the state between 1925 and 1929 were women (241).

Exclusion of Filipinas from entry into US borders would change after the Second World War. Many US servicemen brought Filipina brides home to the USA after the war years, such that by 1960, half of all Filipino immigrants came in as wives of white servicemen (Arnett and Matthaei 1996: 244). In 1947, the War Brides Act eliminated racial discrimination in the war-bride practice established by a 1942 Congressional Act giving foreign veterans the right to naturalise (Arnett and Matthaei 1996: 243). With the War Brides Act, Filipino veterans could now immigrate with their spouses. But as Filipinas' labour and commodified bodies became valued for export on the international market, the Filipina slipped further away from local and even national domestic spaces. Filipinas passed from colonial subjects into a new regime of technical subjection to non-local market values, perhaps best exemplified in the growing flow of Filipina catalogue brides into the USA by the mid-1970s. This gender shift in exported labour materialised through mass-communication technologies functioning as the medium between Filipinas who live in post-colonial poverty zones and first-world American men who, even with meager salaries, have the purchasing capital to afford cheap domestic labour and sexual services in exchange for marriage certificates that promise US citizenship to Filipinas with little economic opportunity at home.

Desirable cheap labour expanded its expression from single rural Filipinos capable of the harshest agricultural stoop labour to single Filipinas capable of providing simultaneous domestic service, sexual entertainment and traditional wifely duties.[18] Buyers transformed from sugar plantation owners to ageing lower and middle-class unmarried US males shopping on the internet. As journalist Robert Draper eloquently put it in an article published in *Gentlemen's Quarterly*, 'The graying, sagging figures who shuffle out of the arrival gates and into the obliging lushness of the Philippines do not constitute the elite of American malehood'

(1998: 228). Asian-American feminist activist Grace Lyu-Vockhausen described these men and their desires more bluntly, 'I consider this an international sex ring. The men who apply, basically they're losers. They cannot make it in this country so they go out and look for women who can be their total slaves' (Arnett and Matthaei 1996: 254). Labour is still cheap in the Philippines, and getting cheaper with the latest currency devaluations. Now, however, labour for export from the Philippines includes not only male construction workers in the Middle East, cheap agricultural labour in Hawaii, and domestic workers in Hong Kong, but a new assemblage of female domestics/sex workers/submissive wives who make their way to the USA through the technical machine of the internet catalogue.

The internet allows American males, who may be old, unattractive and not too successful, and who either can't find US wives or don't want them because of their independence, to buy the devotions of a passive, subdued, often very young and accommodating Filipina bride. Labour and commodity forms merge in a threshold transformation enacted through a series of simple transactions that begin anonymously on the World Wide Web. Within this regime of signs and values, Filipinas become wives and mothers, overseas contract workers, domestic service workers and sex workers in one stroke – called into becoming through the internet and postal systems. The desires and needs of Filipinas and their families are subjected to the substances and forms of expression of the internet shopping mall. The technical machine provides the medium for the transactions involved.

For the first-world man, those transactions include international shopping at the touch of the mouse, contract negotiations with the would-be bride and discipline – during the period prior to marriage and during the first two years of marriage when wives have temporary visas and divorce would mean deportation back to the Philippines. For the third-world woman, transactions look like courtship, negotiations for income often sent back to family members in the Philippines, and a marriage contract. For the catalogue owners, the transactions include free advertising on the World Wide Web and easy international marketing. We should not forget the role that the Hollywood cinema and SkyCable contributes in this system of exchanges by providing the dream fantasies and seductive images of America that lure those young women for whom abject poverty has already taken away their 'choice' to enter into the World Wide Web and the print catalogues as commodities – in spite of the fact that the Philippine government outlawed the mail-order bride practice in 1992 (Chant and McIlwaine 1995: 34). Local legislation had little effect on the 'international personal ads' business, however. *Cherry Blossoms Catalog*, for example, hasn't advertised in the Philippines for more than a decade, but then they don't have to. Filipinas still provide the majority of its photographs (Draper 1998: 230). The reason is local poverty, and that fact is well known by the owners of the catalogues. US journalist Robert Draper interviewed Robert Burrows who owned *Cherry Blossoms* during its high-growth years between 1987 and 1997. When asked why his business had so much response from Filipinas, he replied matter of factly, 'Because there's poverty there' (230).

The power dynamics of these oppressive social relations between Filipinas and US men are further facilitated by internet technologies capable of reaching expanding markets of American and European men who are specifically looking for a third-world woman. J. Bourne, the owner of *Intimate-Liaisons*, gave the following insightful suggestions to e-consumers in his 27 October 1997 advice column (http://www.metagalaxy.com/intimate-liaisons/advice.html).

Some of these ladies are very poor. It would be a very good idea to purchase a few International Reply Coupons (IRCs) and mail them to the lady(ies) after your initial feel me out letter. BUT don't ever send money. Unless you have some 'special' arrangement going where she performs some esoteric sexual act, one common example: sending you hear [sic] panties, nylons, or whatever, taking photos or videos just for you. Some of our members are otherwise married and are members solely for having a lady for those discreet business trips. They don't want to touch the AIDS ridden whores one finds in Bangkok or elsewhere, and some of our ladies are very open-minded.

In a section entitled, 'Some really straightforward advice', Mr Bourne advises clients on how to control the contract proceeding with their prospective mail-order brides to their best advantage.

2. Notice her initial reaction to you and see if she is willing to 'perform' for you. Yes some ladies are shy. But heck if she can't open up during the correspondce [sic] stage then how is she going to come to your hotel room for an afternoon when you have taken the time and expense to travel to say, St Petersburg, Manila or Beijing! And yes friends it always pays to sample the goods first! Martin, on our staff tried 16 ladies when he traveled to their countries to meet them after several months of correspondence, 6 in Manila alone, before he selected

Josefina. So if she is not willing to put out . . . well you'll have to take this into consideration.

3. [. . .] Now this is important: Some of you may just want a simple old fashioned wife. And this is fine as many of our ladies are conservative, religious (particularly from the Philippines) or shy/modest. So disregard this next missive. But some of you want a lady who will fit your needs and fetishes and here's where the following additional advice can help.

a) when writing to a lady and trying to find out if she would be willing to accommodate your desires/fetishes, for example: to wear stiletto heels, nylons and garters around the house or just model for you, don't ask her right away in the first 1 or 2 letters, BUT by the 3rd or 4th go for it. We have found that in the 3rd or 4th letter, you can really open up with her. I suppose this goes for any realionship [sic], but particularly with foreign women, from the Phillipines [sic], and Russia. (China and Korea and some others do not hold to this for some reason). Agaion [sic] this information is relative to our experinces [sic]. So bear this in mind when targeting a particular country. Also, that is another reason why you would want to write to as many ladies as possible.

In spite of the fact that most of the women who list in the catalogues specify age limits, Bourne encourages potential clients to disregard the women's specifications, reminding men that bargaining power lies ultimately in their hands. Everything about these catalogues reminds the men involved that these women are disempowered and dependent – setting the tone for relationships of domination that typically follow the initial correspondences.

Your age really does not matter. Even though many ladies have used an age range as a preference. We have found that this usually does not hold steadfast. It is not uncommon to find beautiful Filipinas married to a man 30 years older than she. Or a fox like my Soon married to a dog like myself. The secret is showing an interest in their culture. Heck, I learned to like Kim chi and now I get a really nice 'desert' [sic] if I mention a simple complementary comment on my lady's cooking. You don't have to be a Nobel prize winner to realize that women from all over the world want a man to pay attention. The difference with a foreign lady from Russia or Asia proper is that they go the extra mile to reciprocate with their numerous charms.

There's no question that the value of Filipina internet-order brides for this market audience has increased in relation to the growth of the women's movement in the USA. Economically dependent and devalued Filipinas are seen as a viable solution to the problem of independent first-world women who have become demanding, self-assertive and presumably too choosy to appreciate the value of these men. Ironically, these overtly exploitative relations are reified in internet-order-bride discourse as a return to 'traditional' values.

One thing is clear, you are far more likely to find a lady who will please you and not give you the level of grief one finds today in American or other Western cultured women. And this goes for Asian and Russian women who have become Americanized by living her [sic] since their early youth. Our research into this has shown that foreign customs are geared more toward loyalty, with the nuclear family being paramount. Yet, one does not have to be an Einstein to figure this out, just look at the comparative divorce rates between the Philippines, China and Russia as compared to the USA. Something is wrong with this picture.

Indeed, something is definitely wrong with this picture. But not exactly what the writer has envisioned as the problem.

Over the course of the century, Filipinas have materialised within the global economy in a lineage that moves from civilian war victims to bar girls and military prostitutes to international sex-tour workers to overseas contract workers to brides for purchase on the international marketplace. Within this system of 'global' values, Filipinas have contributed their hard-earned share to the national economy, including a share of the US$8 billion sent home to the Philippines annually by Filipinos abroad. But the price paid in human terms has been high.

The overt violence of the colonial war years has hardly disappeared from the imperialist relations between Filipina brides and US men. Rather it resurfaces, channelled into other forms of oppression within the private sphere, in the form of battering, abuse, neglect and spousal homicides. This was the case with Emilita Villa, a catalogue bride from Cebu City who had the misfortune to marry Jack Reeves, a US Vietnam veteran who would murder her just as he had his previous two wives.[19] Emilita's family had submitted her picture to *Island Blossoms Catalog*, and had helped select Reeves, who had submitted a photograph ten years out of date, because he sent money to the family. Emilita's older sister later confided to a journalist covering the story that she had encouraged her sister to stay in the marriage when it was obviously in trouble: 'Stay in the marriage,' the older sister admonished her. 'You have a child' (Draper 1998: 283). Emilita's father was a street vendor whose income wasn't enough to support his wife and eight children. Her mother's stroke had left the family with a hospital bill they couldn't pay (232).

In Australia, statistics showed Filipinas were six times more likely to be victims of spousal homicide than Australian women (Draper 1998: 234). Such a study in the USA has yet to be completed.

Against the weight of this history, feminist organisations struggle to build resources of support and to draw public attention to the issue of violence against Filipinas, including the National Organisation of Pan Asian Women, the National Network of Asian-Pacific Women, Asian American Women United, Asian/Pacific Lesbian Network and the Center for the Pacific-Asian Family (Arnett and Matthaei 1996: 255). In 1993 the Asian Women's Shelter in San Francisco successfully lobbied for legislation to grant immigrant

Figure 9.16: Emilita Villa in the November–December 1986 issue of *Island Blossoms Catalog*. Denied permission by Cherry Blossoms, Inc.[20]

women the right to petition for immigration status independently of husbands or sponsors (Arnett and Matthaei 1996: 256). Local feminist production, including media production, will play a crucial role in counterbalancing the effects of globalisation on the lives and bodies of Filipinas who live and work in transnational zones where local values are transformed into international profit. Only locally based value production can prevent the Emilitas of transnational space from being disposable commodities in the global marketplace by providing safety spaces, however nascent, where choice is possible.

NOTES

1. Filipinos who took up arms or advocated armed resistance against the USA, or who gave food or shelter to those who did, were subject to execution according to the military proclamation of 20 December 1900 put into effect by General Arthur MacArthur, which authorised capital punishment for 'insurgency' (Blount 1913: 319–25). In 1902 the Americans imposed a Sedition Law authorising the death penalty or long imprisonment for anyone advocating independence from the USA (Chant and McIlwaine 1995: 236). Many military historians attribute the eventual US victory in the Philippines during the colonial war to these laws.

2. US racism was not just directed at foreign bodies far from home. The Bud Dajo massacre occurred in the same year as the 1906 Atlanta Riots in the Jim Crow South in the USA. During these racially motivated riots, angry whites launched a violent backlash in the streets against emancipated blacks, setting fire to a thriving post-Reconstruction African–American business community and cultural district. See Tera Hunter's discussion of the effects of racial violence on women during the postbellum era in *To 'Joy My Freedom: Southern Black Women's Lives and Labors after the Civil War* (1997).

3. The water cure involved forcing water into the victim's mouth until the stomach was distended. Many did not survive the procedure, used by US troops as a way to gather information from captured 'insurgents'.

4. As it was, the USA granted independence to the Philippines only after the war, in 1946, with Manila in ruins and the country devastated by the violence of modern warfare. Economic dependence, however, was maintained through a series of trade agreements favouring US interests and through the military base agreements.

5. Agoncillo cites Leonard Wolff's recounting of US soldiers' testimonies and press reports regarding the Balangiga massacre in *Little Brown Brother* (1961):

Lieutenant Bissell Thomas of the 35th Infantry was convicted of

211

striking prisoners, one of whom was lying on the ground and bleeding from the mouth. The officer was reprimanded and fined three hundred dollars. Just before Mr Root took office, Robert Collins of the Associated Press was permitted to cable: 'There has been, according to Otis himself and the personal knowledge of everyone here, a perfect orgy of looting and wanton destruction of property.' Private Jones of the 11th Calvalry wrote that his troop, upon encountering a wedding party, fired into the throng killing the bride and two men, and wounding another woman and two children.

6. Note the distress in this Igorot woman's face. Visual anthropologist and filmmaker Marlon Fuentes points out in his film *Bontoc Eulogy* (1995) that Igorots in the 'Philippine Reservation' of the Fair were not allowed to leave the compound, nor were they allowed to return home to the Philippines. Fuentes' grandfather was one of those who never found his way back from the St Louis World's Fair to his homeland or his pregnant wife and family. Fuentes suspects that he died on the reservation.

7. The fact is ironic because the US functions symbolically as a successful model of democracy, while in reality its 'democratisation' follows in the wake of the destruction by its war machine.

8. Australian media critic McKenzie Wark is careful to distinguish between the popular memory and the telesthetic memory of the 'democracy movement' and 'massacre' of Tiananmen Square in *Virtual Geography* (1994). On the differentiation between street truth, mediated truth and official truth, he writes, 'The tactical use of memory in the territory is always a different thing from either the tactical deployment of memory in the media vector or the strategic stockpiling of memory in the official archives and memory crypts of the state. Telesthesis creates quite distinct forms of memory of events when compared to proximate memory' (106).

9. This uneven development is embodied in the rapid overbuilding of commercial high-rises, elite private condominiums and tourist attractions in lieu of health care, education, infrastructure and low-income housing development.

10. Not only is speed a factor in electronic markets, but also agent-operated decision making which is beyond the realm of human values. 'E-commerce' using programmed agents rather than humans is a hot research and development item at IBM Corporation's research labs. A reporter for *Inter@ctive Week* noted, 'Because agents operate at lightning speed, the agent's owners could lose a lot of money or even start a market crash before anyone noticed' (Jones 1998: 32). IBM senior researcher in charge of agent research Jeff Kephart stated, 'The agent economy is evolving quickly today. More and more, business is relying on rules and embedded processes – decisions made

automatically by application talking to application' (Jones 1998: 32).

11. Shintaro Ishihara argued that Japan should no longer acquiesce to US foreign policy and strategic planning, but rather should play its high technology card and take a leadership position with what he called the Pacific Age Newly Industrialised Economies including South Korea, Taiwan, Hong Kong, and Singapore (Shintaro 1991: 61). He also called for greater Japanese military responsibility for regional defence of sea lanes in the Pacific (54).

12. See David Sanger (1998).

13. As if US investors and bankers have no memory of the US savings and loan crash of the 1980s.

14. *The New York Times* wanted US$400 to reproduce this image for academic usage. The cost was too prohibitive to include the image here. Ironically, this American-made representation of the Asian economic crash, even in its secondary usages, is explicitly a commodity for sale in a profit-driven marketplace.

15. The regional enunciations took several forms of expression: if it is time for international investment capital to flee a legacy of overdevelopment in Thailand, it is time to pull out of the Philippines as well, regardless of real differences in the countries' banking practices. Or, if the Indonesian rupiah falls in value, the surrounding currencies must fall as well in order to remain competitive on the international export market.

16. The industry is commonly referred to as 'mail-order bride' services, but catalogue owners disown that label, arguing that they provide 'international personal ads'. Cherry Blossoms Inc. granted permission to reproduce images from their catalogue provided I used the latter language.

17. This premise about the manageability of single Filipino men did not prove entirely true, however. In spite of recruitment policies targeting rural men without families, organised resistance to the harsh working and living conditions on the sugar plantations led to nine strikes among Filipino labourers in Hawaii between 1909 and 1925, causing one plantation owner to write: '[Filipinos were] the most unsatisfactory of any unskilled laborers we ever hired. They were the very essence of independence, taking every advantage to cause the employer trouble' (Arnett and Matthaei 1996: 237).

18. Certainly, this description does not correspond to all marriages that began through international personal ads. But to the extent that this description does correspond to many mandates a critique of the practice.

19. Reeves' war-zone experiences no doubt set the tone of the relation with his Filipina bride. 'When he was in Vietnam,' his half-sister Pat Goodman told me, 'he sent me photos of dead people, women lying there nude' (Draper 1998: 235).

20. Her photograph can be seen in Draper's article in the June 1998 *GQ*.

10

Deleuze's Bergson: Duration, the Virtual and a Politics of the Future

ELIZABETH GROSZ

I. PAST AND FUTURE

There is a paradoxical desire at work in a feminist politics that aspires to change, to innovation, to the future (and it seems clear that any politics that seeks the designation of 'feminist' must have this as a minimal defining condition): to think the new entails some commitment to and use of the past and the present, of what prevails, what is familiar, the self-same. The terms by which something can be judged new, radical or innovative must involve some repetition, and some recognition of the old, such that this new departs from it. How can the new, the radical, the transgressive – the 'post-feminist' – be understood except as a departure from what is, and thus in the terms of what is? This is the general challenge of any political transformation or upheaval, and most especially, that to which feminist, anti-racist and other minoritarian struggles are directed: to somehow generate a new that is not entirely disconnected from or alien to the old, which nevertheless overcomes its problems, its oppressions, conflicts or struggles. Politics is in fact always intimately bound up, in ways that are not always self-recognised, with the question of time, becoming, futurity and the generation of the new.

This question of the new can be readily retranscribed into a set of terms that have their own quite recent feminist history: instead of the production of the new, the question of revolution, of the future feminist upheaval/overthrow of patriarchy, could have been raised. Is this concept, revolution, a term that seemed to flourish in the zeal of the 1960s, an old-fashioned idea, an idea that isn't as 'revolutionary', as provocative of the new, as its heralding discourses (Marxism, socialism, anarchism, feminism) once proclaimed? Is it in fact a short-hand formulation for the *contrary* of revolution or upheaval; that is, predictable transformation, transformation that follows a predetermined or directed goal (the rule of the proletariat, autonomous self-regulation, an equal share for women in social organisation), that is, controlled and directed transformations? Or does revolution or upheaval entail the more disconcerting idea of *un*predictable transformations, upheavals in directions and arenas which cannot be known in advance and whose results are inherently uncertain? This is clearly a dangerous and disconcerting idea, seeing that revolution can carry no guarantees that it will improve the prevailing situation, ameliorate existing conditions, or provide something preferable to what exists now.

Are feminists forced, through a lack of viable alternatives, to accept a more pragmatic, expedient and internal relation to the structures of global patriarchy, corporate capitalism, international racism or local governmental regulation, working within them and accepting their conditions as we struggle against them? Instead of directing feminism to the new, perhaps it should be focusing on living with, and negotiating our way through, the complex and ambiguous structures we inhabit now (as Foucauldian pragmatism implies)? Should feminists, following some of the strategies provided by Gilles Deleuze in his reading of Henri Bergson, to be explored below, give more impetus and energy to reclaiming a concept of futurity, while wrestling it away from the tired discourses and ritualised practices that surround its associated political struggles? Can the notion of the future be severed from a direct connection with the utopian or the atopian? The utopic is (definitionally) conceived as a place, a space with definite contours and features; its inverted other, the atopic, is not a definite place, but rather, a non-place, an indeterminate place, but place and space nonetheless. What Deleuze and, through his innervation and interpretation, Bergson offer is a way of conceptualising the future in the terms most appropriate to its formulation: duration or temporal flow. The new, the future, what is yet to come, is the mutual horizon of both feminist political struggles, and those discourses that are most directed to a pragmatics of action in the world, a philosophy of force and effectivity, such as that offered by the tradition of

William James, John Dewey, Bergson, C. S. Peirce and Deleuze.

It is not clear whether we have a choice between an orientation to the present and the past, which is a directedness towards that which is fixed and inert but nonetheless both grounds and frames our practical needs and actions; and an orientation to the future, in which we are always out of our element, which we can only approach through anticipation, hope, or wish, where we cannot and do not live, yet to which we are drawn even in spite of ourselves. Should feminists focus too strongly on the question of the new, the future, the actualisation of virtualities hitherto undeveloped, they would lose sight of the day-by-day struggles necessary to provide the conditions under which the terms, categories, concepts necessary to think and to make the new can be developed. However, if they were directed only to the pragmatics of day-by-day struggles, they would remain locked within their frame, unable to adequately rise above or displace them, stuck in the immediacy of a present with no aspirations to or pretensions of something different, something better. Without some conception of a new and fresh future, struggles in the present cannot or would not be undertaken or would certainly remain ineffective.

While Deleuze is no feminist, he may prove to be one of the few philosophers committed to the task of thinking the new, of opening up thought and knowledge to the question of the future while nonetheless contesting and providing alternative readings, positions and goals to those of philosophical orthodoxy. His writings on Bergson, who appears throughout Deleuze's writings with a predictable insistence, testify to the ongoing interest he has in the question of futurity and the productivity which may help provide some of the conditions under which we can access and live with a concept of the future open to the potentialities of divergence of the present.[1]

Deleuze's understanding of the pragmatic productivity of thought involves his conception that thought is always generated by problems, for problems function as the provocation for thinking, and it is thought that is manifest, in the various forms that responses to the problem take (which are not always or even usually conceptual in form). Problems can be addressed pictorially (in the visual arts), rhythmically (in music or poetry), spatially (in architecture) as well as graphically (in science) and conceptually (in philosophy). Thought, genuinely innovative thought, as much as radical politics, involves harnessing the power of the virtual. Deleuze's concept of the virtual will be linked with a notion of the future, and thus to the question of the ethics and politics of feminist revolution or dynamic change. This question of revolution, transformation and radical futures seems to be the unspoken heart of feminist politics: feminist politics cannot see itself except as a form of overcoming and transformation, yet the very logic of change, the capacity to initiate a pragmatics of change, is central to its formulation as a political and theoretical practice. The problem is that there is so little work being done under the *aegis* of feminist theory on the question of time and futurity, and so much work, relatively speaking, on the question of time, memory and history. Feminist theory needs to find more adequate resources by which to think the radical openness of the future through new conceptions of duration and becoming if questions fundamentally oriented to the status of the future are not to be understood only in terms of the status and forms of the past.

Bergson's analysis of the entwinement of the pragmatics of perception, scientific knowledge and space, and its disjunction from duration and the pull of the future is the focus of Deleuze's reading, and will be the object of discussion for the bulk of this chapter. His conception of duration may provide some of the more incisive tools for a feminist reconfiguration of time which makes primary the force and pull of the future.

II. PERCEPTION AND ACTION

Deleuze focuses on a number of Bergson's key texts, primarily *Matter and Memory* (1988), *Creative Evolution* (1944), and *The Creative Mind: An Introduction to Metaphysics* (1992), where Bergson develops a position, unique in the history of philosophy, which refigures the relations between objectivism and subjectivism, matter and consciousness, space and duration.[2] Commonly represented as an unrequited metaphysician by a positivist and scientistic philosophical tradition dating from Russell and Whitehead, and largely ignored in the late twentieth century, Bergson poses a peculiar and unexpected combination of vitalist phenomenology, scientific pragmatism and psychophysiological interests that makes his work difficult to classify accurately. Deleuze's reading of Bergson can, for the purposes of this chapter, be divided into three central components: Bergson's understanding of matter and its relation to memory; his account of the relations between past, present and future; and his understanding of the distinction between the virtual and the possible.

Bergson's opening statement in *Matter and Memory*, which defines matter as an aggregate or series of images, makes clear his distinction from both philosophical idealism and materialism. His position encapsulates ingredients of both at the same time:

> Matter, in our view, is an aggregate of 'images'. And by 'image' we mean a certain existence which is more than that which the idealist calls a *representation*, but less than that which the realist calls a *thing* – an existence placed half-way between the 'thing' and the 'representation' . . . the object exists in itself, and, on the other hand, the object is, in itself, pictorial, as we perceive it: the image it is, but a self-existing image. (Bergson 1988: 9–10)

Matter is a multiplicity or aggregate of images. This involves both a realism (insofar as the object exists in itself, independent of any observer) and an idealism (insofar as matter coincides with and resembles its various images). Bergson is drawn to the question of memory because it is to be located at the point of intersection of mind and matter. He defines perception and memory, the key attributes of mind, our modes of access to the present and the past, in operational or pragmatic terms: the present is that which is acting, while the past can be understood as that which no longer acts (Bergson 1988: 68). Perception is linked to nascent or dawning action, action-in-potential. Perception does not fade or recede into the past to produce memory, as is commonly assumed. Rather memory is fundamentally different in kind to perception. While perception is always a mode of linking the present to an immediate future, memory must be regarded as ideational, inactive, virtual. 'The past is only idea, the present is ideo-motor' (1988: 68). Perception propels us towards the real, to space, to objects, to matter, to the future; while memory impels us towards consciousness, to the past, and to duration. If perception directs us to action and thus to objects, then to that extent objects reflect my body's possible actions upon them.

If matter is an aggregate of self-subsisting images, then in the perception of matter there is not a higher order image – the image of an image – but rather, the same images oriented towards the organising force of the image of my body. The difference between matter and perception is not the difference between an object and a subject (which simply begs the question of in what that difference consists), rather, the subject must be understood as a peculiar sort of object, linked to its body's central organising position in framing the rest of matter. My body is one material object among all the

218

others that make up the world. What differentiates my body from other objects is, in the first instance, the way in which the image that is my body has a peculiarly privileged relation to action:

I call *matter* the aggregate of images, and *perception of matter* these same images referred to the eventual action of one particular image, my body. (Bergson 1988: 22)

My body is distinguished from other objects not because it is the privileged location of my consciousness, but because it performs major changes on other objects. As Bergson himself remarks, the images that constitute my perception, and those which constitute the universe are the same images with a different orientation. Those organising the universe subsist in their own indifference to each other, while those organising the body cohere and organise the others. The question governing much of Bergson's writings is the crucial one: how do these two types of images, the universe and the body, the inanimate and the animate, coexist? How can the same images belong to and function within these two quite different types of system, one with a centre, the other without? In other words, what is the relation between mind and matter, and what is the manner of their coexistence?

Bergson sees this relation as one of mutual occupation. Scattered throughout the system of linked images that constitute the material world are living systems, *centres of action*, zones of inde-termination, points where images are capable of mobilising action by subordinating other images to the variations and fluctuations, changes of position and perspective afforded by these centres of action. Life can be defined, through a difference in kind from matter, by the necessity of prolonging a stimulus through a reaction. The more simple the form of life, the more automatic the relation between stimulus and response. In the case of the protozoa, the organs of perception and the organs of movement are one and the same. Reaction seems like a mechanical movement. However, in the case of more complex forms of life, there is interposed both a delay, an uncertainty, between a perceptual reaction and a motor response;[3] and an ever-widening circle of perceptual objects which in potential promise or threaten the organism, which are thus of 'interest' to the organism.

This notion of life, mind and perception as both the organisation of images around an organising nucleus and as the interposition of a temporal delay in stimulus and response distinguishes Bergson's position from any form of humanism or anthropomorphism. Mind or life are not special substances, different in nature to matter. Rather mind or life partake of and live in and as matter. Matter is organised differently in its inorganic and organic forms: this organisation is dependent on the degree of indeterminacy that life exhibits relative to the inertia of matter. It may be for this reason that Bergson develops one of his most breathtaking hypotheses: the brain does not make humans more intelligent than animals; the brain is not the repository of ideas, of mind, of freedom or creativity. It stores nothing, it produces nothing and organises nothing. Yet it is still part of the reason for the possibility of innovation, creativity and freedom insofar as it is the mechanism for the interposition of a delay between stimulus and response, perception and action, the explanation for a capacity for rerouting and reorganisation:

In our opinion . . . the brain is no more than a kind of central telephone exchange: its office is to allow communication or to delay it. It adds nothing to what it receives . . . That is to say that the nervous system is in no sense an apparatus which may serve to fabricate, or even to prepare, representations. Its function is to receive stimulation, to provide motor apparatus, and to present the largest possible number of these apparatuses to a given stimulus. The more it develops, the more numerous and the more distant are the points of space which it brings into relation with ever more complex motor mechanisms. In this way the scope which it allows to our action enlarges: its growing perfection consists in nothing else. (Bergson 1988: 31)

The brain intercedes to reroute perceptual inputs and motor outputs. It links, or does not link, movements of one kind (sensory or perceptual) with another kind (motor). The brain functions, in his conception, not to produce images, or to reflect on them, but rather to put images directed from elsewhere into the context of action – to *dislocate* perception from automatic action. The more developed the organism, the wider in nature are the perceptual or sensory inputs and the broader the range of objects which make up the scope of the organism's action. The brain does not sort images or store them. It inserts a gap or delay between stimulus and response which enables but does not necessitate a direct connection between perception and action. The brain enables multiple, indeterminable connections between what the organism receives (through perception or affection) and how it acts, making possible a genuine freedom from predictability. It is precisely this delay or interval that lifts the organism from the immediacy of its interaction with objects to establish a distance which allows perceptual images to be assessed and served in terms of their interest, utility or expedience for the subject.[4]

The object can be understood to contain both real action, the indiscriminate action of its various features upon whatever surrounds it, and comes into causal connection with it, as well as virtual action, that potential to exert specific effects on a living being of the kind which the being seeks or may interest it. This cerebral delay allows the object's indiscriminate actions on the world to be placed in suspension, and for the living being to see only particular elements of the object:

To obtain this conversion from the virtual to the actual, it would be necessary, not to throw light on the object, but on the contrary, to obscure some of its aspects, to diminish it by the greater part of itself, so that the remainder, instead of being encased in its surroundings as a *thing*, should detach itself from them as a *picture* . . . There is nothing positive here, nothing added to the image, nothing new. The objects merely abandon something of their real action in order to manifest their virtual influence of the living being upon them. (Bergson 1988: 36–7)

The 'zones of indetermination' introduced into the universe by life produce a kind of sieve or filter, which diminishes the full extent of the object's real effects in the world in order to let through its virtual effects. What fills up this cerebral interval, these 'zones of indetermination' that are indices of life, and interposes itself between sensation and action to enrich and complicate both are affections, body-memories (or habit-memory) and pure recollections (duration). By their interposition, they become 'enlivened', and capable of being linked to nascent actions, drawn out of their inertia.

III. MEMORY AND PERCEPTION

Bergson speaks of two different kinds of memory, one bound up with bodily habits, and thus essentially forward-looking insofar as it aims at and resides in the production of an action, the other inherently bound with the past. Habit-memory is about the attainment of habitual goals or aims (driving a car, typing, activities in which the body 'remembers' what it is to do). It has a kind of 'natural' place in the cerebral interval between perception and action for it is the most action-oriented, the most present- and future-seeking of memories from the inert past. Bergson distinguishes this habit-memory from recollection or memory proper, which for him is always spontaneous, tied to a highly particular place, date and situation, unrepeatable and unique, perfect in itself (incapable of developing).[5] If habit-memory is future-oriented, memory proper is always and only directed to the past. Where habit-memory interposes a body-schema between sensation and action, memory proper is directed towards an idea. If the cerebral delay could be indefinitely postponed, Bergson suggests, precise, concrete memory- images would serve to fill the breach. This is precisely what occurs in the case of sleep, which severs perception from action, and more readily tolerates the interposition of memory-images. Movement and action drive the memory-image away.

If memory can be carried along the path to action, it is significant that for Bergson we can also pass in the reverse direction, from movements and actions to memory, a movement which is needed to 'complete' perception of the object, which has been stripped of manifold connections in reality to serve as a point of interest for perception and action. Perception can never be free of memory, and is thus never completely embedded in the present. This movement from the multiple circles of memory must occur if a productive circuit between perception and memory, where each qualifies the other occurs: that is, if there is to be the possibility of a reflective perception or a directed recollection. Bergson thinks this circuit in terms of a return movement from the object to recollection in increasingly concentrated or dilated circles. Memory is fundamentally elastic: it is capable of existing in a more or less contracted or dilated state. The whole of memory is contained within each circuit in concentric degrees of concentration.[6]

IV. PAST AND PRESENT

The present is that which acts and lives, which functions to anticipate an immediate future in action. The present is a form of impending action. The past is that which no longer acts, yet, although it lives a shadowy and fleeting existence, it still is; it is real. The past remains accessible in the form of recollections, either as motor mechanisms in the form of habit-memory, or, more correctly, in the form of image-memories. These memories are the condition of perception in the same way that the past, for Bergson, is a condition of the present. Where the past in itself is powerless, if it can link up to a present perception, it can be mobilised in the course of its impulse to action. In this sense, the present is not purely in itself, self-contained; it straddles both past and present, requiring the past as its precondition, while oriented towards the immediate future. Perception is a measure of virtual action upon things. The present, as that which is oriented to both perception and action, is the threshold of their interaction, and thus the site of duration. For Bergson as for Deleuze, the present functions in the domain of the actual, while the past functions as virtual.

The past cannot be identified with the memory-images which serve to represent or make it useful to us; rather, it is the seed which can actualise itself only in memory. Memory is the present's mode of access to the past. The past is preserved in time, while the memory-image, one of its images or elements, can be selected according to present interests. Just as perception leads me to objects where they are, outside of myself and in space, and just as I perceive affection (which Deleuze would refer to as intensity) where it arises, in my body (Bergson 1988: 57), so too, I recall only by placing myself in the realm of the past, where memory subsists. Memory, the past, is thus, paradoxically, not *in us*, just as perception is not *in us*. Perception takes us outside ourselves, to where objects are (in space); memory takes us to where the past is (in duration).

Bergson seems to problematise a whole series of assumptions regarding our conceptions of the present and the past. We tend to believe that when the present is somehow exhausted or depleted of its current force it somehow slips into the past, where it is stored in the form of memories. It is then replaced by another present. Against this presumption, Bergson suggests that a new present could never replace the old one if the latter did not pass while it is still present. This leads to his postulate of the *simultaneity* of past and present. The past is contemporaneous with the present it has been. They exist at the 'same' time. The past could never exist if it did not coexist with the present of which it is the past:

The past and the present do not denote two successive moments, but two elements which coexist: One is the present, which does not cease to pass, and the other is the past, which does not cease to be but through which all presents pass . . . The past does not follow the present, but on the contrary, is presupposed by it as the pure condition without which it would not pass. In other words, each present goes back to itself as past. (Deleuze 1991b: 59)

Bergson argues that the past would be inaccessible to us altogether if we can gain access to it only through the present and its passing. The only access we have to the past is through a leap into virtuality, through a move into the past itself, seeing that the past is outside us and that we are in it rather than it being located in us.

The past exists, but it is in a state of latency or virtuality. We must place ourselves in it if we are to have recollections, memory-images: and this we do in two movements or phases. First, we place ourselves into the past in general (which can only occur through a certain detachment from the immediacy of the present) and then we place ourselves in a particular region of the past. Bergson conceives of the past in terms of a series of planes or segments, each one representing the whole of the past in a more or less contracted form.[7]

Each segment has its own features although each contains within itself the whole of the past. Memories drawn from various strata may be clustered around idiosyncratic points, 'shining points of memory', as Bergson describes them, which are multiplied to the extent that memory is dilated (Bergson 1988: 171). Depending on the recollection we are seeking, we must jump in at a particular segment; in order to move on to another, we must do so through another leap: 'We have to jump into a chosen region, even if we have to return to the present in order to make another jump, if the recollection sought for gives no response and does not realise itself in a recollection-image' (Deleuze 1989: 99). For Deleuze, this provides a model for Bergson's understanding of our relations to other systems of images as well (and hence Bergson's suitability to Deleuze's analysis of cinema).

It is only through a similar structure that we can detach ourselves from the present to understand linguistic utterances or make conceptual linkages. The structure of the time-image also contains that of the language-image and the thought-image. It is only by throwing ourselves into language as a whole, into the domain of sense in general, that we can understand any utterance; as it is only by leaping into a realm of ideas that we can understand problems.[8] In all three cases, this leap involves landing in different concentrations of the past, language or thought, which nonetheless contain the whole within them in different degrees of expansion or intensity.

Along with the simultaneity or coexistence of each moment of the present with the entirety of the past there are other implications in Bergson's paradoxical account. Each moment carries a virtual past with it; each present must, as it were, pass through the whole of the past. This is what is meant by the past in general: the past does not come after the present has ceased to be, nor does the present somehow move into the past. Rather, it is the past which is the condition of the present, it is only through a pre-existence that the present can come to be. Bergson does not want to deny that succession takes place – one present (and past) replaces another; but such real or actual succession can only take place because of a virtual coexistence of the past and the present, the virtual coexistence of all of the past at each moment of the present. This means that there must be a relation of repetition between each segment, whereby each segment or degree of contraction/dilation is a virtual repetition of the others, not identical, certainly, but a version. The degrees of contraction or dilation which differentiate segments constitute modes of repetition in difference.[9]

V. THE ACTUAL AND THE VIRTUAL

Bergson claims that a distinction between subjective and objective (or, what amounts to the same thing, duration and spatiality) can be formulated in terms of the distinction between the virtual and the actual. Objects, space, the world of the inert, are entirely actual; they contain no elements of the virtual. If everything about matter is real, if it has no virtuality, this means that the object's existence is spatial. The object, while it exists in duration, while it is subject to change, does not reveal more of itself in time: it is 'no more than what it presents to us at any given moment'. By contrast, what duration, memory and consciousness bring to the world is the possibility of an unfolding, a narrative, a hesitation. Not every thing is presented all at once. Matter can be placed on the side of the actual and the real, and mind, life or duration can be placed on the side of the virtual. What life (duration, memory, consciousness) brings to the world is the new, the movement of the actualisation of the virtual, the existence of duration:

Thus the living being essentially has duration; it has duration precisely because it is continuously elaborating what is new and because there is no elaboration without searching, no searching without groping. Time is this very hesitation. (Bergson 1992: 93)

Deleuze devotes a good deal of attention to Bergson's distinction between the two oppositions, between the virtual and the actual, and the possible and the real. In the couples virtual/actual and possible/real, the possible can never be real but may be actual; the virtual precludes the actual, but it must be considered real. Possibilities may be realised (in the future); while virtualities are real (in the past) and may be actualised in the present. Like Bergson, who rejects the possible/real couple in favour of the virtual/actual pair, Deleuze argues that there is a closure in the process of realisation which is opened up in the process of actualisation. The passage from virtual to actual only occurs on the field of duration. In another terminology, thus the process from virtual to actual could be called 'becoming'.

Realisation is governed by two principles, resemblance and limitation. The real not only resembles the possible, it is an exact image, with the addition of the category of existence or reality. Conceptually, in other words, the real and the possible are identical (since, as Kant argued, existence is not a quality or attribute). Moreover, realisation involves the limitation, the narrowing down of possibilities, so that some are rejected and others are selected. The field of the possible is wider than that of the real. Deleuze suggests that implicit in this pairing is a preformism: the real is already preformed in the possible. The possible passes into the real through limitation, the culling of other possibilities. Through resemblance and limitation, the real comes to be seen as *given*:

Everything is already *completely given*: all of the real in the image, in the pseudo-actuality of the possible. Then the sleight of hand becomes obvious: If the real is said to resemble the possible, is this not in fact because the real was expected to come about by its own means, to 'project backwards' a fictitious image of it, and to claim that it was possible at any time before it happened? In fact it is not the real that resembles the possible, it is the possible that resembles the real, because it has been abstracted from the real once made, arbitrarily extracted from the real like a sterile double. (Deleuze 1988: 98)

The possible is both more than but also less than the real. It is more insofar as the real selects from a number of possibles, limiting their ramifying effects; but it is less insofar as it is the real minus existence. Realisation is a process in which creativity and production are no longer possible and cannot thus provide an appropriate model for understanding the innovation and creativity that marks evolutionary change. Making the possible real is simply giving it existence without adding to or modifying its conception. Deleuze asks whether the possible produces the real, or whether the real projects itself backwards to produce the possible? The processes of resemblance and limitation that constitute realisation are, according to Bergson, subject to the philosophical illusion which consists in the belief that there is *less* in the idea of the empty than the full; and less in the concept of disorder than order, where in fact the ideas of nothing and disorder are *more* complicated than of existence and order. To reduce the possible to a pre-existent

226

phantom-like real is in effect to curtail the possibility of thinking the new, of thinking an open future, a future not bound to the present:

[I]ts possibility, which does not precede its reality, will have preceded it once the reality has appeared. The possible is therefore the mirage of the present in the past; and as we know the future will finally constitute a present and the mirage effect is continually being produced, we are convinced that the image of tomorrow is already contained in our actual present, which will be the past of tomorrow, although we did not manage to grasp it. (Bergson 1992: 101)

In *Difference and Repetition* (1994a), Deleuze claims that the virtual must be distinguished from the possible on three counts. First, in talking of the possible rather than the virtual, the status of existence is what is in question. Existence, the acquisition of reality by the possible, can only be understood as both an inexplicable eruption and a system of all or nothing – either it 'has' existence, in which case it is real, or it 'lacks' existence, in which case it is merely possible. But if this is true, then it is hard to see what the difference is between the existent and the non-existent, seeing the possible has all the characteristics of the existent. Existence is generally understood as the occurring in space and time, in a definite situation or context. But given this understanding of the possible, the real seems absolutely indifferent to its context of emergence. By contrast, it is only the reality of the virtual that produces existence in its specific context and space and time of emergence. The actual is contingently produced from the virtual.

Second, if the possible is thought in place of the virtual, difference can only be understood as restriction, the difference between the possible and the real, a difference of degree not kind. The possible refers to a notion of identity which the virtual renders problematic, the self-identity of the image, which remains the same whether possible or real.

Third, the possible, as already discussed, is produced by virtue of resemblance, while the virtual never resembles the real that it actualises. It is in this sense that actualisation is a process of creation that resists both a logic of identity and a logic of resemblance to substitute a movement of differentiation, divergence and innovation (see Deleuze 1994a: 211–12).

The possible must be in excess of this restrictive understanding, for it makes both a reality which corresponds to it possible, and also makes possible the projecting back of the present reality into a modality of the past.[10] A different, more positive sense is required to add the dimension of creativity and productivity to this otherwise smooth transition from the possible to the real.

Actualisation is a process of genuine creativity and innovation, the production of singularity or individuation. Where the possible/real relation is regulated by resemblance and limitation, the virtual/actual relation is governed by the principles of difference and creation. For the virtual to become actual, it must create the conditions for actualisation. The actual in no way resembles the virtual; rather, the actual is produced through a mode of differentiation from the virtual. Actualisation involves the creation of heterogeneous terms, for the lines of actualisation are divergent, creating multiplicities and varieties. This is a movement of the emanation of a multiplicity from a virtual unity, divergent paths of development in different series and directions.

The movement from a virtual unity to an actual multiplicity requires a leap of innovation or creativity, surprise. Realisation is the concretisation of a pre-existent plan or programme; by contrast, actualisation is the opening up of the virtual to what befalls it. Indeed, this is what life, *élan vital*, is of necessity: a movement of differentiation of virtualities in the light of the contingencies that befall it.

If there is a movement of differentiation from a virtual unity, the unity of the past as a whole contracted in different degrees in the process of actualisation, Deleuze (unlike Bergson at this point) suggests that there is also a complementary movement from the actual multiplicity to the virtual underlying it: 'The real is not only that which is cut out according to natural articulations or differences in kind; it is also that which intersects again along paths converging toward the same ideal or virtual point' (Deleuze 1988: 29). This point of convergence, reconfiguring the movements of divergence and differentiation that made a process of actualisation of the virtual occur, is the point at which memory is reinserted into perception, the point at which the actual object (re)meets its virtual counterpart.[11]

Insofar as time, matter, history, change and the future need to be reviewed in the light of this Bergsonian disordering, perhaps the openendedness of the concept of the virtual may prove central in reinvigorating the notion of a transgressive, radical future, a political future without specification, by refusing to tie it to the realisation of possibilities (the following of a plan) and linking it to the unpredictable actualisation of virtualities. This understanding of virtuality as the impetus for incipient action is itself a dynamising concept, one which may serve feminist, anti-racist and other political movements by making clear that there is always a leap, an unexpectedness that the new brings with it, and that it is the goal of politics to initiate such leaps, precisely without a clear plan in mind. This leap, like the very gap between perception and action, is the movement by which paths of divergence and bifurcation, the impetus of the virtual in the actual, bring about the new. This leap is the one that feminism, and any political discourse committed to change, must both entice and theorise. But its extraordinary elusiveness – in a sense nothing is more intangible than the future – means that the theoretical resources needed to be open to futurity must be chosen with care. Bergson, and following him Deleuze, provide some of the more subtle and complex tools by which to raise the future to a living question, a problem, if not the problem, that politics seeks to address.

VI. FEMINIST FUTURES?

Historical research is commonly based on the belief that we can learn from the past, and by reflecting on it, we can improve the present. The past is fundamentally like the present, and insofar as this similarity continues, the past will provide a pre-eminent source for the solution of contemporary problems. The more and the better we understand the past, the more well armed we are to face a future which is to a large extent a copy or reformulation – the variation on a theme (e.g., the continuity of patriarchy) – of historical events. It is for this reason that memory has tended to be cultivated, as the art, and scholarship appropriate to memorialise the past.

It is precisely such a view that Bergson, and Deleuze's reading of him, problematises. Such a view of history can at best understand the present in terms of realisation, and can only see the future in terms of tendencies and features of the present. The future can only be understood as a prospective projection of the present. This produces a predictable future, a future in which the present can still recognise itself, instead of a future open to contingency and to transformation. What is needed in place of such a memorial history is the idea of a history of singularity and, particularly, a history that defies repeatability or generalisation. Only such a history would be commensurate with a politics directed to the pragmatics of change. Such a history, through its repetitions and traces, is

229

mobilised not by bringing out the resonances, structures or regularities of historical processes and events, but to bring out the latencies, the potentiality of the future to be otherwise than the present.

What Bergson's understanding of duration provides is an understanding of how the future, as much as the present and past, is bound up with the movement and impetus of life, struggle and politics. While duration entails the coexistence of the present with the past, it also entails the continual elaboration of the new, the openness of things (including life) to what befalls them. This is what time *is* if it is anything at all: not simply mechanical repetition, the causal effects of objects on objects, but the indeterminate, the unfolding and emergence of the new:

[T]ime is what hinders everything from being given at once. It retards, or rather it is retardation. It must, therefore, be elaboration. Would it not then be a vehicle of creation and of choice? Would not the existence of time prove that there is indetermination in things? Would not time be that indetermination itself? (Bergson 1992: 93)

What Bergson, through Deleuze, shows is that life and duration, and thus history and politics, are never either a matter of unfolding an already worked out blueprint, or the gradual accretion of qualities which progress stage by stage or piecemeal over time. Duration proceeds not through the accumulation of information and the growing acquisition of knowledge, but through division, bifurcation, dissociation – by difference, through sudden and unpredictable change, which overtakes us with its surprise. Duration differs from itself while matter retains self-identity. It is the insertion of duration into matter that produces movement; it is the confrontation of duration with matter as its obstacle that produces the impetus for action, which is also the impetus to innovation and change, evolution and development.

What relevance do these rather abstract reflections on duration have for feminist theory? They may have (at least) one major implication. That unless feminist theory becomes more self-aware of the intellectual and political resources it relies on, and the potentialities of these resources to produce the impetus to propel the present into a future not entirely contained by it, it risks being stuck in political strategies and conceptual dilemmas that are more appropriate to the past than the future. Unless it is capable of thinking the complexities of time and becoming, which involves a careful consideration of the ways in which the past, present and future are entwined, it risks losing its practical efficacy as a politics of the future. Bergsonism, of the kind elaborated and developed in Deleuze's writing, may serve as a crucial guide for feminist theory to develop a more nuanced and subtle understanding of the intrications of matter and mind, time and becoming, history and the future.

NOTES

1. There are only a few authors who seem to take seriously the degree of Deleuze's commitment to Bergsonism. See, in particular, Ronald Bogue (1989), *Deleuze and Guattari*; Paul Douglass (1992), 'Bergson's Deleuze: Bergson Redux'; Michael Hardt (1993), *Gilles Deleuze: An Apprenticeship in Philosophy*; and Brian Massumi (1992), *A User's Guide to* Capitalism and Schizophrenia: *Deviations from Deleuze and Guattari.*

2. Deleuze's reading of Bergson is not confined to the text specifically devoted to him, *Bergsonism* (1991b), but is developed, often in scattered references to virtuality and the intuition in *Cinema 2: The Time-Image* (1989); *Difference and Repetition* (1994a); and, with Félix Guattari, *What is Philosophy?* (1994).

3. Bergson's claim seems to be that the more complex the form of life, the more unpredictable the response, the more interposing the delay or gap:

   In a word, the more immediate the reaction is compelled to be, the more must perception resemble a mere contact; and the complete process of perception and of reaction can then hardly be distinguished from a mechanical impulsion followed by a necessary movement. But in the measure of that the reaction becomes more uncertain, and allows more room for suspense, does the distance increase at which the animal is sensible of the action of that which interests it. By sight, by hearing, it enters into relation with an ever greater number of things, and is subject to more and more distant influences; and, whether these objects promise an advantage or threaten a danger, both promises and threats defer the date of their fulfilment. The degree of independence of which a living being is master, or, as we shall say, the zone of indetermination which surrounds its activity, allows, then, of an a priori estimate of the number and distance of the things with which it is in relation. (1988: 32)

4. By way of confirmation, Bergson claims that this principle of action indicates that perception is not primarily epistemic in its orientation, aimed at providing or securing knowledge, but at movement and change:

   But, if the nervous system is thus constructed, from one end of the animal series to the other, in view of an action which is less and less necessary, must we not think that perception, of which the progress is regulated by that of the nervous system, is also entirely directed toward action, and not toward pure knowledge? (Bergson 1988: 31)

5. Bergson suggests that it makes perfect sense for a dog, for example, to be bound up with habit-memory, which has potentially immediate effects. The dog may also have access to memory- images, 'pure memory', but it makes no sense to see the animal detaching from its immediate present to make creative use of them:

When a dog welcomes his master, barking and wagging his tail, he certainly recognizes him; but does this recognition imply the evocation of a past image and the comparison of that image with the present perception? Does it not rather consist in the animal's consciousness of a certain special attitude adopted by his body, an attitude which has been gradually built up by his familiar relations with his master, and which the mere perception of his master now calls forth in him mechanically? We must not go too far; even in the animal it is possible that vague images of the past overflow into the present perception; we can even conceive that its entire past is virtually indicated in its consciousness; but this past does not interest the animal enough to detach it from the fascinating present, and its recognition must be rather lived than thought. (Bergson 1988: 82)

6. See Figure 1 from Bergson 1988: 105.

7. The present can be understood on such a model as an infinitely contracted moment of the past, the point where the past intersects most directly with the body. It is for this reason that the present is able to pass.

8. [T]his time-image extends naturally into a language-image, and a thought-image. What the past is to time, sense is to language and idea to thought. Sense as past of language is the form of its pre-existence, that which we place ourselves in at once in order to understand images of sentences, to distinguish the images of words and even phonemes that we hear. It is therefore organized in coexisting circles, sheets or regions, between which we choose according to actual auditory signs which are grasped in a confused way. Similarly, we place ourselves initially in the idea; we jump into one of its circles in order to form images which correspond to the actual quest. (Deleuze 1989: 99–100)

9. In Deleuze's reading Bergson systematically develops a series of para-doxes regarding the past and present which run counter to a more common, everyday understanding. They are:

1. we place ourselves at once, in a leap, in the ontological element of the past (paradox of the leap); 2. there is a difference in kind between the present and the past (paradox of Being); 3. the past does not follow the present that it has been, but coexists with it (paradox of coexistence); 4. what coexists with each present is the whole of the past, integrally, on various levels of contraction and relaxation (*détente*) (paradox of psychic repetition). (Deleuze 1988: 61–2)

These Bergsonian paradoxes, which are only paradoxical if duration is represented on the model of space, are all, Deleuze claims, a critique of more ordinary theories of memory, whose propositions include:

(1) we can reconstitute the past with the present; (2) we pass gradually from the one to the other; (3) that they are distinguished by a before and an after; and (4) that the work of the mind is carried out by the addition of elements (rather than by changes of level, genuine jumps, the reworking of systems). (Deleuze 1988: 61–2)

10. For Bergson,

One might as well claim that the man in flesh and blood comes from the materialization of his image seen in the mirror, because in that real is everything to be found in this virtual image with, in addition, the solidity which makes it possible to touch it. But the truth is that more is needed here to obtain the virtual than is necessary for the real, more of the image of the man than for the man himself, for the image of the man will not be portrayed if the man is not first produced, and in addition one has to have the mirror. (Bergson 1992: 102)

11. Deleuze wants to make this moment of convergence central to his understanding of what he calls the 'crystal structure' of the time-image in cinema. The crystal-image is the coalescence of an actual image with 'its' virtual image, a two-sided image, with one face in perception, and thus directed towards the present, the actual, while the other is steeped in recollection, in the past, the virtual:

What constitutes the crystal-image is the most fundamental operation of time: since the past is constituted not after the present that it was but at the same time, time has to split itself in two at each moment as present and past which differ from each other in nature, or, what amounts to the same thing, it has to split the present in two heterogeneous directions, one of which is launched towards the future while the other falls into the past . . . In fact the crystal constantly exchanges the two distinct images which constitute the actual image of the present which passes and the virtual image of the past which is preserved:

233

distinct and yet indiscernible, and all the more indiscernible because distinct, because we do not know which is one and which is the other. (Deleuze 1989: 81)

The crystal-image, a central mechanism in modernist cinema, is of the very essence of time: it is duration itself which splits every image into a duality of actual and real. It is this duality of the image, the fact that as it is created each image is placed simultaneously in time (duration) and space (the present), that is the very mark of its temporal existence. The past can in this sense be seen as a dilated present, while the present can be regarded as an extremely contracted form of memory. The actual contracts virtual states within itself, and, similarly, the virtual dilates the actual. (See Massumi 1992: 63–4.)

Notes on Contributors

Rosi Braidotti is Professor and Chair of women's studies and Director of the Netherlands Research School of Women's Studies at Utrecht University. Her publications include *Patterns of Dissonance* (1991) and *Nomadic Subjects* (1994). She has also co-authored *Women, the Environment and Sustainable Development* (1994) and edited, with Nina Lykke, *Between Monsters, Goddesses and Cyborgs* (1996). She has published extensively on feminist theory, poststructuralism and psychoanalysis.

Claire Colebrook teaches at the Centre for Comparative Literature and Cultural Studies at Monash University in Melbourne. She has published articles on William Blake, feminist ethics, Heidegger, Foucault, Derrida, Irigaray, and philosophy and literature. Her book *New Literary Histories* (1997) examined the relationship between poststructuralism and new historicism. *Representation and Ethics* (1999) concerns the relationship between political representation and representation in language. She is currently completing a third book on irony.

Verena Andermatt Conley teaches in the Literature Program at Harvard University. Her publications include *Hélène Cixous: Writing the Feminine* (1984 and 1991). She has also published an edited volume, *Rethinking Technologies* (1993) and *Ecopolitics: The Environment in Poststructuralist Thought* (1997). She is currently working on problems of transformations of space in contemporary culture.

Catherine Driscoll lectures in English and Cultural Studies at the University of Adelaide. Her research and teaching interests bring together feminism, youth studies, modernism, and late modern history and philosophy. Her current research combines all of these in the book *Girls: Feminine Adolescence in Popular Culture and Cultural Theory*.

Jerry Aline Flieger is Professor of Comparative Literature at Rutgers University, where she also teaches theory, cultural studies and women's studies. She is the author of *The Purloined Punch Line: Freud's Comic Theory and the Postmodern Text* (1990), and *Colette and the Fantom Subject of Autobiography* (1991). She is completing a book on psychoanalytic theory at the millennium (*Is Oedipus Online? Siting Freud in Millennial Culture*), which will appear in 2000.

Camilla Benolirao Griggers is the Director of Women's Studies at Carlow College in Pittsburgh. She is the author of *Becoming-Woman* (University of Minnesota Press, 1997) and founding editor of the e-journal *Cultronix* on the World Wide Web. She has produced and directed several videos including *Alienations of the Mother Tongue* (1995) and *The Micropolitics of Biopsychiatry* (1996). She is currently completing a documentary on the Philippine–American War of 1899 entitled *Memories of a Forgotten War*, for which she has received a Pennsylvania Council of the Arts Media Fellowship.

Elizabeth Grosz is the author of *Sexual Subversions: Three French Feminists* (1989), *Jacques Lacan* (1990), *Volatile Bodies* (1994) and *Space, Time and Perversion* (1995). She has also edited and co-edited several anthologies on feminist theory. She is currently working on architectural theory.

Eleanor Kaufman is a fellow at the Society for the Humanities at Cornell University. She is co-editor of *Deleuze and Guattari: New Mappings in Politics, Philosophy, and Culture* (1998).

Dorothea Olkowski is Associate Professor of Philosophy at the University of Colorado, Colorado Springs, where she founded the Women's Studies Program and served as its Director until 1995. She is the author of *Gilles Deleuze and the Ruin of Representation* (1999) and co-editor with Constantin V. Boundas of *Gilles Deleuze and the Theater of Philosophy* (1994).

Nicole Shukin is a doctoral student in the Department of English at the University of Alberta, Canada. She is currently researching theories of representation and the animal.

Works Cited

Acker, Kathy (1987), *Blood and Guts in High School, Plus Two*, London: Pan Books.

Agoncillo, Teodoro (1990), *History of the Filipino People*, 8th edn, Quezon City: Garotech Publishing.

Amis, Martin (1987), *Einstein's Monsters*, London: Penguin.

Arbus, Diana (1972), *Diana Arbus*, New York: Millerton.

Arnett, Teresa and Julie Matthaei (1996), *Race, Gender and Work: A Multi-cultural Economic History of Women in the United States*, Boston: South End Press.

Atwood, Margaret (1985), *The Handmaid's Tale*, Toronto: Seal Books.

Bair, D. (1986), 'Simone de Beauvoir: Politics, Language, and Feminist Identity', *Yale French Studies–Simone de Beauvoir: Witness to a Century*, 72, pp. 149–62.

Balsamo, Anne (1996), 'Panic Postmodernism and the Disappearance of the Body', *Technologies of the Gendered Body: Reading Cyborg Women*, Durham and London: Duke University Press.

Barr, Marleen S. (1993), *Lost in Space: Probing Feminist Science Fiction and Beyond*, Chapel Hill: University of North Carolina Press.

Bataille, Georges (1957), *L'Érotisme*, Paris: Union Générale d'Éditions, 10/18, 1974.

Baudrillard, Jean (1995), *The Gulf War did not Take Place*, Sydney: Power Publications.

Beauvoir, Simone de (1964), *The Blood of Others*, trans. Yvonne Moyse and Roger Senhouse, Harmondsworth: Penguin.

Beauvoir, Simone de (1966), *A Very Easy Death*, trans. Patrick O'Brien, New York: Putnam.

Beauvoir, Simone de (1972), *The Second Sex*, trans. and ed. H. M. Parshley, Harmondsworth: Penguin.

Benhabib, Seyla (1995), 'Feminism and Postmodernism: An Uneasy Alliance', in Linda Nicholson (ed.), *Feminist Contentions: A Philosophical Exchange*, New York: Routledge.

Bergson, Henri (1944), *Creative Evolution*, trans. Arthur Mitchell, New York: Random House.

Bergson, Henri (1988), *Matter and Memory*, trans. N. M. Paul and W. S. Palmer, New York: Zone Books.

Bergson, Henri (1992), *The Creative Mind: An Introduction to Metaphysics*, trans. Mabelle L. Andison, New York: Citadel Press.

237

Works Cited

Blanchot, Maurice (1969), *L'Entretien Infini*, Paris: Gallimard.
Blount, James (1913), *American Occupation of the Philippines 1898/1912*, New York: G. P. Putnam and Sons.
Bogue, Ronald (1989), *Deleuze and Guattari*, New York: Routledge.
Bordo, Susan (1995), *Unbearable Weight: Feminism: Western Culture and the Body*, Berkeley: University of California Press.
Boundas, Constantin V. (1993), 'Introduction', in C. V. Boundas (ed.), *The Deleuze Reader*, New York: Columbia University Press.
Boundas, Constantin V. (1996), 'Deleuze-Bergson: An Ontology of the Virtual', in Paul Patton (ed.), *Deleuze: A Critical Reader*, Oxford: Blackwell.
Bourne, J. (1997), *Intimate-Liaisons* (http://www.metagalaxy.com/intimate-liaisons/advice.html).
Braidotti, Rosi (1989), 'The Politics of Ontological Difference', Teresa Brennan (ed.), in *Between Feminism and Psychoanalysis*, London: Routledge.
Braidotti, Rosi (1991), *Patterns of Dissonance*, trans. Elizabeth Guild, Cambridge: Polity Press.
Braidotti, Rosi (1994a), 'Toward a New Nomadism: Feminist Deleuzian Tracks; or Metaphysics and Metabolism', in Constantin V. Boundas and Dorothea Olkowski (eds), *Gilles Deleuze and the Theater of Philosophy*, New York: Routledge.
Braidotti, Rosi (1994b), *Nomadic Subjects: Embodiment and Sexual Difference in Contemporary Feminist Theory*, New York: Columbia University Press.
Brecht, Bertold (1978), 'On Music and Gest', in *Brecht on Theatre: The Development of an Aesthetic*, trans. John Willett, London: Methuen.
Breitbart, Eric (1997), *A World on Display: Photographs from the St Louis World's Fair, 1904*, Albuquerque: University of New Mexico Press.
Brossard, Nicole (1990), 'Corps d'énergie/Rituels d'écriture', trans. Alice Parker, *Public 3*, Public Access Collective.
Buchanan, Ian (1997), 'The Problem of the Body in Deleuze and Guattari, Or, What Can a Body Do?', *Body and Society*, 3.3, September, pp. 73–91.
Butler, Judith (1987), *Subjects of Desire: Hegelian Reflections in Twentieth-Century France*, New York: Columbia University Press.
Butler, Judith (1990), *Gender Trouble: Feminism and the Subversion of Identity*, New York: Routledge.
Butler, Judith (1993), *Bodies That Matter: On the Discursive Limits of 'Sex'*, New York: Routledge.
Butler, Judith (1997), *The Psychic Life of Power: Theories in Subjection*, Stanford, CA: Stanford University Press.
Canguilhem, Georges (1966), *Le normal et le pathologique*, Paris: Presses Universitaires de France.
Carroll, Lewis (1978), *Alice's Adventures in Wonderland and Through the Looking Glass*, London: Octopus Books.
Carter, Angela (1981), *The Bloody Chamber and Other Stories*, Harmondsworth: Penguin.
Castells, Manuel (1996), *The Rise of the Network Society*, Cambridge: Blackwell.
Chant, Sylvia and Cathy McIlwaine (1995), *Women of a Lesser Cost: Female Labour, Foreign Exchange and Philippine Development*, London: Pluto Press.
Chanter, Tina (1995), *Ethics of Eros, Irigaray's Rewriting of the Philosophers*, New York: Routledge.
Chodorow, Nancy (1978), *The Reproduction of Mothering: Psychoanalysis and the Sociology of Gender*, Berkeley: University of California Press.
Chow, Rey (1993), *Writing Diaspora: Tactics of Intervention in Contemporary Cultural Studies*, Bloomington: Indiana University Press.

Cixous, Hélène (1974a), *Prénoms de personne*, Paris: Seuil.
Cixous, Hélène (1974b), 'Character of Character', trans. Keith Cohen, *New Literary History*, 5 (Winter), pp. 384–402.
Cixous, Hélène (1975), 'Sorties' in *La Jeune Née*, Paris: Union d'Editions Générales, 10/18, trans. Betsy Wing (1986), *The Newly Born Woman*, Minneapolis: University of Minnesota Press.
Cixous, Hélène (1991), 'Interview with Hélène Cixous', in Verena Andermatt Conley, *Writing the Feminine*, Nebraska: University of Nebraska Press, pp. 163–78.
Corea, Gena. (1985), *The Mother Machine: Reproductive Technologies from Artificial Insemination to Artificial Womb*, New York: Harper and Row.
Cornell, Drucilla (1991), *Beyond Accommodation: Ethical Feminism, Deconstruction and the Law*, New York: Routledge.
Cornell, Drucilla (1992), *The Philosophy of the Limit*, New York: Routledge.
Cornell, Drucilla (1996), 'Enabling Paradoxes: Gender Difference and Systems Theory', *New Literary History*, 27.2 (Spring), pp. 185–97.
Creed, Barbara (1993), *The Monstrous Feminine: Film, Feminism, Psychoanalysis*, London, New York: Routledge.
De Landa, Manuel (1997), *A Thousand Years of Non-Linear History*, New York: Zone Books.
Deleuze, Gilles (1953), *Empirisme et subjectivité: Essai sur la nature humaine selon Hume*, Paris: PUF.
Deleuze, Gilles (1972), *Proust and Signs*, trans. Richard Howard, New York: George Braziller.
Deleuze, Gilles (1983), *Nietzsche and Philosophy*, trans. Hugh Tomlinson, London: Athlone.
Deleuze, Gilles (1988), *Foucault*, trans. Sean Hand, London: Athlone.
Deleuze, Gilles (1989), *Cinema 2: The Time-Image*, trans. Hugh Tomlinson and Robert Galeta, London: Athlone.
Deleuze, Gilles (1990a), *Pourparlers*, Paris: Minuit.
Deleuze, Gilles (1990b), *The Logic of Sense*, trans. Mark Lester, Constantin V. Boundas (ed.), New York: Columbia University Press.
Deleuze, Gilles (1991a), *Empiricism and Subjectivity: An Essay on Hume's Theory of Human Nature*, trans. Constantin V. Boundas, New York: Columbia University Press.
Deleuze, Gilles (1991b), *Bergsonism*, trans. Hugh Tomlinson and Barbara Habberjam, New York: Zone Books.
Deleuze, Gilles (1992), *Expressionism in Philosophy: Spinoza*, trans. Martin Joughin, New York: Zone Books.
Deleuze, Gilles (1993), *The Fold: Leibniz and the Baroque*, trans. Tom Conley, Minneapolis: University of Minnesota Press.
Deleuze, Gilles (1994a), *Difference and Repetition*, trans. Paul Patton, New York: Columbia University Press.
Deleuze, Gilles (1994b), *Critique et clinique*, Paris: Minuit.
Deleuze, Gilles (1997), *Essays Critical and Clinical*, trans. Daniel W. Smith and Michael A. Greco, Minnesota: University of Minnesota Press.
Deleuze, Gilles and Félix Guattari (1977), *Anti-Oedipus: Capitalism and Schizophrenia*, trans. Robert Hurley, Mark Seem and Helen R. Lane, New York: Viking Press.
Deleuze, Gilles and Félix Guattari (1986), *Kafka: Toward a Minor Literature*, trans. Dana Polan, Minneapolis: University of Minnesota Press.
Deleuze, Gilles and Félix Guattari (1987), *A Thousand Plateaus: Capitalism and Schizophrenia*, trans. Brian Massumi, London: The Athlone Press.

Deleuze, Gilles and Félix Guattari (1994), *What is Philosophy?* trans. Hugh Tomlinson and Graham Burchill, London: Verso.

Deleuze, Gilles and Claire Parnet (1987), *Dialogues*, trans. Hugh Tomlinson and Barbara Habberjam, New York: Columbia University Press.

Derrida, Jacques (1976a), *Writing and Difference*, trans. Alan Bass, London: Routledge.

Derrida, Jacques (1976b), *Of Grammatology*, trans. Gayatri Chakravorty Spivak, Baltimore: Johns Hopkins University Press.

Derrida, Jacques (1983), 'Geschlecht: Sexual Difference and Ontological Difference', trans. R. Berezdivin, *Research in Phenomenology*, 13, pp. 65–83.

Derrida, Jacques (1988), *Limited Inc*, trans. Samual Weber, Evanston: Northwestern University Press.

Derrida, Jacques (1989), 'How to Avoid Speaking: Denials', trans. Ken Frieden, in Sanford Budick and Wolfgang Iser (eds), *Languages of the Unsayable: The Play of Negativity in Literature and Literary Theory*, New York: Columbia.

Derrida, Jacques (1994), *Specters of Marx: The State of Debt, the Work of Mourning and the New International*, trans. Peggy Kamuf, New York: Routledge.

Diacritics (1984), Diacritics: Nuclear Criticism.

Douglass, Paul (1992), 'Bergson's Deleuze: Bergson Redux', in Frederick Burwick and Paul Douglass (eds), *The Crisis in Modernism: Bergson and the Vitalist Controversy*, Cambridge: Cambridge University Press, pp. 368–88.

Draper, Robert (1998), 'Death Takes a Honeymoon', *Gentlemen's Quarterly*, vol. 68, no. 6, June: 228–35, 281–5.

Driscoll, Catherine (1997), 'The Little Girl', *Antithesis*, 8.2, 1997; in a revised form as 'Becoming-Girl' in C. Boundas and D. Olkowlski (eds) (2000), *Deleuzian Becomings*, New York: Routledge.

Fiedler, Leslie (1979), *Freaks: Myths and Images of the Secret Self*, New York: Simon and Schuster.

Flieger, Jerry Aline (1991), *The Purloined Punch Line: Freud's Comic Theory and the Postmodern Text*, London and Baltimore: Johns Hopkins University Press.

Foucault, Michel (1966), *Les Mots et les choses*, Paris: Gallimard.

Foucault, Michel (1977), 'Foreword', in Deleuze and Guattari, *Anti-Oedipus*: x–xiv.

Foucault, Michel (1984), 'Theatricum Philosophicum', in D. F. Bouchard (ed.), *Language, Counter-Memory, Practice: Selected Essays and Interviews*, Ithaca: Cornell University Press, pp. 165–96.

Francisco, Luguiminda Bartalome and Jonathan Shepard Fast (1985), *Conspiracy for Empire*, Quezon City: Foundation for Nationalist Studies.

Franklin, Sarah, Celia, Lury and Jackie Stacey (1991), *Off-Centre: Feminism and Cultural Studies*, London: Harper and Collins.

Freud, Sigmund (1905) 'Jokes and their Relation to the Unconscious', in James Strachey (ed.) (1965), *Standard Edition of the Works of Sigmund Freud*, vol. 8, New York and London: Norton.

Freud, Sigmund (1911), 'Psychoanalytic Notes on an Autobiographical Account of a case of Paranoia', in James Strachey (ed.) (1965), *Standard Edition of the Works of Sigmund Freud*, vol. 12, New York and London: Norton.

Freud, Sigmund (1920), 'Beyond the Pleasure Principle', in James Strachey (ed.) (1965), *Standard Edition of the Works of Sigmund Freud*, vol. 18, New

York and London: Norton.

Freud, Sigmund (1921), 'Group Psychology and the Analysis of the Ego', in James Strachey (ed.) (1965), *Standard Edition of the Works of Sigmund Freud*, vol. 18, New York and London: Norton.

Fuss, Diana (1989), *Essentially Speaking*, New York: Routledge.

Gatens, Moira (1996a), *Imaginary Bodies: Ethics, Power and Corporeality*, London: Routledge.

Gatens, Moira (1996b), 'Through a Spinozist Lens: Ethology, Difference Power', in Paul Patton (ed.), *Deleuze: A Critical Reader*, Oxford: Blackwell.

Griggers, Camilla Benolirao (1997), *Becoming-Woman*, Minneapolis: University of Minnesota Press.

Grosz, Elizabeth (1989), *Sexual Subversions: Three French Feminists*, Sydney: Allen and Unwin.

Grosz, Elizabeth (1993a), 'Nietzsche and the Stomach for Knowledge', in Paul Patton (ed.), *Nietzsche, Feminism and Political Theory*, London: Allen and Unwin, pp. 49–70.

Grosz, Elizabeth (1993b), 'A Thousand Tiny Sexes: Feminism and Rhizomatics,' *Topoi* 12, pp. 167–79.

Grosz, Elizabeth (1994a), *Volatile Bodies*, Sydney: Allen and Unwin.

Grosz, Elizabeth (1994b), 'A Thousand Tiny Sexes: Feminism and Rhizomatics', in C. V. Boundas and D. Olkowlski (eds), *Gilles Deleuze and the Theater of Philosophy*, New York: Routledge, pp. 187–210.

Grosz, Elizabeth (1995), *Space, Time and Perversion*, Sydney: Allen and Unwin.

Grosz, Elizabeth and Elspeth Probyn (eds) (1995), *Sexy Bodies: The Strange Carnalities of Feminism*, London, New York: Routledge.

Guattari, Félix (1989), *Les Trois Écologies*, Paris: Galilée.

Guattari, Félix (1995), *Chaosmosis: An Ethico-aesthetic Paradigm*, trans. Paul Bains and Julian Pefanis, Bloomingdale: Indiana University Press.

Haraway, Donna (1991), 'A Cyborg Manifesto: Science, Technology and Socialist-Feminism in the Late Twentieth Century', in *Simians, Cyborgs and Women*, New York: Routledge, pp. 149–82.

Haraway, Donna (1996), *Modest_Witness@Second_Millennium: FemaleMan _Meets_OncoMouseTM: Feminism and Technoscience*, New York: Routledge.

Harding, Sandra (1991), *Whose Science? Whose Knowledge?*, Milton Keynes: Open University Press.

Hardt, Michael (1993), *Gilles Deleuze: An Apprenticeship in Philosophy*, Minneapolis: University of Minnesota Press.

Hofmann, Michael (1997), 'The Emperor of Nonsense', *The New York Times Book Review* (21 December).

Hunter, Tera (1997), *To 'Joy My Freedom: Southern Black Women's Lives and Labors after the Civil War*, Boston: Harvard University Press.

Hurley, Vic (1936), *Swish of the Kris: The Story of the Moros*, New York: E. P. Dutton & Co. [Reprinted with a foreword by Renato Constantino, Manila: Cacho Hermanos, Inc., 1985.]

Ileto, Reynaldo Clemeña (1997), *Payson and Revolution: Popular Movements in the Philippines, 1840-1910*, 4th edn, Manila: Ateneo de Manila University Press.

Irigaray, Luce (1985a), *This Sex Which is Not One*, trans. Catherine Porter, Ithaca: Cornell University Press.

Irigaray, Luce (1985b), *Speculum of the Other Woman*, trans. Gillian C. Gill, Ithaca: Cornell University Press.

Irigaray, Luce (1989), 'Sexual Difference', in Toril Moi (ed.), *French Feminist Thought: A Reader*, Oxford: Basil Blackwell.

Works Cited

Irigaray, Luce (1993a), *Je, Tu, Nous: Toward a Culture of Difference*, trans. Alison Martin, New York: Routledge.

Irigaray, Luce (1993b), *An Ethics of Sexual Difference*, trans. Carolyn Burke and Gillian C. Gill, Ithaca: Cornell University Press.

Irigaray, Luce (1996), *I Love to You: Sketch of a Possible Felicity in History*, trans. Alison Martin, New York: Routledge.

Jameson, Frederic (1983), 'Postmodernism and Consumer Society', in Hal Foster (ed.), *The Anti-Aesthetic: Essays on Postmodern Culture*, Washington: Bay Press, pp. 111–25.

Jameson, Frederic (1997), 'Marxism and Dualism in Deleuze', *South Atlantic Quarterly*, 96:3, Ian Buchanan (ed.), Summer, pp. 393–416.

Jardine, Alice (1985), *Gynesis: Configurations of Woman and Modernity*, Ithaca: Cornell University Press.

Johnson, Barbara (1982), 'My monster/Myself', *Diacritics*, 12.2.

Jones, Kevin (1998), 'Researchers Explore "Bot" Downside' *Inter@active Week*, vol. 5, no. 28 (27 July): 32.

Juno, Andrea and V. Vale (eds) (1991), *Angry Women, Re/Search*,13, San Francisco: Re/Search Publications.

Kaufman, Eleanor (1999), 'Klossowski or Thoughts-Becoming', in Elizabeth Grosz (ed.), *Making Futures*, Ithaca: Cornell University Press.

Klossowski, Pierre (1997), *Nietzsche and the Vicious Circle*, trans. Daniel W. Smith, Chicago: University of Chicago Press.

Kolbowski, Silvia (1995), 'A Conversation on Recent Feminist Art Practices', *October*, 71, pp.49–69.

Kristeva, Julia (1975), *Polylogue*, Paris: Editions du Seuil.

Kristeva, Julia (1980), 'Postmodernism?', in H. R. Garvin (ed.), *Romanticism, Modernism, Postmodernism*, Lewisburg: Bucknell University Press.

Kristeva, Julia (1982), *Powers of Horror*, trans. Leon S. Roudiez, New York: Columbia University Press.

Kristeva, Julia (1984), *Revolution in Poetic Language*, trans. M. Walter, New York: Columbia University Press.

Kristeva, Julia (1986), *The Kristeva Reader*, ed. Toril Moi, Oxford: Basil Blackwell.

Kroker, Arthur and Marilouise Kroker (1987), *Body Invaders: Panic Sex in America*, New York: Saint Martin's Press.

Lefanu, Sarah (1988), *In the Chinks of the World Machine*, London: The Women's Press.

Levi-Strauss, Claude (1955), *Tristes Tropiques*, Paris: Plon.

Levi-Strauss, Claude (1969), *The Raw and the Cooked: Introduction to a Science of Mythology 1*, trans. John and Doreen Weightman, New York: Harper and Row.

Lispector, Clarice (1972), 'Love', in *Family Ties*, trans. Giovanni Pontiero, Austin: University of Texas Press.

Lloyd, Genevieve (1996), *Spinoza and the Ethics*, New York and London: Routledge.

Marks, Elaine and Isabelle de Courtivon (1981), *New French Feminisms*, New York: Schocken Books.

Massumi, Brian (1992), *A User's Guide to Capitalism and Schizophrenia: Deviations from Deleuze and Guattari*, Cambridge, MA: MIT Press.

Moi, Toril (1985), *Sexual/Textual Politics: Feminist Literary Theory*, London: Methuen.

Morgenson, Gretchen (1998), 'The Man Behind the Curtain: Hedge Fund

Wizard or Wall St Gambler Run Amok', *The New York Times*, 2 October, C1.
Morris, Meaghan (1996), 'Crazy Talk is Not Enough', *Environment and Planning: Society and Space*, 14.4, pp. 384–94.
Mullarkey, John (1997), 'Deleuze and Materialism: One or Several Matters?', in Ian Buchanan (ed.), *A Deleuzean Century*, Special Issue of *The South Atlantic Quarterly*, 96.3 (Summer), pp. 439–63.
Neil, David (1998), 'The Uses of Anachronism: Deleuze's History of the Subject', *Philosophy Today* (Winter), 42.4, pp. 418–32.
Nietzsche, Friedrich (1967), *On the Genealogy of Morals and Ecce Homo*, trans. Walter Kaufmann and R. J. Hollingdale, Walter Kaufmann (ed.), New York: Vintage Books.
Nietzsche, Friedrich (1969), *On the Genealogy of Morals*, trans. Walter Kaufmann, New York: Vintage Books.
Nixon, M. (1995), 'Bad enough mother', *October*, 71, pp. 71–92.
Novalis, Friedrich von Hardenberg (1973), *The Encyclopaedia*, Bk 9, trans. Karl Siegler, Vancouver: Archai Publications.
Nye, Andrea (1990), *Words of Power: A Feminist Reading in the History of Logic*, New York: Routledge.
Olkowski, Dorothea (1994), 'Nietzsche's Dice Throw: Tragedy, Nihilism, and the Body Without Organs', in Constantin V. Boundas and Dorothea Olkowski (eds), *Gilles Deleuze and the Theater of Philosophy*, New York: Routledge.
Penley, Constance and Andrew Ross (eds) (1991), *Technoculture*, Minneapolis: University of Minnesota Press.
Pister, Patricia (1997), 'Cyborg Alice; or, Becoming-Woman in an Audiovisual World', *Iris*, 23 (Spring), pp. 148–63.
Rich, Adrienne (1987), *Bread, Blood and Poetry*, London: Virago.
Ronell, Avital (1989), *The Telephone Book: Technology, Schizophrenia, Electric Speech*, Nebraska: University of Nebraska Press.
Ronell, Avital (1994), *Finitude's Score: Essays for the End of the Millennium*, Nebraska: University of Nebraska Press.
Rose, Gillian (1993), *Feminism and Geography: The Limits of Geographical Knowledge*, Minneapolis: University of Minnesota Press.
Sanger, David (1998), 'IMF Remedies Played a Role in Asia's Panic', *International Herald Tribune*, Hong Kong, 14 January: 1.
Santner, Eric. L. (1996), *My Own Private Germany: Daniel Paul Schreber's Secret History of Modernity*, Princeton: Princeton University Press.
Schor, Naomi (1989), 'This Essentialism Which is Not One: Coming to Grips With Irigaray', *Differences*, 1:2 (Summer).
Scott, William Henry (1986), *Ilocano Responses to American Aggression, 1900–1901*, Quezon City, Philippines: New Day Publishers.
Seem, Mark (1977), 'Introduction', in Deleuze and Guattari, *Anti-Oedipus*: pp. xv–xxiv.
Shelley, Mary Wollstonecraft (1980), *Frankenstein: or, The Modern Prometheus*, M. K. Joseph (ed.), Oxford: Oxford University Press.
Shintaro, Ishihara (1991), *The Japan That Can Say No*, New York: Simon and Schuster.
Socialist Workers' Party Resolution (1994), 'What the 1987 Stock Market Crash Foretold', *New International: A Magazine of Marxist Politics and Theory*, no. 10: 101–201.
Sofoulis, Zoe (1992), 'Virtual corporeality: a feminist view', *Australian Feminist Studies*, 15.

Sontag, Susan (1966), *Against Interpretation*, New York: Farrar, Straus and Giroux.

Soros, George (1997), 'The Capitalist Threat', *The Atlantic Monthly* (February): 45–58.

Spinoza, Benedict de (1955), *Ethics*, trans. R. H. M. Elwes, New York: Dover.

Stacey, Jackie (1997), *Teratology*, London/New York: Routledge.

Stevens, Wallace (1997), *Wallace Stevens: Collected Poetry and Prose*, Frank Kermode and Joan Richardson (eds), New York: The Library of America.

Stone, Roseanne Allucquere (1995), *The War of Desire and Technology at the Close of the Mechanical Age*, Cambridge, MA: MIT Press.

Tolentino, Roland B. (1996), 'Bodies, Letters, Catalogs: Filipinas in Transnational Space', *Social Text* 48, vol. 14, no. 3: 49–76.

Tucker, Marcia (1994), 'The Attack of the Giant Ninja Mutant Barbies', in *Bad Girls*, New York: The Museum Of Contemporary Art/MIT Press, pp. 14–46.

Twain, Mark (1992), 'A Defence of General Funston', in Jim Zwick (ed.), *Mark Twain's Weapons of Satire: Anti-Imperialist Writings on the Philippine-American War*, Syracuse: Syracuse University Press, 1992.

Vance, Carole S. (1990), 'The pleasures of looking: The Attorney General's commission on pornography versus visual images', in Carol Squiers (ed.), *The Critical Image*, Seattle: Bay Press, pp. 38–58.

Virilio, Paul (1989), *War and Cinema: The Logistics of Perception*, trans by Patrick Camiller, London: Verso Press.

Wark, McKenzie (1994), *Virtual Geography: Living with Global Media Events*, Bloomington: Indiana University Press.

Warner, Marina (1994), *Managing Monsters: Six Myths of Our Time, The 1994 Reith Lectures*, London: Vintage Press.

Weldon, Fay (1983), *The Life and Loves of a She-Devil*, London: Coronet.

West, C. (1994), *Prophetic Thought in Postmodern Times*, Monroe: Common Courage Press.

Whitford, Margaret (1991), *Luce Irigaray: Philosophy in the Feminine*, New York: Routledge.

Wilcox, Marrion (ed.) (1900), *Harper's History of the War in the Philippines*, New York: Harper and Brothers Publishers.

Wollstonecraft, Mary (1989), 'Vindication of the Rights of Woman With Strictures on Political and Moral Subjects', in Janet Todd and Marilyn Butler (eds), *The Works of Mary Wollstonecraft*, vol. 5, London: William Pickering.

Woolf, Virginia (1928), *Orlando: A Biography*, London: Hogarth Press.

Woolf, Virginia (1952), *Three Guineas*, London: Hogarth Press.

Woolf, Virginia (1972), *A Room of One's Own*, Harmondsworth: Penguin.

Woolf, Virginia (1988), *Between the Acts*, London: Grafton Books.

Wright, Elizabeth (1992), *Feminism and Psychoanalysis: A Critical Dictionary*, Oxford: Blackwell.

Wyatt, Edward (1998), 'A Volatile Day Turns Wall St to Uneasy St', *The New York Times*, 9 October, A1, 19.

Zwick, Jim (ed.) (1992), *Mark Twain's Weapons of Satire: Anti-Imperialist Writings on the Philippine-American War*, Syracuse: Syracuse University Press.

Index

Index